The *Cercle Social*,
the Girondins, and the
French Revolution

GARY KATES

The *Cercle Social,* the Girondins, and the French Revolution

PRINCETON UNIVERSITY PRESS

Princeton, New Jersey

Copyright © 1985 by Princeton University Press
Published by Princeton University Press, 41 William Street, Princeton,
New Jersey 08540
In the United Kingdom: Princeton University Press, Guildford, Surrey

All Rights Reserved

Library of Congress Cataloging in Publication Data will be found
on the last printed page of this book

ISBN 0-691-05440-1

Publication of this book has been aided by the Paul Mellon Fund
at Princeton University Press

This book has been composed in Linotron Granjon

Clothbound editions of Princeton University Press books
are printed on acid-free paper, and binding materials are chosen
for strength and durability

Printed in the United States of America by Princeton
University Press, Princeton, New Jersey

The photograph on the title page,
an interior view of the Palais Royal, is reprinted
courtesy of the Boston Athenaeum

For

Lucian Marquis
Professor of Political Studies, Pitzer College

and

Werner Warmbrunn
Professor of History, Pitzer College

teachers, mentors, friends

This Cercle Social, for which Brissot chants in sincere timber-tones ... what is it: Unfortunately wind and shadow.

Thomas Carlyle

Nothing could be more confused than the bibliography of the various pamphlets, periodic or otherwise, of Fauchet, Bonneville, and their group.

Alphonse Aulard

It is regrettable that no monograph has been devoted to the internal history of the ... Cercle Social.... One would surely find in a study of its membership, and in the discussions that occurred there, precious bits for appreciating the movement of ideas during the first years of the Revolution.

Sigismond Lacroix

CONTENTS

x   CONTENTS

ILLUSTRATIONS

ABBREVIATIONS

Bdf	*Bouche de fer*
BAV	*Bulletin des Amis de la Vérité*
Cdm	*Chronique du mois*
CdP	*Chronique de Paris*
FHS	*French Historical Studies*
ICS	Imprimerie du Cercle Social
JMH	*Journal of Modern History*
Moniteur	*Moniteur universel. Réimpression de l'ancien Moniteur; seule histoire authentique et inaltérée de la Révolution française; depuis la réunion des Etats-Généraux jusqu'au Consulat (mai 1789-novembre 1799)*, 32 vols. (Paris: Plon, 1847-79).
Pf	*Patriote français*
RFB	*Révolutions de France et de Brabant*
RdP	*Révolutions de Paris*
Rf	*Révolution française*

ACKNOWLEDGMENTS

IT IS A PLEASURE finally to acknowledge the debt I owe to many friendly colleagues whose supportive criticism helped to bring this book to completion. My gratitude begins with Keith Baker, who guided me through the obstacle course known as a Ph.D. candidacy. Certainly no dissertation adviser has ever been more fair, honest, and intellectually stimulating than he. In its first life as a Ph.D. dissertation, the manuscript was also carefully read by William H. McNeill, Carroll Joynes, and Jamie Melton.

Between 1978 and 1983 I revised the dissertation thoroughly. Jack Censer labored over every page and helped me to understand the difference between a dissertation and a book. Betty Eisenstein read the manuscript and offered important suggestions at a crucial stage of revision. I also wish to thank Jeremy Popkin for reading Part III. Ken Margerison closely read a draft and offered criticisms which were so intelligent that I found myself making major changes in the table of contents late in the revision process. Finally, Tim Tackett and Jonathan Dewald offered gracious and cogent analyses of the finished version.

Trinity University has also been very supportive of this research. Colleagues Char Miller and John Martin read various versions with interest and wit and provided several useful suggestions. Nina Ekstein helped with some difficult translations. Dorothy Williams went well beyond her role as Department of History secretary and became an excellent copy editor (and, increasingly, an admirer of Claude Fauchet). Linda Clark typed the manuscript with good humor, despite stubborn resistance from a new word processor. Funds for this project were provided by the Department of History, the Dean of Humanities and Fine Arts, a Maddux Library Faculty Research Collection grant, and a Faculty Development Committee Summer Research Stipend.

Special gratitude is owed to my close friend, Judith Lipsett, who spent many hours helping to edit the manuscript. Her useful suggestions, editorial skill, and interest in the project made re-writing always rewarding and often fun.

Finally, this project would have never gotten off the ground without the love and support of Lynne Diamond, friend and wife, who worked hard to support our family while I took a leave of absence to complete this book.

San Antonio, Texas
1 June 1984

The *Cercle Social*,
the Girondins, and the
French Revolution

INTRODUCTION

THIS BOOK presents the first history of the Cercle Social.
Although thousands of volumes have been devoted to the
French Revolution, no one has charted the evolution of the
Cercle Social from a clique of Parisian politicians and then a
club of a few thousand members to the most prominent Girondin
publishing company. This lacuna is particularly striking because
the Cercle Social is mentioned in most major histories of the
French Revolution, and in scores of monographs, as having
played a vital role in the development of political thought during
the Revolution's early years. Historians have made many claims
about the Cercle Social: that it embodied a radical theory of
democracy at a very early stage of the Revolution; that it adapted
Masonic ideas and rituals to political and social radicalism; that
it developed a notion of socialism that presaged Saint-Simon
and Marx. Feminist historians see the Cercle Social as one of
the most important centers of feminist thought; Rousseau scholars see it as a headquarters for a renewed cult of Rousseau; and,
most recently, James Billington has claimed that the Cercle Social

represented one of the first efforts of a small circle of intellectuals
systematically to propagate radical social ideas to a mass audience ...
[It] launched the idea of an inner intellectual "circle" as the controlling
unit of a secret international movement. [It] seems even to have an-
ticipated the future eastward migration of this idea through the German *Kreis* and the Polish *kota* to the Russian *kruzhok*.[1]

[1] James H. Billington, *Fire in the Minds of Men: The Origins of the Revolu-
tionary Faith*, pp. 40-41. Examples of standard views on the Cercle Social are
P.J.B. Buchez and P. L. Roux, *Histoire parlementaire de la Révolution française*,
7: 447; Jules Michelet, *Histoire de la Révolution française*, 1: 474-75; Alphonse
Aulard, *The French Revolution: A Political History*, 1: 230; Albert Mathiez, *The
French Revolution*, p. 122; Jacques Godechot, *Les institutions de la France sous
la Révolution et l'Empire*, p. 62; Norman Hampson, *A Social History of the
French Revolution*, p. 100; J. M. Thompson, *The French Revolution*, p. 234;
George Lefebvre, *The French Revolution. Volume I: From its Origins to 1793*,
p. 181.

The limitation of these claims (and perhaps one reason why no history of the group has been completed) is that they all are rooted in the realm of ideas. The Cercle Social is thought to have been the source of unusual and seminal ideas, but no one has looked at how those ideas grew out of the political and social context of revolutionary France, and, conversely, how those ideas may have affected the course of the Revolution. While historians have acknowledged the intellectual value of the Cercle Social, most have dismissed its members as wild-eyed utopians, with little grounding in the political realities of revolutionary Paris. This historiographical tradition began during the early nineteenth century, and was made into a kind of orthodoxy, ironically enough, by Karl Marx. In his *Holy Family* of 1844, Marx remarked that the Cercle Social was the first truly "revolutionary" group, one of the earliest precursors of his own ideas. Unfortunately, Marx's remark was taken literally by his followers, and is still today the standard view of the Cercle Social.[2]

The problem with Marx's contention becomes evident when the leaders of the Cercle Social are allowed to emerge from behind their rhetoric. Marxists tend to find their heroes among the Revolution's most radical politicians, ranging from Robespierre and Marat to Babeuf and the Enragés. But very few of these radicals or their allies played important roles in the Cercle Social. Indeed, most of the Cercle Social's leaders, including Brissot, Roland, and Condorcet, became enemies of their more radical colleagues, and have incurred the wrath of Marxist historians. The Cercle Social offers a clear example of the pitfalls inherent in examining ideas from a strictly theoretical viewpoint; in this case that approach has obscured the organization's political role.

This book does not evaluate Cercle Social ideas for their own sake; instead, it situates those ideas within the social and political struggles that make up the French Revolution. This approach, what Peter Gay has called the "social history of ideas," has only

[2] Karl Marx, *The Holy Family or Critique of Critical Criticism*, p. 161; V. Alexeev-Popov, "Le Cercle Social (1790-1791)," *Recherches soviétiques* 4: 89-150; R. B. Rose, "Socialism and the French Revolution: The Cercle Social and the Enragés," *Bulletin of the John Rylands Library* 41: 139-164.

recently come into its own. In an important essay, François Furet has called upon historians to stop analyzing French revolutionary ideas from an exclusively ideological framework and to restore "to the French Revolution its most obvious dimension, the political one."

> The Revolution replaced the conflict of interest for power with a competition of discourses for the appropriation of legitimacy. Its leaders' "job" was not to act; they were there to interpret action. The French Revolution was the set of new practices that added a new layer of symbolic meanings to politics.[3]

Furet argues that ideas must not be treated as independent factors imposed upon politics, but rather as developing within particular political contexts for strategic purposes. He seeks to integrate the study of revolutionary ideology by charting in precise ways the influence of one upon the other. This study of the Cercle Social responds to Furet's call by showing how the group's ideas developed and changed under the pressure of particular political events.

The relations between ideology and politics must be seen from the vantage point of the people involved. In the Cercle Social there were ten members, the most committed activists, who may be considered the core of the group, and it is with them that any history must begin. These men were: Nicolas Bonneville, an aspiring philosophe known for his translations of German literature; the abbé Claude Fauchet, a bishop in the Constitutional Church; Jacques-Pierre Brissot, the most astute and powerful politician of the group; Jean-Marie Roland, minister of the interior; Condorcet, the last of the great Enlightenment philosophes; Henri Bancal, a dreamy-eyed thinker who tried to start a branch of the Cercle Social in London; François Lanthenas, a physician who made himself an expert on revolutionary clubs; Jean-Philippe Garran-Coulon, one of the most popular politicians in revolutionary Paris; Jacques Godard, a local politician famous for his advocacy of civil rights for Jews; and Jacques-

---

[3] François Furet, *Interpreting the French Revolution*, trans. Elborg Forster, pp. 27, 48-49; Peter Gay, *The Party of Humanity: Essays in the French Enlightenment*, p. x.

Antoine Creuzé-Latouche, the only one who served in the Constituent Assembly.

These men shared many characteristics. Most of them were from provincial middle-class families, usually in a small retail business or one of the professions. Each was given a solid education and a good start in life. By an early age they all considered themselves intellectuals, and most of them had already published books or pamphlets before the Revolution. But what held them together more than intellectual pursuits or socioeconomic background, was the intricate network of friendships among them, some of which went back to the 1770s. Bancal, Lanthenas, Garran-Coulon, Creuzé-Latouche, and Jean-Marie and Manon Roland had identified themselves as a small group of friends for years, and by the eve of the Revolution, Brissot had become part of their circle. In 1790 they dreamed up the idea of cooperatively buying a farm in the countryside, where together they would eventually retire, growing crops by day and discussing philosophy by moonlight. Their dream included establishing a press on the farm, which they hoped would become a source of enlightenment for the rural poor.[4]

They were also interested in politics. Even before the Revolution they had absorbed the radical ideas of the Enlightenment and had already envisioned a liberal democratic state. In 1789 they became particularly active in the Paris Municipal Revolution. Seven of the ten were elected to the new municipal legislature, the Paris Communal Assembly, where they became a loosely organized political group that campaigned for a municipal constitution based upon representative democracy. In 1791, five were elected to the Legislative Assembly, and one year later, seven were elected to the Convention. Their old friendships facilitated political cooperation in the assemblies, and during the fall of 1791, they emerged at the center of the political group known as the Girondins. Six of the seven Cercle Social leaders who were elected to the Convention have been classified as part of the Girondins' "Inner Sixty" (those sixty deputies closest to

[4] Claude Perroud, "Projet de Brissot pour une association agricole" *Rf* 42: 260-65.

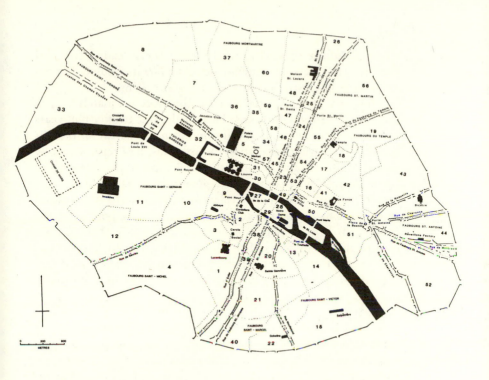

PARIS AND ITS DISTRICTS, 1789–1790

Redrawn from R. B. Rose, *The Making of the Sans-Culottes: Democratic Ideas
and Institutions in Paris, 1789-92* (Manchester University Press)

Brissot).[5] Of the remaining three Cercle Social leaders (Godard died in 1791), there is clear evidence that Garran-Coulon, Bonneville, and obviously Roland were also Girondins.

The story of the Cercle Social is therefore intimately tied to the history of the Girondins. During the last twenty-five years historians have taken renewed interest in the nature of the Girondins. An earlier generation of historians, best represented by Albert Mathiez, saw the Girondins as a political party that stood for a liberal and decentralized government, laissez-faire economic policies, and greater toleration for royalists and priests, in contrast to the more radical and centralizing policies of the Montagnards. In a meticulously researched study of the Girondins published in 1961, Michael Sydenham argued that the Girondins were not in any sense a political party. He claimed that they did not vote as a bloc and that the idea of a Girondin political faction was only a myth developed by the Jacobins. At most, Sydenham wrote, the Girondins constituted nothing more than "Brissot's circle of friends" and "should be regarded as a small and loose-knit group or coalition of individualists who rapidly become representative of resistance of the majority to Robespierre, their personal independence remaining unqualified." During the 1960s and 1970s several historians argued with Sydenham, claiming that the Girondins exhibited a distinct political identity and behavior.[6] In seeking to determine the nature of the Girondins, these historians have focused on the Girondins' behavior in the Legislative Assembly and Convention. But it may be more useful to discuss the range of their activities out of this context, including participation in clubs, publishing ven-

---

[5] M. J. Sydenham, *The Girondins*, p. 229.

[6] Albert Mathiez, *Girondins et Montagnards*; Sydenham, *Girondins*, pp. 194, 208. See also Sydenham, "The Montagnards and Their Opponents" *JMH* 43: 287-93; "The Girondins and the Question of Revolutionary Government" *FHS* 10: 342-48; Alison Patrick, *The Men of the First Republic: Political Alignments in the National Convention of 1792*; "Political Divisions in the French National Convention 1792-1793" *JMH* 41: 421-74; "The Montagnards and Their Opponents: Some Comments" *JMH* 43: 293-97; Theodore Di Padova, "The Girondins and the Question of Revolutionary Government" *FHS* 9: 432-50; "The Question of Girondin Motives: A Response to Sydenham" *FHS* 10: 349-52; Albert Soboul, ed., *Actes du colloque Girondins et Montagnards (Sorbonne, 14 decembre 1975)*

tures, and the like. If the Girondins were essentially a group of friends, their experience in the national assemblies may form only a phase, albeit a crucial one, of their development.

Part of the problem surrounding the discussion of the nature of the Girondins is precisely that no one has focused on the role played by the Cercle Social. On the one hand, the Cercle Social has traditionally been viewed as a group of utopian dreamers whose ideas were later adopted by nineteenth-century socialists, so there has been little reason to include them in analyses of political behavior. On the other hand, the Girondins are often described as "the representatives of the propertied middle classes, the commercial and industrial bourgeoisie."[7] How could a group of Girondins produce "socialist" ideas? In the Cercle Social we encounter the paradox of a group whose ideas were seemingly at variance with its members' political behavior. Reconciling this problem requires a renewed focus on the nature and development of the Girondins as well as on the relationship between political thought and behavior.

Another reason that the Cercle Social has not been previously linked to the Girondins is that historians have concentrated on the Cercle Social's incarnation as a club. But the Cercle Social met as a club only until the summer of 1791, when it was closed following the massacre at the Champ de Mars. The Cercle Social was then transformed from a club into a publishing company. Far from signaling the end of the Cercle Social, the change marked the beginning of its last and most interesting stage, a period that saw the rise of the Girondins in national politics. The Imprimerie du Cercle Social claimed it was "established on foundations which are much larger than the ordinary bookstore."

The writings and principles of the Directors of the Imprimerie du Cercle Social are known throughout Europe. Their authors are certainly not any less famous; and their revolutionary writings, published in all dialects, are found in Italy, Spain, Vienna, Berlin, and in the

---

[7] Albert Soboul, *The French Revolution 1787-1799: From the Storming of the Bastille to Napoleon*, p. 276.

two Indies, attesting well enough that their subscribers are actively propagating liberty.[8]

The Cercle Social thought of its publishing company as a political institution whose authors shared a common outlook and similar approaches to public issues. Through a program of well-financed journals, books, pamphlets, posters, and art, a publishing company like the Imprimerie du Cercle Social could wield enormous influence upon political events and therefore must be seen as something more than simply a business. This was especially true during the early years of the Revolution, when political journalism established itself in France. As Brissot saw so clearly in 1791, the Cercle Social was much more effective as a publishing company than as a club in disseminating information and developing a political consciousness among the people.[9] Historians have largely ignored the role played by publishers during the Revolution. But through an analysis of the Cercle Social and its extensive publishing program, this study will focus on the specific relationship between the Imprimerie du Cercle Social and the Girondins. As François Furet suggests, the Girondins' importance was not simply as a group who acted in politics, but was more fundamental: they gave actions a new set of political meanings. In this respect, the Cercle Social became the Girondins' most enduring attempt to develop a discourse that claimed to speak for the nation.

THIS BOOK is organized around the three successive transformations the Cercle Social underwent between 1790 and 1793. Part I charts how the Cercle Social was begun by a group of Parisian politicians, led by Nicolas Bonneville and Claude Fauchet, who advocated representative democracy during the Paris Municipal Revolution of 1789-1790. At this point the Cercle Social was a small, secretive group of fifteen or twenty men who published a journal aimed at strengthening the position of the Paris Communal Assembly.

This first phase ended during the summer of 1790, when

[8] *BAV*, 1 January 1793, p. 2.
[9] *Pf*, 2 August 1791, p. 135.

Bonneville, Fauchet, and their friends were defeated in the municipal elections. They temporarily retreated from municipal politics and founded a large club, the Confédération des Amis de la Vérité (Confederation of the Friends of Truth), which is the subject of Part II. This Confédération became one of the largest clubs of the Revolution (3,000-6,000 members) and was famous for its radical views on land reform, religion, women's rights, and democracy. Along with the Cordeliers club, the Confédération led the movement to establish a democratic republic after the flight of King Louis XVI in June 1791, and was suppressed after the massacre at the Champ de Mars.

Part III takes the Cercle Social from the summer of 1791 to the summer of 1793, focusing on its extraordinary publishing company, the Imprimerie du Cercle Social. The same men who began the Cercle Social in 1790, and who had been leaders in its Confédération des Amis de la Vérité, now directed and wrote for the publishing company. Part III first analyzes the philosophy and personnel of the Imprimerie, and then devotes separate chapters to its three most significant journals: The *Chronique du mois*, which was aimed at intellectuals, the *Sentinelle*, posted on Paris streets for sans-culottes, and the *Bulletin des Amis de la Vérité*, a daily newspaper. The Imprimerie du Cercle Social was suppressed at the beginning of the Terror.

The Origins
of the Cercle Social,
1789-1790

Philosophy has directed a great revolution in France. The reign of liberty and equality has been established on the ruins of despotism and all other abuses.

Bulletin des Amis de la Vérité, 11 April 1793, p.3.

1

Bonneville, Fauchet, and the Paris Municipal Revolution

Jean-Philippe Garran-Coulon (1748-1816). Elected to the Paris Communal Assembly, Legislative Assembly, and Convention; municipal judge; *Chronique du mois* editor for legal affairs. A popular politician in Paris during the Revolution's early years, Garran was close friends with Brissot, and published sharply anti-Jacobin pamphlets during the trial of Louis XVI. But he managed to avoid arrest during the Girondin purge of 1793, and went on to have a successful political career under the Directory and Napoleon.
Courtesy of The Newberry Library, Chicago

Intellectuals in the lower income groups are termed the intellectual proletariat, a phenomenon which arises as a consequence of an over-abundance of persons offering their knowledge in the market. Always a pathological condition, it is caused by an intellectual overestimation of formal education in general. . . . They are sworn enemies of government policies, eternally restless spirits which lead the bourgeois opposition and even revolutionary proletarian parties.

Robert Michels, "Intellectuals," *Encyclopedia of the Social Sciences*, 15 vols. (New York: MacMillan, 1932), 4:122.

T HE ORIGINS of the Cercle Social are difficult to discover, but at least the reason for the difficulty is clear: the founders of the Cercle Social shrouded their first activities in secrecy, preventing historians from learning much about the group. The task has been further complicated by the practice engaged in by Cercle Social leaders of constantly playing with the names of their various projects, so that it is easy to mistake one for another. For example, the term "Cercle Social" was at various times used as the name for a small group of men, a very large weekly club, and a journal. It is expedient, then, to refer to the entire organization as the Cercle Social, just as contemporaries eventually did. But for the purposes of charting the origins of the group, it is necessary to note an important distinction between the Cercle Social and its later club, the Confédération des Amis de la Vérité. The first was a small, secret clique of Parisian politicians, established during the early months of 1790. It was not until October of that year that this tiny coterie started the Confédération and became its directoire (steering committee). Since the Confédération became famous for its progressive ideas and attempts to revive Enlightenment classics, the original group and its largely political roots have been ignored.

The beginnings of the Cercle Social are embedded in the struggles for political power within the new Parisian municipal government. The group first constituted a political entity in opposition to the administration of Mayor Jean-Sylvain Bailly. The extent to which this faction included future leaders of the Girondins is remarkable. This view of the Cercle Social's origins is in sharp contrast to the one found in textbooks on the Revolution, which sees in the group's origins merely "a mixture of Freemasonry and 'social' Christianity."[1] Yet if one is to understand the Cercle Social's later political role as a mouthpiece for moderate republicanism, it is necessary to pay close attention to its municipal beginnings.

Within this political faction, two men were particularly influential in founding the Cercle Social. The first, Nicolas Bonneville, was a young writer and a disciple of the Enlightenment. The other, Claude Fauchet, was a priest noted for his powerful sermons and religious writings. While their personalities were very different, the two became close associates in the Paris Communal Assembly during the first year of the Revolution. Their leadership was the most important factor in shaping the direction and spirit of the Cercle Social, so an appreciation of their careers and their collaboration is vital to an understanding of the group.

THE FRENCH Revolution began as a struggle between the monarchy and the aristocracy over the government's inability to pay its bills. By the late 1780s, the national debt had reached some 110 million livres, and, without some basic reforms of a woefully inadequate tax system, the government would continue on its road to bankruptcy. There were essentially three ways out of this quagmire. The first was simply to collect more taxes from the peasants. But by the end of the eighteenth century the French peasants were already oppressed by various feudal taxes and no effort to increase these significantly could hope to succeed. Second, the government could cut its own expenses. The problem with this solution was that even if the king could streamline his administration, it was unlikely that the savings would be enough to relieve the massive debt. Therefore, the government decided upon a third method: a land tax on all subjects, including the hitherto privileged members of the First and Second Estates (the clergy and the nobility).[2]

In 1787 the king's minister, Calonne, called a meeting of influential priests, noblemen, officeholders, and financiers, known

---

[1] Norman Hampson, *A Social History of the French Revolution*, p. 100.
[2] On events between 1787-1789, see William Doyle, *The Origins of the French Revolution*, and Jean Egret, *The French Pre-Revolution 1787-1788*.

as the Assembly of Notables. Calonne hoped to persuade the Notables to approve the land tax. After several weeks it was clear this strategy had failed. Most members did not believe that the debt was very large and insisted that the monarchy cut its own expenses. The king dismissed Calonne and replaced him with the Archbishop Brienne, who fared no better.

By the summer of 1788 the local parlements were refusing to register any new laws, and a revolt of the nobility had begun. Noble leaders accused the king of despotism. In various pamphlets and proclamations the king was accused of trying to subvert the fundamental laws of the land and replace them with his own arbitrary will. The leaders of the parlements argued that only a meeting of representatives from the three estates could approve major tax reforms. The king and his ministers were backed into a corner. The fiscal crisis was worsening and the nobility was becoming more inflexible. In August the king yielded to the demands of the parlementaires, and called for a meeting of the Estates General.

Until this point the Third Estate (comprising all commoners) had supported the aristocracy in its claim that the real issue behind the fiscal crisis was the despotism of the crown. The Third Estate hoped that the Estates General would go beyond tax reform and discuss major reforms of other feudal laws. On 25 September 1788 these hopes were dashed when the Parlement de Paris ruled that the Estates General should be constituted just as it had been at its last meeting in 1614, that is, in three separate chambers, each possessing one vote, and each with the same number of members.

The leaders of the Third Estate now emerged as an independent group with their own ideas and plans. They realized that the Parlement's decree meant that the aristocracy (First and Second Estates) could always outvote the Third Estate. "The public debate has changed," the journalist Mallet du Pan wrote in January 1789. "Now the king, despotism, the constitution are merely secondary; it is a war between the Third Estate and the two other orders."[3] The new desires of the Third Estate were best stated in the abbé Sieyès pamphlet, *What Is the Third Estate?*,

[3] Cited in Doyle, *Origins*, p. 147.

which not only demanded that the numerical strength of the Third Estate's representation be doubled and all votes counted individually, but also envisioned the abolition of feudalism and the introduction of a new kind of regime based upon "a body of associates living under *common* laws and represented by the same *legislative assembly*."[4]

In addition to Sieyès hundreds of other writers were publishing pamphlets, books, and journals with the same message. Even if 1789 was not remembered as the year of revolution, historians would still recall it as a year that witnessed an explosion in political journalism. One of Sieyès' better known followers was Nicolas Bonneville, who began his own journal, the *Tribun du peuple*, during the early months of 1789. Bonneville had grown up in Normandy, the son of a provincial attorney. He had been expelled from a local college for reading portions of Rousseau's *Emile* aloud to other students, and he came to Paris to cut a figure as a man of letters. Like so many young writers living in Paris during the 1780s, such as Brissot, Carra, and Mercier, Bonneville dreamed of becoming a great philosophe. Unfortunately, despite the publication of a few books on history and Freemasonry, Bonneville eked out a living translating German and English classics into French. In 1789 he was twenty-nine years old, and if his career was not yet a failure, neither was it a success. The Revolution swept him up into the new world of political journalism and electoral politics.[5]

In the *Tribun du peuple* Bonneville expressed the hope that the Estates General would not merely reform taxes but would initiate a complete reorganization of political institutions, a reorganization that would recognize the aspirations of the Third Estate. Where the leaders of the First and Second Estates had equated despotism with abuses in the monarchy, the *Tribun du peuple* equated despotism with "exclusive and hereditary privileges."[6] Bonneville warned the nobility to avoid obstructing the

[4] Emmanuel Sieyès, *What Is the Third Estate?*, p. 58.
[5] Philippe Le Harivel, *Nicolas de Bonneville, pré-romantique et révolutionnaire, 1760-1828*; Gary Kates, "The Cercle Social: French Intellectuals and the French Revolution," pp.17-23.
[6] *Le Tribun du peuple, ou Recueil des lettres de quelques électeurs de Paris,*

desires of the Third Estate, which he regarded as the sovereign authority in France. "The Third Estate, which really is the whole nation in its entirety and the sole legislative authority, creates or deposes officials and kings as it pleases."[7]

The *Tribun du peuple* was important because it helped spread radical political ideas some three or four months before the taking of the Bastille. But the ideas presented in it also mark a turning point in Bonneville's own life: the transformation of a philosophe into a revolutionary. Before 1789, Bonneville had studied literature, language, and philosophy, rather than political theory, government, and economics. If he immersed himself in Montesquieu and Rousseau, it was generally for their literary and philosophical reflections. His training prepared him for an active career in what d'Alembert had called the Republic of Letters, not for leading a revolution. All of his previous writings had been intended for a small, highly literate audience. But in the *Tribun du peuple* he wrote in plain language designed to reach as many readers as possible. "Oh Montesquieu! Oh Voltaire! And you, my dear Rousseau! Teach me the art of sweetening healthful drinks! For the truth itself has its pretty side; and it is only by showing that side that one can present the truth to men in such a way that they are sure to absorb it. Otherwise, it will not be pleasing, and will often be rejected."[8]

Bonneville did more than spread revolutionary ideas; he became a politician. During the spring of 1789, the Paris Third Estate was divided into sixty electoral districts. These districts were to choose electors who would sit in a Paris-wide Assembly of Electors, who would in turn elect twenty deputies to the Estates General. Bonneville became president of his district, Carmes Déchausés, which then selected him to represent them in the Assembly of Electors.

For reasons beyond its control, the Assembly of Electors did not meet until 26 April, and did not complete its task of selecting

avant la Révolution de 1789, pour servir d'introduction aux feuilles de la bouche de fer (Paris: ICS, 1790), p. 5. This is actually the third edition of the *Tribun du peuple* of 1789.
 [7] Ibid., p. 12.
 [8] Ibid., p. 33.

twenty deputies and composing a list of grievances until 23 May. By that date the Estates General had already been in session for over two weeks, and it was apparent that the aspirations of the Third Estate were not getting very far. The Electors decided to reconvene on 7 June in order to keep abreast of events at Versailles. Since the government had organized the districts and the Assembly of Electors for the exclusive purpose of selecting deputies to the Estates General, and that task had been completed, the royal authorities declared that the Electors had no authority to meet again. Nonetheless, after some delay, the Assembly of Electors reconvened at the Hotel de Ville on 25 June in direct violation of the ruling of the Paris authorities.[9]

Meanwhile, the situation at Versailles became considerably more tense. On 17 June the representatives of the Third Estate voted to call themselves the National Assembly; two days later a majority of the clergy voted to fuse with this Assembly; and on 20 June these men took the famous Tennis Court Oath, reiterating their claim to be the National Assembly and vowing to remain in session until a constitution was written. These events had a profound impact upon the Paris Electors, and no one was more affected than Nicolas Bonneville. He needed no popular uprising to convince him that France had undergone a revolution. Bonneville saw in these events nothing short of the transformation of a feudal kingdom into a free nation composed of citizens whose political and civil rights were recognized. "We have just witnessed the first *national, public, and popular* activity after fourteen centuries of servitude. Happy month of June! . . . Today I begin to live!" he exulted.[10]

When the Paris Assembly of Electors reconvened on 25 June, Bonneville was among the first to claim that the great events at Versailles implied a new role for the Electors. In a fiery speech interrupted by loud applause from the public gallery, he urged

[9] *Procès-verbal des séances et déliberations de l'Assemblée générale des Electeurs de Paris*, 1: 1-100; Henry E. Bourne, "Improvising a Government in Paris in July, 1789" *American Historical Review* 10: 280-308; and more generally, Marcel Reinhard, *Nouvelle histoire de Paris: La Révolution 1789-1799*.

[10] *Tribun du peuple* (1789), pp. 140-42.

his colleagues to lead a municipal revolution.[11] He argued that the districts and the Assembly of Electors were much more than temporary electoral devices; they were the basis for new political institutions. "The deputies [of the National Assembly] are only the delegates of the electors, just as the electors are only the representatives of the districts, villages, towns, and cities."[12] He called for the Assembly of Electors to become the legislative assembly for Paris. The Electors would act as intermediaries between the districts and the National Assembly. The districts would meet "one or two times a week," and would then inform their Electors of local problems, complaints, and the like.[13] The Electors would debate solutions to these problems in their Assembly, sending instructions on to the deputies at the National Assembly. Bonneville ended his speech with a motion for the establishment of a citizen militia (*garde bourgeoise*) that would protect the new government against any aristocratic or royal attacks.[14]

Bonneville's plan went further toward democracy than anything said or done in the National Assembly. In its declaration of 17 June, for example, the National Assembly had followed Sieyès in asserting the sovereignty of the nation over the crown. But it also asserted that the National Assembly "alone" had the right "to interpret and present the general will of the nation."[15] No mention was made of the National Assembly's relationship to other more local assemblies. Several of Bonneville's fellow Electors interpreted this to mean that only the National Assembly had the authority to transform electoral assemblies into permanent bodies.[16]

Bonneville responded by invoking a radical and democratic interpretation of popular sovereignty. He realized that representatives of a national assembly had a certain amount of freedom

---

[11] The speech was reprinted in *Tribun du peuple* (1789), pp. 145-51, but mistakenly dated 21 June 1789.

[12] Ibid., p. 145.

[13] Ibid., p. 149.

[14] The motion is found in Archives Nationales C I 1 fol. 95.

[15] "Declaration Constituting the National Assembly," D. I. Wright, ed., *The French Revolution. Introductory Documents*, p. 38.

[16] *Procès-verbal des . . . Electeurs*, 1: 156-65.

to develop laws for the nation. But he claimed that they also had a responsibility to carry out the wishes of their constituents; if the Electors made demands of their deputies, "they [the deputies] do not have the right to refuse you [the Electors]."[17] Bonneville believed that a mere change from control by the crown to control by an assembly was not enough; real political power had to be placed in the hands of ordinary citizens, "otherwise you will have substituted a despotism of the many in place of a despotism of one minister."[18]

Bonneville's arguments were rejected by the Electors, who were not at all ready to begin a struggle over democracy with the National Assembly. Likewise, his plan for a citizen militia was dropped for the time being. But in the long run this speech did more for Bonneville's career than anything else, and throughout the early years of the Revolution colleagues repeatedly praised him for it. "M. de Bonneville is one of the great bards of liberty," wrote Brissot in his newspaper. "And he doesn't limit himself to just singing about it. He is among the first who defended it in his speeches and with his sword. He is the author of the motion for a citizen militia and for the reorganization of the districts. He truly merits the title Tribun du peuple."[19] Bonneville himself recognized the motion's importance, continuing to praise himself for years as the "author of the motion for the National Guard" (the name of the citizen militia was soon changed to National Guard).[20]

While the majority of Electors were against him, a small group of radicals clustered around Bonneville at the end of June and the beginning of July. Among them was Jean-Philippe Garran-Coulon. He had studied medicine and then law in Poitiers and Orléans and had written plays, poems, and essays on a variety of topics. Although forgotten by historians today, Garran was very popular among Parisian radicals, almost winning a seat in

[17] *Tribun du peuple* (1789), pp. 150-51.
[18] Ibid., p. 145.
[19] *Pf*, 2 July 1790, p. 4; see also [Claude Fauchet, ed.], *Tableux de la Révolution française ou Collection de quarante-huit gravures*, p. 13.
[20] Nicolas Bonneville, *L'Année M DCC LXXIX, ou Les Tribuns du peuple*, p. x.

the Estates General. Even Jean-Paul Marat, who rarely had a kind word to say about anyone, praised Garran-Coulon for being a "generous citizen."[21] Another of these radicals was Henri Bancal, who grew up in Clermont-Ferrand, but moved to Paris as a notary in 1783. He became one of the first members of the antislavery club, the Société des amis des noirs, and became friendly with several important Parisian radicals, including Garran-Coulon.[22] Finally, there was Claude Fauchet.

By THE EARLY 1900s historians had come to regard Fauchet as one of the most important priests of the Revolution.[23] A compelling orator, gifted writer, incisive thinker, and skilled politician, Fauchet was ambitious, self-confident, and charismatic. He was a person who was not well liked but was always respected and often admired. An egotist, Fauchet was unable to be part of a group without being its leader, for he refused to take orders from anyone. Fiercely independent, he made many more enemies than friends, and died under the guillotine as an outlawed Girondin in 1793.[24]

Born in 1744, Fauchet was the son of a wealthy landowner. As soon as he was of age, his family directed him into the Church, where at sixteen he gave his first sermon and at twenty he took his vows. Six years later he was ordained and began his career as a tutor for the children of a wealthy nobleman. In 1774, Fauchet had the good fortune to be invited to deliver the annual panegyric of Saint Louis before the French Academy. The subsequent publication of the address established his reputation as a thinker.[25] Soon he began to attract the attention of the literary

[21] *Ami du peuple*, 14 November 1789, p. 77; see also *Pf*, 19 February 1790, p. 3; and X. Barbier de Montault, "Papiers de Garran de Coulon (1756-1788)" *Revue d'archéologie Poitevine* 3: 315-18; "Mémoires de Garran de Coulon" *Revue illustrée des provinces de l'Ouest* 2(1890): 256-64, 3(1891): 31-40, 5(1892): 214-19. These memoirs unfortunately stop at 1782.

[22] Francisque Mège, *Le Conventionnel Bancal des Issarts. Étude biographique. Suivi de lettres inédites.*

[23] Elphège Boursin, *Dictionnaire de la Révolution française*, p. 2.

[24] Jules Charrier, *Claude Fauchet: Evêque constitutionnel du Calvados, Député à l'Assemblée Legislative et à la Convention 1744-1793.*

[25] *Journal des beaux-arts et des sciences*, November 1774, p. 283.

world, and the influential *Mémoires secrets* cited him as a rising star.[26]

During the 1780s Fauchet had gained distinction as an orator and was sought by provincial churches to give guest sermons. Even those listeners who were critical of Fauchet recognized his rhetorical talents. "I heard the abbé Fauchet," wrote Etienne Dumont in 1788.

He slightly resembles a charlatan who sells two drugs, one which he calls Hell, and the other which he calls Paradise. He gesticulates with great skill, but his delivery seems to me to be too harsh, and never a word is spoken which is not calculated. He has a brilliant style and uses antithesis as his principal oratorical tool. But in my opinion he tends to manipulate rhetorical techniques without really being a great orator. His sermon was full of energy, detailed anecdotes, and happy phrases, but it was all a bit overdone.[27]

By 1789, Fauchet was well on his way to a very successful clerical career. Unlike Bonneville, he did not need a revolution to increase his glory. Nonetheless, he had come to many of the same radical conclusions regarding French society as had his younger colleague. In his little-known history of the French Revolution, written in 1790 or 1791, Fauchet analyzed the long-term causes of the Revolution. During the course of the eighteenth century, he asserted, the monarchy mismanaged the government to such an extent that by the 1780s the kingdom was at war with itself:

At that time France offered a unique spectacle. ... One saw in the nation two different nations occupying themselves with the *Encyclopédie* and *billets de confession*; political economy and Jansenist miracles, *Emile* and a bishop's decree, a *lit de justice* and the *Social Contract*, proscribed Jesuits, exiled parlements, and persecuted philosophes.

Into "this chaos" stepped "tyrants called *nobles* and *priests*, who ... formed two privileged castes," and who ruthlessly victimized the poor with an oppressive tax system.[28]

---

[26] *Mémoires secrets pour servir à l'histoire de la république des lettres en France*, 20 May 1776, p. 115.

[27] Cited in J. Benetruy, *L'Atelier de Mirabeau: Quatre proscrits génévois dans la tourmente révolutionnaire*, p. 151.

[28] [Fauchet], *Tableaux de la Révolution française*, pp. i-iii.

Fauchet, then, welcomed the Revolution with open arms, declaring its purpose to be to "annihilate despotism and raise national sovereignty upon the debris."[29] Like Bonneville, Fauchet wasted no time becoming a revolutionary. Just as the Third Estate had been split into electoral districts during the spring of 1789, so too was the Parisian clergy, who chose deputies from the First Estate for the meeting at Versailles. The eighty-five voters in the parish of Saint-Roch elected Fauchet to the Paris First Estate's Assembly of Electors, although he was the fifth to be elected in a delegation of five. On 1 July, Fauchet was the first representative of the First Estate to join the Third Estate's Assembly of Electors, hoping that the Electors would transform themselves into a new municipal legislature.[30] A clergyman's joining the Third Estate was an immensely popular act, and Fauchet immediately became a leader in the Electors. On 4 July, for example, Fauchet, Bancal, and Bonneville were chosen as part of a delegation sent to inform the National Assembly of events in the capital.[31]

Paris had entered a new crisis by the time the Electors met again on 10 July. During the first week of July a great fear swept over the capital. Parisians were concerned that the king would not allow the National Assembly to continue its revolt. They believed that royal troops were massing around Versailles and Paris, ready to arrest the leaders of the National Assembly and take the city. Amidst the political crisis, there were reports that vagabonds were taking advantage of the situation. In George Lefebvre's words, a "bourgeois" revolution was rapidly becoming a "popular" one.[32]

The Electors realized that strong measures had to be taken, if the populace were to be prevented from taking matters into their own hands. Bonneville reiterated his motion of 26 June, calling for the establishment of a National Guard and urging

[29] Ibid., p. 8.
[30] Charles Chassin, ed., *Les Elections et les cahiers de Paris en 1789*, 2: 42 and 3: 446-47.
[31] *Procès-verbal des ... Electeurs*, 1:110.
[32] Georges Lefebvre, *The Coming of the French Revolution*. On the July crisis see Jacques Godechot, *The Taking of the Bastille: July 14th, 1789*.

Electors to declare themselves a provisional communal assembly. The first task of such an assembly would be the drafting of a provisional constitution for Paris. The speech was again interrupted by applause from the public galleries. Fauchet supported Bonneville, asking only that a committee be named for the writing of this constitution, which would then have to be ratified by the districts. Bonneville welcomed these amendments. Bonneville also received support from the future Girondin Jean-Louis Carra, and from Henri Bancal, who called the royal troops the "arm of despotism."[33]

The Electors appointed Fauchet, Bonneville, Bancal, Carra, Garran-Coulon, and four others to a committee to study the proposal. The following day this committee reported back to the Electors, who approved the plan for a national guard, but balked at the idea of declaring themselves to be a communal assembly.[34]

On 12 July the king dismissed his minister of finances, Necker, who had become a national hero for his budgetary reforms. The move was interpreted by the Paris populace as a sign of impending attack by the king's troops. Theaters were closed, armories were looted for guns and ammunition, and demonstrations were held. Bonneville's public reaction to Necker's dismissal was recorded by the elector and future Girondin, Jean Dusaulx:

A young man, M. Bonneville, who expressed himself with great wisdom and maturity, suddenly lost his temper, and seeing what would soon happen to us, cried: "To arms! To arms!" Some reacted in horror, others simply laughed at him, and one retorted: "Young man, it is not yet time."[35]

On the evening of 13 July the electors responded to this crisis by establishing a Permanent Committee. This group was composed of the most important electors and some of the officers of the old Paris government. It was specifically asked to oversee the establishment of the National Guard and the distribution of

---

[33] *Procès-verbal des ... Electeurs*, 1: 130-75; Chassin, *Les Elections* 3: 475-77.
[34] Ibid.
[35] Jean Dusaulx, "L'Oeuvre des sept jours ... ," in *Mémoires de Linguet sur la Bastille et de Dusaulx sur le 14 juillet ...* , p. 271.

food supplies, but it quickly took responsibility for all municipal problems. It was this Permanent Committee—permanent in the sense that it was always in session—that governed Paris during the tumultuous day, 14 July 1789. Among its members were Dusaulx, Bancal, who acted as a liaison with the National Assembly, and Fauchet, who was part of a delegation that courageously attempted to convince the royal troops protecting the Bastille to surrender their arms peacefully to the National Guard.[36]

Great events finally accomplished the aims Bonneville, Fauchet, Garran-Coulon, and Bancal had been espousing since late June. Whatever the misgivings of the more conservative electors, the Assembly of Electors became a de facto municipal legislature with the radicals as its leaders after the taking of the Bastille on 14 July and the subsequent collapse of the old government. During the next week Garran-Coulon presided over the electors, often working around the clock.[37] The electors had three serious problems that required immediate attention: providing adequate food supplies for the city, reestablishing law and order, and creating a new municipal government.

There had been a food shortage in Paris for quite some time. The result was a significant rise in the price of bread. "The price of a four-pound loaf in the Paris markets rose to twelve sous on 8 November [1788], to thirteen sous on the 28th, to fourteen sous on 11 December and, finally, to fourteen and one-half sous on 1 February," writes George Rudé. "It was to remain at this level after the fall of the Bastille."[38] The poor were clearly hurt the most by this shortage. Thus, everyone in the new government agreed that obtaining adequate food supplies was a prerequisite to reestablishing order; without more bread no government could

---

[36] *Procès-verbal des. . . Electeurs*, 1: 188 and ff.; Jean-Sylvain Bailly, *Mémoires de Bailly*, 1: 347, 364-65, 370, 2: 47; Jean Dusaulx, "La Prise de la Bastille, discours historique," in *Mémoires de Linguet sur la Bastille et de Dusaulx sur le 14 juillet . . ., p. 335; see also* Bourne, "Improvising," *and* Godechot, *The Taking of the Bastille.*

[37] J. A. Creuzé-Latouche, "Les Grandes journées de juin et de juillet 1789 d'après le *Journal* inédit de Creuzé-Latouche," *Revue des questions historiques* 123 and 124: 264.

[38] George Rudé, *The Crowd in the French Revolution*, p. 33.

expect order in Paris. "Food provisions," noted one elector, "were the principal aim of the disturbances and riots."[39]

The situation was critical, but not hopeless. The government had secret reserves of 15,000 to 20,000 milliers of rice, which one leader estimated could feed 800,000 people for four or five days.[40] But obtaining more grain for the capital was very difficult. The countryside was in disarray; bandits controlled many roads, river routes were disrupted, and peasants were refusing to take their grain to market. Circumstances were particularly bad in the Seine Valley, between Le Havre and Rouen, a crucial artery for the capital. Many of the smaller Norman towns along the route insisted on adding a surcharge on grain destined for Paris. More important, grain dealers were under pressure from local townspeople to break their contracts with Parisian authorities and keep their grain for the local community.[41]

The electors responded quickly by insisting upon the free circulation of grain. On 16 July they gave Bonneville the awesome responsibility for obtaining grain in Vernon, Mantes, and Meulan, three towns on the Seine between Rouen and Paris. He left immediately and by 20 July had convinced grain dealers to abide by their previously arranged contracts. By that date the electors had established a "Subsistence Committee," whose sole purpose was to oversee food provisions; Garran-Coulon became its president. On 20 July this committee sent instructions for Bonneville to proceed to Rouen and Le Havre to secure the purchase of 55,900 sacks of wheat, barley, and rye, which had previously been committed for the capital. This mission was also a success, and even the electors of Rouen publicly thanked Bonneville for doing such a good job. Finally, on the 29th, the Subsistence Committee sent Bonneville a group of National Guardsmen to help him to organize convoys of grain shipments to Paris. Thus Bonneville was instrumental in restoring order

[39] Jacques Godard, *Exposé des travaux de l'Assemblée générale des Représentants de la Commune de Paris, depuis le 25 juillet 1789 jusqu'au mois d'octobre 1790*, p. 23.

[40] Bailly, *Mémoires* 2: 357.

[41] Bourne, "Improvising," p. 307.

to the grain trade in the Seine valley and helping to alleviate the severe food shortage in Paris.[42]

The electors next had to reestablish law and order in the city. But this problem, compounded by the other tasks facing the electors, proved too great for the Permanent Committee. On 18 July the electors decided to reorganize the Permanent Committee into four separate and independent committees, charged directly with reestablishing law and order.[43]

Claude Fauchet became the first president of the Police Committee and its most important member. The Committee worked tirelessly for four months and, in the words of one contemporary, "rendered to the capital and to France inestimable services."[44] Fauchet himself described the Committee's activities as "the justice of savage peoples, exercised by enlightened men, who were not allowed a moment's rest and of whom would not have been pardoned the slightest uncertainty or the least delay."[45]

The Police Committee performed a variety of tasks, including controlling the influx of people that daily poured into the city, regulating the price and distribution of bread, and prohibiting gambling in the center of town. In August, after many children had been accidentally wounded or had even killed themselves, the Committee even posted placards around the city, warning parents of the danger of allowing their children to play Bastille games with their fathers' weapons.[46] But the most interesting and controversial policies initiated by the Committee concerned publishing.

Fauchet and the members of the Police Committee clearly believed in freedom of the press. But they also recognized that

[42] *Procès-verbal des . . . Electeurs* 2: 8, 12, 13, 244, 245, 419-22; Godard, *Exposé*, pp. 10, 95-100; *RdP*, 2 August 1789, pp. 18-19; Nicolas Bonneville, *Lettre de Député de la Ville de Paris à MM. les volontiers-patriotes de la Commune de Rouen* (Rouen: Ferrand, 1789).

[43] *Pf*, 10 August 1789, p. 4. On the disorders see *Pf*, 3 September 1789, p. 3; *RdP*, 16 August 1789, p. 5; *Journal de Paris*, 19 July 1789, pp. 900-901; Bailly, *Mémoires* 2: 343-44; Godard, *Exposé*, pp. 18, 77.

[44] *Journal des amis de la constitution*, 8 May 1791, pp. 81-82.

[45] Godard, *Exposé*, pp. 12-15. See also Dorimon, "L'Abbé Claude Fauchet, membre de la Commune de Paris," *Revue de la Révolution* 10: 161.

[46] *Cdp*, 24 August 1789, p. 4; Archives de la Seine, 3 AZ 250 and 4 AZ 931 and 932.

journalists and authors had great influence over Parisian readers and were concerned that irresponsible authors would incite the people to further violence. Therefore, in late July the Committee ruled that every publication had to carry the name of its publisher, and that if an author could not be identified, the publisher would be held accountable for the contents of the work.[47] The Committee executed this rule in a relatively responsible fashion. For example, in September it ordered the arrest of one Jeudy de l'Houmand, who had printed pamphlets attacking the government for mismanaging food provisions. He accused officials of corruption and claimed that a policy supporting total freedom of circulation would only plunge the people into profound misery. These charges undercut the effectiveness of the Subsistence Committee, which clearly was working diligently.[48]

Most journalists respected the Police Committee's wishes, and nowhere do we find criticism of arrests of men like Jeudy de l'Houmand.[49] But at least one radical journalist, Louis-Marie Prudhomme, believed that Fauchet was subverting the freedom of the press. "The provisional Police Committee," he wrote in his *Révolutions de Paris*, "has inflicted on the publisher an ordinance more annoying than all the absurd regulations of the inquisitional police which existed before the Revolution. . . . This ordinance is unjust, oppressive, and contrary to the first principles of law."[50] Prudhomme believed that the ordinance was unjust for three reasons: first, it restricted the people's legitimate right to information; second, it limited the author's right to circulate his ideas freely; and finally, and most important, it gave publishers too much control over authors. "Can we ignore the fact that there exists a pact between bookstores and publishers against men of letters?" Prudhomme asked. Bookstores and

[47] *Rdp*, 2 August 1789, pp. 9-10; Bailly, *Mémoires* 2: 209-10.

[48] Sigismond Lacroix, ed., *Actes de la Commune de Paris pendant la Révolution. 1st series, 25 juillet à 8 octobre 1790* 2: 70; Jeudy de L'Houmand, *Le Pain à bon marché, ou Le Monopole terrassé et le peuple vengé* (Paris: Laurens and Cressdonnier, n.d.); *Les Monopoleurs terrassés ou Le Danger éminent de faire manger au peuple de mauvais pain* (Paris: Laurens, n.d.).

[49] *Courrier de Versailles à Paris*, 26 July 1789, p. 1; *Journal d'Etat et du citoyen*, 20 August 1789, p. 32.

[50] *RdP*, 2 August 1789, pp. 9-10.

publishers would take advantage of the situation and force writers "to pay the very expensive printing costs, or to share their profits with the bookstores."[51] In a subsequent issue, Prudhomme attacked Fauchet personally. After criticizing one of Fauchet's speeches, he said that "it was only because M. l'abbé Fauchet is president of the Police Committee that we have severely criticized his speech."[52] The Police Committee was willing to tolerate these criticisms up to a point, but when they became personal attacks upon Fauchet, the Committee members threatened to suspend the paper and ordered its editor to appear before it. But the Police Committee asked only for a public retraction; and once this was agreed to, the Committee approved the continued publication of the *Révolutions de Paris*.[53]

The third great task that lay before the Assembly of Electors in July and August 1789 was the establishment of an acceptable communal government. Already on 15 July the electors had asked Jean-Sylvain Bailly to become mayor of Paris, a position he held through the summer of 1791. Bailly is another example of an intellectual turned revolutionary. Before the Revolution he had established an international reputation as an astronomer. During the 1780s he became Condorcet's main rival for leadership of the Paris Academy of Sciences and belonged to a somewhat conservative faction within the academic community. Thus, while Bailly fully supported the great events of June and July 1789, he was not what might be called a man of the people. In many ways, he had far more in common with the privileged classes who were to become the victims of the Revolution.[54]

Bailly held strongly antidemocratic views concerning the formation of a municipal government. He wanted a centralized administration, in which the mayor possessed executive control as well as legislative initiative. He particularly distrusted the Assembly of Electors, whom he regarded as usurpers of municipal power. Nobody had authorized the electors to take over

[51] Ibid., p. 42. Prudhomme may have been speaking for the Cordelier district. See Lacroix, *Actes* 1: 355.
[52] *RdP*, 5 September 1789, p. 16.
[53] Ibid., 27 October 1789, pp. 4, 13-14, 34.
[54] Gene A. Brucker, *Jean-Sylvain Bailly: Revolutionary Mayor of Paris*.

municipal affairs, he reasoned; and while they had been useful in leading Paris through the crisis of 14 July, a reorganization was long overdue.[55] This view was also supported by the districts, many of which believed that the electors were intentionally reducing the districts' powers. Thus when Bailly proposed a committee of 180 (three men from each district) to write a new municipal constitution, the districts welcomed the idea.[56]

On 25 July the Committee of 180 was constituted and four days later replaced the Assembly of Electors as the new municipal legislature, calling itself the Provisional Communal Assembly. Immediately it appointed a commission to write a municipal constitution. Bailly had hoped that the Communal Assembly would follow his leadership. But he clearly underestimated the influence of the democratic leaders who had played such an important role in the Municipal Revolution. The Communal Assembly ignored the mayor, and the constitutional commission would have nothing to do with him.

Instead, the constitutional commission came under the influence of Jacques-Pierre Brissot, who was largely responsible for writing the commission's Plan de municipalité. Before the Revolution, Brissot had published several books on a variety of topics, including one complimentary work on the United States. Like Bonneville, he had tried hard to make a career as a writer, but had not been very successful. On the eve of the Revolution, he had to pick up odd jobs, including spying for the police. By 1789 he had developed strong democratic views, and was good friends with several radical electors, including Garran-Coulon and Bancal, with whom he often dined.[57]

The Plan de municipalité proposed dividing the government

[55] Ibid., pp. 29-38.

[56] On these events see Lacroix, *Actes* 2; Georges Garrigues, *Les Districts parisiens pendant la Révolution française*; Dale Clifford and Jane Decker, "July to September: The Critical Months of the Parisian Municipal Revolution"; "District Sovereignty and the Parisian Soldat-Citoyen, 1790: The Struggle Over Permanence" (abstract), *The Consortium on Revolutionary Europe: Proceedings*, pp. 229-32.

[57] Eloise Ellery, *Brissot de Warville: A Study in the History of the French Revolution*; Robert Darnton, *The Literary Underground of the Old Regime*, pp. 1-41.

into three branches. The first was the Communal Assembly, composed of three hundred representatives, five chosen from each of the sixty districts. The second branch was the Town Council, which formed the "executive branch of the municipality." It included sixty members chosen from the Communal Assembly. Finally, the mayor, the commander of the National Guard, and eighteen assistants formed the third branch, the Town Bureau. These three branches were ultimately responsible to the sixty districts, who also formed assemblies of their own.[58]

The importance of this plan is that it skillfully embodied the principles of representative democracy developed by Bonneville and Fauchet during June and July. On the one hand, it recognized the sixty districts as the possessors of popular sovereignty. District voters included all males who had reached age twenty-five and who paid direct taxes of any amount. These voters met in assemblies, which had the right to meet any time and to debate freely any concerns, and had the responsibility of sending five representatives to the Communal Assembly. "All power," Brissot wrote, "derives from the people; all power must be delegated, entrusted by it. ... It is above all by the creation of the sixty district assemblies that one preserves the rights of the people."[59]

But the Plan de municipalité also renounced direct democracy in favor of representative democracy by granting all real power to the Communal Assembly. First, while Brissot acknowledged the right of district assemblies to meet whenever they wished, he believed that, if the Communal Assembly acted correctly, district assemblies would exercise this right only during elections. Second, while Brissot allowed districts to supervise and comment upon the sessions and policies of the Communal Assembly, the plan explicitly denied a district the important right to recall its representative if it disapproved of his activities. "Every representative belongs to the entire commune; no one can be recalled

[58] *Projet du Plan de municipalité de la ville de Paris ... Présenté à l'Assemblée générale des Représentants de la Commune, par ses commissaires, le 12 août 1789* (Paris: Lottin, 1789).
[59] Jacques-Pierre Brissot, *Motifs des commissaires ...* , pp. 9-10.

by the district assemblies."⁶⁰ This, in effect, prevented districts from exercising any control over their representatives, and thus gave real authority to the Communal Assembly, except during elections. Brissot was more candid in his newspaper, *Patriote français*: ". . . it is necessary to give the districts of this city a subordinate role in the administration and in the police."⁶¹ Third, having Town Council members elected by the Communal Assembly instead of by the districts further restricted the power of the districts. Finally, although Brissot conceded that the districts would have the right to ratify the constitution, once it had been ratified, the Plan gave the Communal Assembly the right to make constitutional amendments without the approval of the districts.

But the real loser in this scheme was the mayor, whose powers were severely restricted. The Plan gave the Communal Assembly complete control over legislation—the mayor's approval was never needed. More significantly, the mayor's control over the executive branch of government was limited by the Town Council, which supervised his activities. Since Town Council members were also representatives to the Communal Assembly, and chosen by that body, the intention of the plan was clear: Brissot hoped the Communal Assembly would gain enough power to control the executive branch. In the Plan de municipalité, the mayor was little more than a ceremonial figure.

The Plan de municipalité thus marked the culmination of a two-month struggle by a group of radical electors to carry through a municipal revolution according to the principles of representative democracy. Included in this group were Bonneville, Fauchet, Bancal, Garran-Coulon, Brissot, and several other lesser-known municipal politicians. Five months later, when it looked as if their political schemes were in danger, this same group established the Cercle Social. But in mid-August 1789 this danger did not yet exist. When the Plan de municipalité was presented to the Provisional Communal Assembly on 12 August, Brissot

⁶⁰ *Projet du Plan de municipalité*, p. 8.
⁶¹ *Pf*, 15 August 1789, p. 6.

predicted that the Assembly would approve it without major changes.[62] But before the Assembly could act, the Plan was undermined by both Mayor Bailly and the districts, each of whom had completely different visions of how municipal government should operate.

[62] Ibid., 23 August 1789, p. 3, 24 August 1789, p. 4.

2

The Fauchetins:
Advocates of Representative
Democracy

CLAUDE FAUCHET (1744-1793). Elected to the Paris Communal Assembly, Legislative Assembly, and Convention; Constitutional Bishop of Calvados; Procureur-général of the Confédération des Amis de la Vérité. Brilliant and charismatic speaker, Fauchet's speeches and writings, most notably his commentaries on Rousseau's *Social Contract*, personified the revolutionary clergy's hope for ecclesiastical and political reform during the Revolution's early years. His association with the Girondins cost him his life in 1793.
Courtesy of The Newberry Library, Chicago

During the early period of a revolution mistakes are likely enough to be committed—mistakes in principle or in practice; or perhaps, mistakes both in principle and practice. When men are in the early stage of freedom, they are not all sufficiently instructed to be able to inform one another mutually of their several opinions and so they become the victims of a sort of timidity that hinders them from reaching at a single bound that elevation which they have the *right* to attain. We have witnessed symptoms of this imperfection at the beginning of the present revolution.

Tom Paine, *Complete Writings*, ed. Phillip Foner, 2 vols. (New York: Citadel, 1945), 2:1317.

M OST HISTORIANS agree that between the summers of 1789 and 1790 the French Revolution went through a period of relatively quiet and constructive reorganization. This may have been true at the national level, but the opposite was the case for Parisian politics. During that year, a three-way struggle over the nature of the new municipal government seriously retarded the development of Parisian political institutions. The fundamental issue in this struggle was the degree to which popular sovereignty could be incorporated into a new municipal constitution. Each faction had a different view of just how democratic Paris could become. First, Mayor Bailly rejected democracy altogether, hoping to establish a municipality in which the mayor and a few assistants ruled for the people, but certainly not on specific instructions from the people. Directly opposing this concept of government were many district leaders, who wanted a system of direct democracy in which sovereignty would be held and exercised by the people in the sixty district assemblies. In their view, the Communal Assembly was no more than an association of delegates, each of whom was personally accountable to his district. Between these two groups stood a group of militant members of the Communal Assembly, who believed that only representative democracy, with considerable weight given to a central assembly, could avoid what in their view were the anarchistic tendencies of direct democracy, as well as the tyrannical notions of Mayor Bailly. The origins of the Cercle Social stem directly from this third group.

By mid-August 1789 the Communal Assembly was on the verge of passing a municipal constitution—Brissot's Plan de municipalité—which would have taken a great deal of power away from the mayor and the districts. Naturally Mayor Bailly opposed this plan and was determined to quash it. He realized, of course, that he had no influence with the Assembly; if the Plan was to be defeated, he would have to make a bold appeal directly to the districts.[1]

On 30 August Bailly sent to the sixty districts a letter calling on each district to elect five deputies to a new municipal body that would develop a better municipal constitution.[2] Bailly claimed that the Communal Assembly's Plan was not realistic, because three hundred deputies could never effectively govern a city. He argued that the Plan, if passed, would lead to anarchy. In contrast to the ideology of representative democracy, Bailly likened a well-ordered municipal government to a constitutional monarchy. "The powers in the city of Paris," he wrote, "are of the same nature as in the Kingdom. There is a legislative power and an executive power."[3] Naturally this meant that the mayor, like the king, needed to have complete control of the executive branch. "Executive power will reside in the municipal administration. ... It is essential that executive authority always be ready for action; nothing must ever stop it or obstruct its way from being the least divided and the most centralized that is possible."[4] As for legislative authority, if one kept to the analogy of a constitutional monarchy, a Communal Assembly, albeit restricted, would fit the bill. But Bailly shrewdly ignored the Assembly, insisting that legislative authority come directly from the districts. "It is to you," he wrote to the districts, that the responsibility "belongs to make the particular Laws and Reg-

[1] Jean-Sylvain Bailly, *Mémoires de Bailly*, 2: 258-63, 3: 316-25.

[2] Jean-Sylvain Bailly, *Lettre ... à Messieurs des districts*, dated 30 August 1789; Jacques Godard, *Exposé des travaux de l'Assemblée générale des Représentants de la Commune de Paris, depuis le 25 juillet 1789 jusqu'au mois d'octobre 1790*, pp. 29-31.

[3] Ibid., p.5.

[4] Ibid.

ulations for this city; it is for you to revise them and to supervise their execution."[5]

This letter was nothing other than a cleverly worded attempt to undermine the powers of the Communal Assembly. What Bailly wanted was a governmental system that allowed him to run the administration as he wished, without a strong central body to "obstruct his way."[6] The letter makes it appear that Bailly supported the democratic right of the districts to run their own affairs, but that was actually far from true. Bailly was well aware that many of the districts were also hostile toward the Assembly's Plan, and he sought to use the districts to ruin the Assembly. He believed that sixty independent districts would be easier to dominate than a central assembly.[7]

Bailly admitted that 30 August "was the beginning of an endless war between the Representatives of the Commune and myself."[8] The letter to the districts caught the Communal Assembly completely by surprise, and its members responded with complaints and denunciations. Brissot charged that the letter was "illegal." "The mayor," he wrote in his newspaper, "has neither the right to address nor to convoke the districts without the participation of the [Communal] Assembly." Brissot claimed that adherence to this letter could mean the eventual collapse of the Municipal Revolution itself; the 30 August letter, he charged, "contains a system which fundamentally violates all the principles of liberty, since it tries to concentrate all authority in the hands of a few individuals who would be dependent upon one man."[9] But the Communal Assembly was caught in a bind. It could not instruct the districts to ignore Bailly's letter, for this would appear as a violation of the districts' own right to assemble. Therefore the Assembly merely asked the districts to proceed with the new elections called for by Bailly, and explicitly to charge its new deputies with overseeing the executive branch.[10]

[5] Ibid.
[6] Ibid.
[7] Brucker, *Jean-Sylvain Bailly, Revolutionary Mayor of Paris*, pp. 29-30.
[8] Bailly, *Mémoires* 2: 317.
[9] *Pf*, 1 September 1789, p. 2.
[10] The best source for the Communal Assembly's activities is Lacroix, ed., *Actes de la Commune de Paris*, 1st series.

Bailly's letter was successful insofar as it effectively squashed Brissot's Plan and led to the establishment of yet a new Communal Assembly, which met from September 1789 to October 1790, and which now had the purpose of framing a municipal constitution. But if the results of the elections are any indication, Bailly's attempted "coup d'état" was a failure.[11] Most of the new deputies had been members of either the Assembly of Electors or of the first Communal Assembly, and virtually all of the democratic leaders, including Bonneville, Fauchet, Garran-Coulon, and Brissot, were reelected.[12] More important, this group became more aggressive in its attacks upon the mayor. For example, on 5 October, less than three weeks after the new Communal Assembly had convened, its representatives accused Bailly of trying to establish a dictatorship. The Assembly "lodges a complaint against M. the Mayor of Paris ... for usurping legitimate authority from the General [Communal] Assembly, and for not giving the Law its proper honor."[13]

There is strong evidence that Bonneville, Fauchet, and the other democratic deputies became the leaders of the new Communal Assembly during its first few months. One source of this evidence is the lists of representatives elected to important delegations. On 6 October, Bonneville and Fauchet were included in a group of representatives that welcomed the king (who had been forced to establish residence in Paris during the October Days).[14] On 9 October, Brissot, Garran, and Condorcet were designated to collaborate on an address welcoming the National Assembly to Paris. Brissot delivered this address to the National Assembly the next day, and he, Garran, and Condorcet edited other similar addresses.[15]

Condorcet's inclusion in this democratic group is worth noting. His political behavior between 1789 and 1790 was inconsistent because he tried to maintain good relations with demo-

[11] The term belongs to H. E. Bourne, "Municipal Politics in Paris in 1789" *American Historical Review* 11: 275.

[12] Lacroix, *Actes* 2: 677-92. Henri Bancal was an important exception. He was not reelected, and he returned to Clermont-Ferrand, his hometown.

[13] Cited in Godard, *Exposé*, p. 218.

[14] Lacroix, *Actes* 2: 189.

[15] Ibid. 2: 202, 229, 245-47, 254-60, 295.

crats as well as with more conservative politicians, such as Sieyès and Lafayette.[16] While he served in the Communal Assembly, however, Condorcet was attached to the democratic group. He and Fauchet led the important Committee of 24, which developed a plan for a permanent municipal constitution along the lines of Brissot's earlier Plan.[17] On 2 November 1789, Condorcet had the honor of being elected the first president of the Communal Assembly.[18] His election raised the hopes of his colleagues, as is made clear in a letter written by Brissot to Henri Bancal on 11 November 1789:

We have not yet drafted a municipal plan. But it won't be much longer. Condorcet is our president. The [Communal] Assembly is more badly composed than the 180: gossips and ignoramuses. . . . However, I believe that we will succeed. The important thing is to finish with this Assembly and to have a constitutional one. The democratic party will always dominate it.[19]

Brissot and Garran also held important positions in the new government as the most active members of the powerful Investigations Committee, created in October. Ostensibly formed to investigate "the makers of a conspiracy planned last July against the National Assembly and against the city of Paris," the committee quickly broadened its authority and examined a variety of scandals. For example, in November the Investigations Committee was responsible for the arrest of a group of bandits who had robbed women during the October Days; in February it investigated a group of financiers who had allegedly embezzled from the government.[20]

[16] Léon Cahen, *Condorcet et la Révolution française*; Keith Michael Baker, *Condorcet: From Natural Philosophy to Social Mathematics*, Chapter 5.

[17] The minutes of the Committee of 24 (Archives de la Seine, D12) show that on 4 December Condorcet was elected its president and Fauchet its secretary. It then met almost every day in December 1789 and irregularly between January and 25 May 1790.

[18] Lacroix, *Actes* 2: 529. Although the mayor was theoretically head of the Assembly, in fact every fourteen days it elected a president who presided over the sessions.

[19] Brissot, *Correspondance et papiers*, p. 241.

[20] *Journal de Paris*, 1 December 1789, pp. 1560-61; see also *Mercure National*, 7 March 1790, pp. 664-72; *RdP*, 5 December 1789, pp. 7-9; *CdP*, 27 October 1789, p. 259; Lacroix, *Actes* 2: 369; Godard, *Exposé*, p. 93.

But despite the activities of Brissot, Garran-Coulon, Bonne-ville, and Condorcet, the most important figure in the group was Claude Fauchet. Within the Communal Assembly, he did more to influence specific policies and develop a cohesive political group than any other member. Fauchet's dominance over the affairs of the Communal Assembly is symbolized by the fact that he was the only member of the Assembly to be elected president four times. It is for this reason that the term *Fauchetins* is appropriate for this group of democratic politicians, the group that would later form the core of the Cercle Social.

Considering the controversy surrounding political divisions during the Revolution, one must be very cautious in devising new names for groups. No one at the time used the term Fauche-tins. Indeed, these men were neither a political party nor even a very well-organized political faction. They were a loosely struc-tured group of friends and acquaintances who did not think of themselves as much more than a coterie of individual municipal representatives. Likewise, Claude Fauchet was no leader in any formal sense, but merely the most outspoken and well-known member. Nevertheless, this group of friends was involved to-gether in several political projects, including organizing festivals and publishing journals and pamphlets. More important, they shared a strong belief in the efficacy of representative democracy, an ideology in conflict with their more conservative counterparts in the Communal and National Assemblies, and with their more radical counterparts in the districts.

FAUCHET's reputation as a speaker outside the Communal Assembly propelled him to prominence in this group. During the summer and fall of 1789, Parisians often came together to celebrate masses that were meant to be both religious and patriotic. For example, on 5 August a lavish service was held at the Cathedral of Notre Dame to commemorate those who had died storming the Bas-tille. Fauchet was asked to give the eulogy.[21] In what became his standard rhetorical device, Fauchet wove the Revolution and Christianity so tightly together that they appeared to be part of a larger universal system. The martyrs of the Bastille had not

---

[21] *Journal de Paris*, 4 August 1789, p. 973.

died in vain, he averred. They had destroyed the old nobility, which had been not merely politically offensive but also anti-Christian: "It is the aristocracy who crucified the Son of God." By its heroic efforts "France will be the model of nations and the teacher of true liberty throughout the universe."[22] The press praised the sermon, which was published in English as well as in French.[23] Even Mayor Bailly conceded that the speech "was a very great success; he moved all his listeners. . . . What a man! What things he might have made of himself if he had not used his eloquence merely as a tool for his own ambition!"[24]

In July and August Fauchet repeated these themes at commemorative services sponsored by various districts. Wherever he went his message was the same: the French Revolution is based on principles derived from the gospels; anyone calling himself a good Christian ought to become a patriot. And wherever he went the press followed him. "We are pleasantly surprised to find in this discourse," the *Chronique de Paris* wrote of one sermon, "texts which have been for so long interpreted only by aristocratic priests in a manner favorable to despotism, reinterpreted under the pen of M. l'abbé Fauchet in their true meaning and militating for natural liberty and equality."[25] Even Prudhomme, who had been critical of Fauchet for his activities on the Police Committee, admitted that

never since the establishment of the feudal regime has as good a subject been presented so eloquently by any French orator. ... M. l'abbé Fauchet was so good at keeping the attention of his listeners; their hearts and souls were so satisfied that, seized by a religious and patriotic enthusiasm, the residents of the district awarded him a civic wreath.[26]

In August and September each district organized its own unit of the National Guard and held a ceremony of induction. These services usually included sermons, often by lesser-known priests,

[22] Fauchet, *Discours sur la liberté française*, pp. 8, 15.
[23] For example, *CdP*, 24 August 1789, pp. 1-2, and 4 September 1789, p. 47; Claude Fauchet, *A Discourse on The Liberty of France*.
[24] Bailly, *Mémoires* 2: 222.
[25] *CdP*, 21 September 1789, p. 113; see also 7 September 1789, p. 58, 1 October 1789, pp. 155-56; *Journal d'État et du citoyen*, 27 August 1789, pp. 40-43, 3 September 1789, pp. 65-66; *Pf*, 30 September 1789, p. 2; *Courrier de Lyon*, 27 September 1789, pp. 199-200, 7 October 1789, pp. 267-68.
[26] *RdP*, 2 August 1789, p. 19.

who, under the influence of Fauchet's ideas and reputation, imitated his efforts.[27] On 27 September these activities culminated in a mass at Notre Dame, given by the municipal government for the entire Paris National Guard. Fauchet thought the ceremony so significant that he specifically asked the Communal Assembly for the proper way to address his sermon in the new epoch. (It was decided that "Mr. Mayor, Sirs . . ." would be acceptable.) Among those attending the ceremony were the most prominent citizens of Paris: Mayor Bailly, Commander Lafayette, leaders of the Communal Assembly and the districts, and even a few deputies from the National Assembly. When Fauchet entered the church, people hushed one another and fell silent in anticipation of the sermon. It was another mixture of theology and politics. Leaders of the Revolution were praised, symbols of the aristocracy were attacked, and the congregation was urged to live their lives loyal to their nation and faith. "This discourse," one observer noted, "simultaneously sublime and pathetic, produced the most lively sensations. We forgot where we were as we became totally engaged in what the orator was saying. He was interrupted many times by applause, which demonstrated the effect of the principles which he had the courage to develop."[28]

Thus by the end of the summer Fauchet had become the most popular priest of revolutionary Paris. He had become a favorite of the press, and had attracted a small corps of followers among lesser-known Parisian priests.[29] While many Fauchetins had anticlerical instincts, they nevertheless shared Fauchet's ideas. On 15 October, for example, the Communal Assembly passed a resolution written by Brissot and Condorcet, which amounted to an endorsement of the activities of Fauchet and his followers:

[27] Marcel Reinhard, "Les Drapeaux de la Garde Nationale parisienne," *Mélanges offerts à Victor L. Tapié*; Lacroix, *Actes* 2: 94-96.

[28] Lacroix, *Actes* 3: 89-91; Fauchet, *Troisième discours sur la liberté française*.

[29] Reinhard, *Nouvelle histoire de Paris*, p. 192. For examples of some followers see Richard Chaix, *De l'influence de la religion sur le patriotisme*; Louis Claude de Cressy, *Essai sur les moeurs, ou Point de Constitution durable sans moeurs*; and especially François-Valentin Mulot, *Discours sur le serment civique*. Mulot was an important member of the Communal Assembly and a staunch supporter of Fauchet's views. See also *Courrier de Lyon*, 7 January 1790, pp. 42-43.

Citizens, respect the ministers of your holy religion. In insulting one you insult them all. And what is a people without religion? Abandoned to vice, to crime, without any moral grounding, it soon loses its liberty; because for peoples, there can be no liberty without morality and no morality without religion.

This decree was sent to all Parisian parish priests for them to read from the pulpit.[30]

In October, Fauchet tried to exploit his popularity by waging a campaign to create an official chaplaincy of the municipality, nominating himself for the position. The Police Committee was the first to make the suggestion, citing his sermons and his participation in the taking of the Bastille. He was supported by his own district of Saint-Roch, who proposed that the chaplain would direct "all religious ceremonies relative to the Commune and officiate in the absence of Monsieur the archbishop of Paris ... in everything related to religion, instruction, and general habits."[31] The job would have involved no new major activities for Fauchet, so what he was presumably seeking was the prestige of the title. But the idea raised many objections in the districts and even within the Communal Assembly. While municipal leaders appreciated Fauchet's role in the Revolution, they believed that the creation of an official chaplaincy would not give the municipality any more authority over the Church, but might allow the Church to influence civil affairs. Therefore, the Communal Assembly diplomatically thanked Fauchet for his services to the city, but insisted that such a post was not necessary.[32] Clearly, Fauchet had acquired a great deal of power, but it was by no means unlimited.

THE GREATEST challenge to the Fauchetins came not from the mayor, but from the districts. Ever since the storming of the Bastille, some districts had distrusted the very idea of a municipal legislative body. They resented the way that the Assembly of Electors had simply assumed control of the city without their ap-

[30] Lacroix, *Actes* 2: 309-10; *Pf*, 28 July 1789, p. 4, 19 October 1789, pp. 1-2.
[31] Archives de la Seine, VD D623, 'Extrait du registre des délibérations de l'Assemblée générale de Saint-Roch du 2 octobre 1789."
[32] Lacroix, *Actes* 2: 132-38; Bailly, *Mémoires* 2: 402-403.

proval; some even suggested that the establishment of the Permanent Committee had been illegal. These feelings continued into August, and were a major reason that Bailly was able to sack the first Communal Assembly. Nor did the hostility subside when the second Communal Assembly began to meet in September. Indeed, within two months, several districts launched a major offensive aimed at dismantling the Communal Assembly. As Bailly observed in his memoirs, "the majority of the districts are in open war with the municipality."[33]

This "war" was led by the Cordelier district, an area located on the Left Bank, between the Sorbonne and the Jardin de Luxembourg. It was essentially a working-class neighborhood, but was also a center for print shops and bookstores, where writers often gathered. The Cordeliers became the most militant district in Paris for essentially two reasons: first, district politics were controlled by a group of very astute politicians, including Georges Danton, who established an effective "political machine"; and second, a band of radical journalists lived and worked in the district, and spread the Cordeliers' ideas and policies throughout Paris and the nation.[34]

The Cordeliers wanted to establish a democratic form of government in which the idea of popular sovereignty was carried to its logical conclusion: all power would be held and exercised by all the people. This view was perhaps best expressed in Louis-Marie Prudhomme's newspaper, *Révolutions de Paris*, especially in the issues for September and October, coinciding with the early sessions of the second Communal Assembly. Prudhomme stated that all political authority was vested in the sixty districts, which had established the Communal Assembly only to write a municipal constitution (subject to district approval) and to

---

[33] Bailly, *Mémoires* 3: 297. See also Bourne, "Municipal Politics"; J. A. Dulaure, *Histoire physique, civile, et morale de Paris* 4: 70; Garrigues, *Les Districts parisiens pendant la Révolution française*; Clifford and Decker, "July to September: The Critical Months of the Parisian Municipal Revolution." I owe much to these last two scholars who are preparing a book on the districts during the municipal revolution. Of particular importance is also R. B. Rose, *The Making of the Sans-Culottes*, which unfortunately appeared too late for me to take advantage of it.

[34] Norman Hampson, *Danton*, pp. 26-38; Jack Richard Censer, *Prelude to Power: The Parisian Radical Press 1789-1791*.

execute existing laws and ordinances. Outside of these two specific functions, the Communal Assembly could act only when instructed by the districts. All laws and policies had to come from the district assemblies. "It is therefore to the districts, to the primary assemblies ... that the right to make regulations and to consent to laws belongs."[35] In his view, the Communal Assembly was not really a legislature, but rather a kind of federative association of district leaders.

It is the title of Representatives of the Commune which causes the misunderstanding ... it seems to us that in this sense the word as stated is improper, and that they have cruelly stretched the meaning of words; henceforth, we believe no other word could serve us better than *administrator*.[36]

A "representative" was one who was capable of independent reflection and judgment. But Prudhomme thought the members of the Communal Assembly were more like delegates or administrators, who simply carried out the wishes of their constituents. Since these constituents never gave up any authority, an "administrator" could be revoked by a district as it pleased. In Prudhomme's view, a municipal system based upon representatives (such as envisioned in Brissot's Plan) could only result in a "municipal aristocracy." Prudhomme realized that the principles of representative democracy were appropriate at the national level, but he insisted that direct democracy was both practical and necessary for municipalities.

Our Representatives are absolutely not, as in England, the sovereigns of the nation; it is the nation itself that is sovereign. ... But why are laws made at the national level by representatives? Because it is impossible, or people think it's impossible, to collect individual votes of all Frenchmen in one place, in order to establish the general will, which is law. But what is impossible, or at least very difficult, for the kingdom, is very easy for a city.[37]

Already in September the Cordeliers saw that the second Communal Assembly would be no different in its ambitions from the first. "We rapidly passed from slavery to liberty,"

[35] *RdP*, 24 October 1789, p. 5.
[36] *RdP*, 15 November 1789, pp. 21-23.
[37] *RdP*, 19 September 1789, pp. 14, 32.

Prudhomme exclaimed. "We now are marching even more rapidly from liberty to slavery."[38] By November the Cordeliers had become so disgusted with the government that they organized a direct confrontation. The alarm was sounded by Jean-Paul Marat, who denounced the Communal Assembly "for having usurped a sort of arbitrary authority that will soon pull down the Paris municipality into a pure aristocracy, and that will ultimately transform the deputies of the people into cruel tyrants."[39]

On 11 and 12 November, the Cordelier district passed a decree ordering its five deputies in the Communal Assembly to take an oath that embodied their radical ideas. The oath required each deputy to swear by three points: (1) never to violate the rights of constituents; (2) always to conform to the explicit instructions of the district and never to pass anything without its knowledge or approval; and (3) to recognize the right of the district to recall him.[40]

The Communal Assembly reacted swiftly to this attack upon its authority. Under Condorcet's presidency, it passed a decree "nullifying" the Cordeliers' oath and responding with three points of its own: (1) the oath "injures" the rights of the Communal Assembly members; (2) all representatives of the Commune belong to the entire commune and not to any one district; and (3) any municipal system that recognized the power of the district to revoke its representatives was doomed to "anarchy."[41]

The Cordeliers and their journalists in turn denounced this decree, and the crisis deepened as other districts began choosing sides.[42] Meanwhile, many of the radical districts had formed a "Central Committee," composed of district leaders, which

[38] *RdP*, 27 August 1789, p. 1.
[39] *Ami du peuple*, 9 November 1789, p. 40.
[40] "Extrait du registre des délibérations de l'Assemblée générale du district des Cordeliers, des 11 et 12 novembre 1789," reprinted in Lacroix, *Actes* 3: 638-39.
[41] Lacroix, *Actes* 3: 639-41.
[42] *Ami du peuple*, 21 November 1789, p. 202, 23 November 1789, pp. 215-18; *RFB*, 28 November 1789, pp. 10-13; Lacroix, *Actes* 3: 5-11, 27, 33, 670-75. Brissot called the Cordelier proposal "dangerous" in *Pf*, 24 November 1789, p. 3.

threatened to replace the Communal Assembly altogether. Jacques Godard expressed the feelings of all the Fauchetins in declaring the Central Committee "illegal."[43]

On 20 November, in a speech to the Communal Assembly, Fauchet tried to reconcile the differences between the two groups. Fauchet argued that he and his followers were every bit as democratic as the Cordelier district. "All power comes from the People!" he shouted. "All executors of power are accountable to the People. The People are everything."[44] He went on to argue that the Communal Assembly had nothing to fear from the districts; "they are the real thing, and we are only their representation; power belongs to them, and we only exercise it for them. . . . Resistance to [district sovereignty] is a crime."[45]

Because of its radical rhetoric, this speech is easy to misinterpret as an endorsement of the Cordeliers' position, as the *Chronique de Paris* and later historians have done.[46] But Fauchet was merely reiterating the same belief in representative democracy found in Brissot's *Plan de municipalité* and other Fauchetin writings. The Fauchetins had always believed that the districts had the right to sanction all municipal laws. But the fundamental difference between representative democracy and direct democracy is not who finally *approves* laws, but rather who actually *makes* them. As Prudhomme put it, "It is absurd for a delegate to make a law for his constituent. The people assembled together therefore have the right to revoke their representatives, and to revise, adopt, reject, or correct their work. . . . The right to make regulations . . . belongs only to the districts."[47] Fauchet had a different view of this fundamental point:

A great people cannot exercise legislative power by itself . . . it sends deputies to a central assembly. These deputies, furnished with instructions, compare all of the wishes of the districts, modify them in their

[43] Lacroix, *Actes* 2: 533-34, 541; Godard, *Exposé*, pp. 105-108, 160.

[44] Fauchet, *Motion faite à l'Assemblée générale des Représentants de la Commune, le 20 novembre 1789*, pp. 2-4.

[45] Ibid., p. 6.

[46] *CdP*, 25 November 1789, p. 373; Bourne, "Municipal Politics," p. 281; Rose, *Making of the Sans-Culottes*, p. 127.

[47] *RdP*, 19 September 1789, p. 14, 24 October 1789, p. 5.

wisdom, draft them into laws, present them to the chief of the government, who sends them throughout the provinces: all the provinces receive the decrees, state yes or no to the central assembly, which limits itself to tabulating the votes of the districts; and once a majority of votes of all the People has been secured, the legislation is complete.[48]

The key phrase in this formulation is "modify them in their wisdom." For Fauchet, Representatives of the Commune had the right to modify district instructions in any way they saw fit; districts did not have the right to make laws, nor did they have the right to revoke deputies, nor force them to follow specific instructions; districts only had the right to approve the laws with a "yes" or "no." Thus Fauchet's "representatives" have a great deal more authority than the Cordeliers' "delegates" or "administrators."

Yet, what is most striking about Fauchet's 20 November speech was the absence of any hostility toward the Cordeliers. Instead of denouncing the radical districts, Fauchet tried to persuade their leaders that the Representatives of the Commune had their best interests at heart. This strategy soon became characteristic of all the Fauchetins. No longer would Brissot or anyone else publicly criticize the Cordeliers or their journalists. Indeed, the Fauchetins went out of their way to praise the Cordeliers in the hope of winning them over to representative democracy.

The Fauchetins realized that a more organized campaign for representative democracy had to be waged, and they decided upon a two-pronged strategy. First, on 30 November Brissot proposed that the Committee of 24 (established by the Communal Assembly to write a municipal constitution) meet jointly with the Constitutional Committee of the National Assembly to complete a municipal constitution. Meeting jointly with the National Assembly would insure the success of their plan against any other proposed in the districts. Second, to spread their ideas more effectively, the Fauchetins established a new propaganda center, which was soon called the Cercle Social.[49]

---

[48] Fauchet, *Motion . . . 20 novembre 1789*, pp. 3-4. It makes no difference that Fauchet is here speaking specifically of national government, since, unlike Prudhomme, he did not accept any distinction between municipal and national government with regard to popular sovereignty.

[49] Lacroix, *Actes* 3: 82-83, 113.

DURING the crisis over the Cordeliers' oath, Bonneville published a small pamphlet that was circulated within the Communal Assembly.[50] Bonneville's studies of Rousseau and Mably, as well as his concern with the issues raised by the Cordeliers, had led him to the problem of how a local politician could truly know the will of the people. He sought to bridge the gap between a representative and his constituents, and, in his pamphlet, he claimed to have discovered a way to do so. He invited Communal Assembly Representatives to form a "Cercle Social," which would edit and publish writings on civic affairs anonymously submitted by the public in a conveniently placed box. These denunciations, complaints, proposals, and essays would reveal the people's will.

It appears that the pamphlet was well received, for in January 1790 a group calling itself the Cercle Social was established and began to publish a journal by the same name. The first issue of the journal described fifteen members but kept their names secret.[51] "The Cercle Social ... has believed it crucial to the *Grand Enterprise* which it has conceived to stay absolutely unknown." It had chosen an editor-in-chief for its journal who was obviously Bonneville. Some obscure aliases were given. These include "Tubalcain," an expert in ancient and modern languages; "Fort-par-les-Bras," cited as the "Founder of the Districts"; "Publicist," an admirer of Adam Smith and Adam Ferguson; "Moralist," who was writing a "national catechism"; and "Compagnard," a specialist in religious affairs. While it is impossible to identify particular members with any certainty, the assumption that at least a majority of the members of the Cercle Social were Fauchetins is supported by three pieces of evidence: Bonneville circulated the prospectus for the group only among Communal Assembly Representatives; second, the aliases described above clearly describe certain Fauchetins; and, finally, the Cercle Social itself admitted that its members were "com-

[50] Nicolas Bonneville, *À M. le maire et à M. M. des districts de Paris* reprinted in Lacroix, *Actes* 7: 565-71; for a very similar letter see also *Cercle Social*, letter 7, pp. 42-57.
[51] *Cercle Social*, letter 1, pp. 5-12. See also the prospectus *La Bouche de fer* in the Bibliothèque historique de la ville de Paris, 606020, and *Qu'est-ce que la bouche de fer?* (Paris: ICS, n.d.).

posed of old friends, united by principles and by feelings since long before the birth of the National Assembly."[52]

"The principal aim of the Cercle Social," Bonneville declared, was "to give the voice of the people all of its force.[53] As proposed in the November prospectus, the group placed a public box on the door of Cercle Social headquarters. This box was called the *bouche de fer* (iron mouth), because its front was a metallic sculpture of a lion, and people placed their writings inside the lion's mouth. "The bouche de fer is nothing other than the very *Bouche* of the People, and the voice of the People."[54] Despite this claim, the bouche de fer writings were not themselves considered the voice of the people. If that had been the case, there would have been no need for the Cercle Social, and the articles and suggestions could simply have been published as they were written. But the function of the Cercle Social was precisely to decipher the will of the people through the study of their writings; the group acted as a kind of enlightened window through which the desire of the people could be more clearly seen. To this end, the journal *Cercle Social* included more than reprints of items found in the bouche de fer. Cercle Social members also wrote political essays of a more general nature, which analyzed the bouche de fer writings.

One theme that runs throughout the intellectual history of the French Revolution is the struggle of patriotic thinkers to unite two kinds of truth—one revealed through the scientific

---

[52] *Cercle Social,* letter 1, pp. 2-12; letter 6, pp. 41-42; letter 154, p. 243.

[53] Bonneville, *La Bouche de fer. Cercle Social. Dixième livraison. Introduction à la partie politique des feuilles de la bouche de fer, ou Tableau analytique des principes constitutionnels décrétés par l'Assemblée Nationale* ... (Paris: ICS, 1790), p. 1.

[54] *Bulletin de la Bouche de fer,* No. 8, p. 2; see the four-page prospectus, *La Bouche de fer* (Paris; ICS, n.d.) in the Bibliothèque de l'Arsenal, 8° Jo. 20.107b; Albert Mathiez, "Sur le titre du journal *La Bouche de fer,*" *Annales révolutionnaires* 9 (1917): 685-90; *Moniteur* 3:421. The bouche de fer was apparently first used in Renaissance Venice, where each magistracy had its own *Bocca di verità.* There Venetians would drop denunciations of heretics, spies, etc., for state officials to investigate. We next find the bouche de fer in early eighteenth-century England attached to the Buttons Coffee-House. Joseph Addison, the great publicist, promised to print writings dropped into this box twice a month in his newspaper, the *Guardian.* See Ellis, *The Penny Universities: A History of the Coffee-Houses,* pp. 171-75.

method, and the other, a more democratic truth, arising from popular sovereignty.[55] The Cercle Social was one effort to synthesize these two truths. It tried to reconcile the hierarchical nature of the Enlightenment (where ideas were not inherently equal, but were arranged according to intellectual merit), and democratic notions at the heart of the Revolution. Yet it was a rather crude attempt. While the people were to express their thoughts in writing to the bouche de fer, a small and elitist group was to edit the ideas and articulate them in accordance with the standards of the Enlightenment. It is clear that the members of the Cercle Social thought of themselves as intellectuals as well as politicians, for they invited all "men of letters" to help them edit the bouche de fer writings and hoped "everyone in the Republic of Letters will help us . . . to prepare the birth of an establishment which can only exist among a free people."[56] Yet Bonneville insisted on keeping the membership "few in numbers and composed of the most honored men."[57] Thus this first Cercle Social was something between an academy and a secret society, and certainly had not broken free of Old Regime models of intellectual institutions. Nonetheless, while Old Regime academies had studied the writings of savants and scientists, the goal of the Cercle Social was to discuss the writings of the people.

WHILE the Cercle Social was supposed to reflect the thoughts of all the people, it actually became the principal organ of the Fauchetins. They used the organization to spread their democratic ideas, to praise the work of the Communal Assembly, and to attack conservative policies in the municipal government and even in the National Assembly.

In January 1790 the National Assembly passed a law restricting the suffrage to "active" citizens (those who paid taxes equaling three days' wages), and restricting the right to run for national office to those who could pay the *marc d'argent* (taxes

[55] On this theme see K. M. Baker, "Scientism, Elitism, and Liberalism: The Case of Condorcet" *Studies in Voltaire and the Eighteenth Century* 55: 129-65.
[56] *Cercle Social*, letter 1, p. 4, and letter 7, p. 51.
[57] Ibid., letter 54, pp. 243-244.

equivalent to a mark of silver).[58] To the majority of the National Assembly, this bill made clear that political participation was to be based upon property, a notion implicit in Sieyès *What Is the Third Estate?* But to the Fauchetins, this law contradicted democratic rights secured in the Declaration of the Rights of Man. In an early issue of the *Cercle Social*, Condorcet published an article attacking the bill as "dangerous for liberty."[59] "It establishes," he wrote, "a legal inequality against those you have declared equal in rights."[60] Condorcet argued that basing electoral qualifications upon taxes paid was wrong for several reasons. First, since the National Assembly had authority over fiscal laws, it could change the nature of the electorate simply by manipulating the tax laws. The National Assembly could then easily become a new aristocracy. Second, it assumed that wealthier citizens were more productive than poorer ones, which was not necessarily the case. Many ex-noblemen and clergymen had been wealthy from birth but had not demonstrated any usefulness to the nation; on the other hand, a poor writer or educated farmer could be a very good citizen, even if he did not have much money. Third, the bill penalized people for risking their capital. Why should a person lose his right to vote if he loses his fortune? Fourth, people could legally transfer money to their friends and relatives, who would thus get the vote through no legitimate work of their own. Finally, such a law would make fiscal reform much more difficult, since reform would inevitably offend some political interest. Condorcet closed the article by warning the National Assembly that it had been established "to serve" the people, not to violate their rights.

Condorcet's article also offers an example of how the Fauchetins were trying to accommodate the desires of the Cordeliers, who had campaigned against the new electoral laws. The article had originated in the Committee of 24, which decided to send it to the National Assembly only *after* it had been approved by a majority of districts. In the meantime it was first published in

[58] On the active/passive distinction and the marc d'argent see Aulard, *French Revolution* 1: 178-95.
[59] *Cercle Social*, letter 8, pp. 57-75.
[60] Ibid., p. 61; see also Baker, *Condorcet*, p. 268.

the *Cercle Social*, not as an official decree of the municipality, but simply as Condorcet's own ideas. When it was finally sent to the National Assembly in April, Mayor Bailly refused to support it, an act which angered the Fauchetins.[61]

Renewed anger toward Bailly was an increasingly dominant characteristic of Fauchetin activities during the winter and spring of 1790. The Fauchetins were well aware that the greatest bond they had with the Cordeliers was a shared hatred for Bailly and his government. Ever since the summer of 1789, Cordelier journalists had blasted the mayor for being autocratic, incompetent, and corrupt. In December, Marat even "proposed to abolish the office of the mayor [because] it is useless, it is onerous, [and] it is fatal to liberty."[62]

The Fauchetins began to capitalize on this hostility during Fauchet's first term as president of the Communal Assembly (1-14 March 1790). For example, on 9 March Bailly asked the Communal Assembly to support his efforts to get the National Assembly to allow his administration to take over Parisian Church property. Fauchet criticized him for overstepping his authority and insisted that the districts should negotiate directly with the National Assembly on this matter.[63] A similar situation occurred when the Cordeliers came to the Communal Assembly complaining of the government's lack of concern for the poor. Fauchet took the opportunity to endorse the criticism and praise the Cordeliers: "The Assembly is eager to honor the request of MM of the Cordeliers district. We will make every effort to satisfy the district. We can only applaud the zeal of the district."[64]

[61] Condorcet's speech is in manuscript form in the minutes of the Committee of 24, Archives de la Seine VD12, pp. 48-57 (2 January 1790). See also *RdP*, 30 January 1790, p. 11; *Ami du peuple*, 25 July 1790, pp. 1-8; *Mercure National*, 3 January 1790, pp. 32-35; Lacroix, *Actes* 5: 13, 54-55. Bonneville also attacked the new laws in *Cercle Social*, letter 14, p. 352, and in *La Bouche de fer. Cercle Social. Dixième livraison. Introduction . . . ou Tableau analytique . . .* , p. 51 [of the Tableau].

[62] *Ami du peuple*, 27 December 1789, p. 4; for other examples of Cordelier hostility to Bailly see *RFB*, 2 January 1790, pp. 256-59, 16 January 1790, pp. 381-83; *Journal universel*, 29 December 1789, pp. 294-95; *RdP*, 13 March 1790, pp. 20-21.

[63] Lacroix, *Actes* 4: 351-410.

[64] Ibid., 4: 369-70.

A further example of Fauchetin hostility toward Bailly's government at this time concerned abuses of authority within the hospital administration. In the city-owned Hôpital de la Salpêtrière, the chief priest required that patients confess their sins and swear an oath of loyalty to Catholic dogma. In return, the patient received a *billet de confession*, the document necessary for admittance into a legal and Catholic cemetery. The billet de confession had a controversial history throughout the eighteenth century, for it had become a favorite means whereby Jesuit priests persecuted suspected Jansenists. By the time of the Revolution, the billet de confession symbolized the despotic use of ecclesiastical power.[65] When a young radical priest, Richard Chaix, refused to administer the billet de confession at the Salpêtrière, he was discharged. He appealed to Fauchet, and the stage was set for a confrontation.

In an impassioned speech before the Communal Assembly, Fauchet charged that a group of fanatical priests ran the hospital like a gang of tyrants, and that the billet de confession violated the liberties of both Chaix and the hospital patients. Fauchet demanded not only that Chaix be reinstituted, but that the administrators themselves be dismissed. His attacks were intended to be an indictment of the executive branch as a whole, for only a corrupt government could have allowed such despotism within it. Bailly's government refused to act, but the incident further established Fauchet as a champion of human rights among the Cordeliers and as a popular leader among radical priests.[66]

The most important opportunity for an attack upon Bailly's government and a rapprochement with the Cordeliers came in March when the Châtelet (an old court with police powers) ordered the arrest of Danton, leader of the Cordeliers. The story of Danton's arrest is well known.[67] In January the Châtelet had

---

[65] Daniel Carroll Joynes, "Jansenists and Ideologues: Opposition Theory in the Parlement of Paris, 1750-1775."

[66] *Journal de la municipalité et des districts*, 29 April 1790, pp. 681-82; *Moniteur* 4: 448-49; Lacroix, *Actes* 4: 369, 5: 129, 165, 351, 345, 355, 423, 424, 449-51; Godard, *Exposé*, pp. 167-68; Fauchet, *Contre les billets de confessions*.

[67] Alphonse Aulard, "Danton au district des Cordeliers et à la Commune de Paris," *Rf* 24(1893): 113-44.

issued an arrest warrant for Jean-Paul Marat. The Cordeliers allowed Marat to hide in their district. When 3,000 National Guard troops arrived on 22 January demanding the surrender of the journalist, Danton refused to give him up. The Châtelet accused Danton of inciting an insurrection and, two months later, issued an arrest warrant for him.

On 19 March the Cordeliers informed the Communal Assembly of Danton's arrest. Fauchet immediately demanded that Bailly be called to the Communal Assembly for questioning. As mayor, Bailly supervised all of the Paris administration and was thus accountable for the activities of its various departments. If Bailly admitted he was aware of the arrest, he would seem all the more corrupt and tyrannical; if he claimed ignorance, he would appear incompetent at best, and his more hostile critics would accuse him of lying. Bailly chose the latter course, claiming that the Châtelet had acted without his knowledge.[68]

Fauchet then addressed the Communal Assembly, calling Danton "an ardent zealot of liberty ... who has nothing going against him except a patriotic exhuberance and a surplus of civic virtue."[69] Fauchet reminded his audience that Danton was also a member of the Communal Assembly (he had entered the Communal Assembly as a representative of the Cordeliers on 23 January). This meant that the Châtelet was not simply attacking the rights of a radical district leader, but was violating the integrity of the Communal Assembly as well. Fauchet insisted that this incident proved that Bailly's government was a "mixture of despotism and aristocracy."[70] He ended the speech by calling for the National Assembly to overrule the Châtelet and to replace it with a "Grand Jury."[71]

Fauchet's speech was published in the *Cercle Social*, which also printed several articles praising the Cordeliers and calling for the elimination of the Châtelet. Nearly all of the Cordelier *and* Fauchetin journalists flooded their papers with articles on the incident. Even Brissot, who had criticized the Cordeliers in

[68] Lacroix, *Actes* 4: 452, 464.
[69] *Cercle Social*, letter 40, p. 218; Lacroix, *Actes* 4: 474.
[70] *Cercle Social*, letter 40, p. 219.
[71] Ibid., p. 221.

November, now praised the district, and claimed that the Châtelet had violated Danton's "freedom to think and to speak."[72]

At about the same time, the democrats discovered that the Châtelet was secretly preparing to arrest many radicals who had participated in the October Days. The Cordeliers suspected that the Châtelet's investigation was aimed directly at them, offering further proof of the Châtelet's counterrevolutionary nature. The Cercle Social took great interest in this story. The despotic tendencies of the Châtelet (contrasted with praise for the Communal Assembly and the Cordeliers) became one of the journal's prominent themes. More important, the journal published a long investigative report of its own, focusing on the corrupt activities of the royal troops at Versailles during the October Days. The Cercle Social urged that any police investigation ought to center on the royal troops, not on the democrats. This report was praised in several papers. The Cordelier journalist Camille Desmoulins, for example, told his readers to "read the eighth number of the bouche de fer."[73] In all of these examples Fauchet was implicitly telling the Cordeliers that only a strong Communal Assembly could protect the districts from the "abitrary authority" of Bailly's administration.[74] Without the Communal Assembly, Bailly would be able to manipulate the districts by playing them off against one another. Direct democracy would be easily thwarted.

By April it became clear to the Fauchetins that they had failed to improve the prestige or authority of the Communal Assembly. First of all, Bailly found that he could operate the government largely without the approval of the Communal Assembly, and he managed to maintain fairly good relations with many of the districts. In addition, the districts became increasingly hostile to

[72] *Cercle Social*, letter 40, p. 213-221, letter 3, p. 16, letter 10, pp. 105-106, letter 39, pp. 211-12, letter 66, pp. 495-96; *Bulletin de la bouche de fer*, no. 5, p. 4; *Pf*, 26 March 1790, p. 2, 5 May 1790, p. 3; *RdP*, 29 March 1790, pp. 15-16; *RFB*, 29 March 1790, pp. 108-20; *CdP*, 24 March 1790, p. 330; *Courrier de Lyon*, 30 March 1790, pp. 205-206; *Journal de la municipalité et des districts*, 23 March 1790, p. 555.

[73] *Cercle Social*, letter 154, pp. 251-304, letter 13, pp. 337-41, letter 66, pp. 495-96; *RFB*, 26 April 1790, pp. 415-16, 5 July 1790, p. 354; *CdP*, 22 April 1790, pp. 446-47, 1 May 1790, p. 482; *Pf*, 27 April 1790, p. 3, 28 April 1790, pp. 2-3; *Courrier de Lyon*, 29 April 1790, pp. 419-20; Lacroix, *Actes* 5: 139-64.

[74] *Cercle Social*, letter 40, p. 216.

the Communal Assembly and began to sympathize with the plight of the mayor. In February a group of districts created a rival assembly that drew up its own plan for a municipal constitution and that was supported by the mayor. Although this new assembly was denounced in the Communal Assembly and National Assembly, there was actually very little the Fauchetins could do except complain. The Cercle Social declared that it was "angered to see a central committee composed of imposters, who, without any purpose, without any love for the public welfare, insult the representatives of 900,000 souls."[75] More important, some districts began recalling their own deputies, defying the authority of the Communal Assembly. On 18 March, Filles St. Thomas recalled Brissot, and Fauchet was recalled by his district on 30 March. [76]

As a result of these frustrating developments, in early April the Communal Assembly asked Jacques Godard to write a memorandum to the National Assembly and to the sixty districts, informing them that its members were willing to resign as soon as a new municipal body was convoked. Godard, an attorney and president of the Blancs Manteaux district, had entered the Communal Assembly in December and had quickly become one of Fauchet's most vociferous supporters. He also became famous for his advocacy of civic rights for Jews.[77] In his address, Godard summarized the Fauchetin view of the Communal Assembly's plight:

The actual state of the Representatives of the Commune: stripped of all its rightful authority; placed among defiance, suspicion, and envy; insulted in all the papers, injured in a thousand deputations; mistakenly compared with a rival assembly, which itself is illegal, and where the legal chief of the municipality more than often presides; finally without

---

[75] *Cercle Social*, letter 42, p. 230; Godard, *Exposé*, pp. 150-62. See also *Cercle Social*, letter 44, p. 248.

[76] Lacroix, *Actes* 4: 554-55, 720. The Communal Assembly, of course, invalidated the recalls.

[77] Garrigues, *Les Districts parisiens*, p. 115; Arthur Hertzberg, *The French Enlightenment and the Jews: The Origins of Modern Anti-Semitism*, pp. 347, 361, 362, 366. Lacroix notes that Godard played a crucial role in the Communal Assembly in *Actes* 3: ii. Fauchet himself praised Godard in *Oraison funèbre de Charles-Michel de l'Epée*, p. 48.

authority, it endeavors only to tell it like it is. The picture is one of anarchy and of a confusion of powers, the result of license, and destructive to liberty.[78]

The National Assembly responded by ordering the Representatives to stay in their places until a new municipal government was established.

The best example of the districts' hostility toward the Communal Assembly came in May, when another cold war broke out between Bailly and the Fauchetins over the control of Church property.[79] Bailly had negotiated directly with the National Assembly on this issue, ignoring the Communal Assembly and its earlier warnings. On 15 May Fauchet (then serving his second term as president) publicly reprimanded the mayor in front of the Communal Assembly. Bailly responded by attacking the Fauchetins for obstructing the work of the government. If Fauchet's maneuver was designed to win over the districts, it clearly failed. Out of the sixty districts, at least fifty-one sympathized with the mayor and publicly denounced the Communal Assembly. Even the Fauchetins' own districts were among this group. Fauchet's district, Saint-Roch, called the conduct of the mayor "wise and prudent" and criticized the Communal Assembly for treating the mayor with disrespect.[80]

In fact, we have evidence of only one district's supporting the Communal Assembly against Bailly. But this was no ordinary district; indeed, it is very significant that at this point the only district that came out clearly in support of the Communal Assembly was the Cordeliers. "Everyone knows how boldly the Cordelier district asserted itself against the representative system of the city's deputies," the district wrote in its Proclamation of 9 June.

It based itself on the differences and on the restrictive classes of their mandates. But it has always thought that, according to the plan of the municipality provisionally adopted by the majority of districts, that

[78] *CdP*, 5 April 1790, p. 379. *Pf* 16 April 1790, p. 3; Lacroix, *Actes* 4:619-654.

[79] Lacroix, *Actes* 5: 365 and ff.

[80] Ibid., 5: 399-400, 501-509, 522-24, 493, 462.

this Assembly was truly the General Assembly of the Commune; that it must consequently supervise the administration, making the administration accountable to it, and improving the administration as it sees fit.[81]

This decree is remarkable because it illustrates that, while the Fauchetins failed to convince the majority of districts, they succeeded in winning the Cordeliers over to their viewpoint. Never before had the Cordeliers admitted that a majority of districts had ratified the Brissot Plan de municipalité in August 1789; indeed, in November it had argued the opposite case, claiming that only the districts had the authority to supervise the executive branch. Nor was this decree an isolated occurrence. On 15 June a "deputy of the Cordelier district" reiterated the same points to the Communal Assembly.[82] Moreover, other evidence indicates that a rapprochement between the Cordeliers and the Fauchetins had been successfully achieved, including the frequent mention of the Cordeliers in the *Cercle Social* and the Cordelier journalists' reciprocity in complimenting leading Fauchetins and sometimes even reprinting articles from their papers.[83]

The Cordeliers had built reputations as spokesmen for the districts. Why would they suddenly go against the vast majority of their colleagues and support the Communal Assembly? Some historians have reasoned that Danton's entry into the Communal Assembly in January provides the answer.[84] But there was more to it than that. The Cordeliers was the only district to have its leaders arrested by the municipal government. It perceived the Châtelet's secret investigation to be a scheme against the district

[81] "Proclamation de District des Cordeliers. Extrait du registre des délibérations du 9 juin 1790," reprinted in ibid., 5: 493-96.

[82] Ibid., 6: 81.

[83] Examples include *RFB*, 9 August 1790, pp. 618-19; *Journal d'Etat et du citoyen*, 20 August 1789, pp. 28-30, 8 October 1789, p. 180, 31 December 1789, p. 31, 31 January 1790, pp. 189-200, 7 March 1790, p. 664, 16 May 1790, pp. 315-22, 13 June 1790, p. 441; *Mercure National et Révolutions de l'Europe*, no. 17, (n.d.), pp. 533-39, 29 October 1790, p. 1210; *Pf*, 9 July 1790, p. 3, 2 August 1790, p. 3; 3 August 1790, pp. 2-3, 13 September 1790, p. 4. This evidence shows that relations between Brissot and the Roberts were particularly close.

[84] See Lacroix, *Actes* 5: 496-97.

itself, and it found the Fauchetins to be the most vociferous protectors of the Cordeliers against Bailly's government. Thus during the spring of 1790, the Cordeliers came to agree with the Fauchetin belief that the greatest threat to the municipal revolution came from the despotic designs of the mayor.

The accord between the Cordeliers and the Fauchetins at this time, particularly with regard to the threat posed by Mayor Bailly, illustrates the extent to which the two groups cooperated during the early years of the Revolution. While they disagreed over a few fundamental issues, both saw the Revolution as essentially democratic, a view which was still considered quite radical in 1790. Until the antidemocratic factions were eliminated from public life in 1792, these two groups were on very friendly terms, and together the Cordeliers and the Fauchetins neary toppled the monarchy during the summer of 1791.

DESPITE its success with the Cordeliers, by the summer of 1790 the Communal Assembly had become an impotent force in municipal politics, and its members waited for elections to take place for a new government. Most of the Fauchetins focused their attention on matters outside the Communal Assembly. Fauchet prepared a eulogy to Ben Franklin; the Cercle Social asked Bonneville to begin a second journal, which was no different in its content than the first; and Brissot devoted himself to his *Patriote français*.[85] Within the Communal Assembly, most Representatives simply sat and listened to the Fauchetin Jacques Godard read his *Exposé des travaux de l'Assemblée générale des représentants de la Commune de Paris* (*An Account of the Works of the General Assembly of the Representatives of the Commune of Paris*), which he had been asked to write as a history of the Communal Assembly from a Fauchetin point of view. Claude Fauchet was the hero of the book, Mayor Bailly the archvillain, and the struggle between the districts and the Communal Assembly now became a tragic misunderstanding. A committee that included Fauchet edited and approved the *Exposé* in Sep-

---

[85] Fauchet, *Elôge civique de Benjamin Franklin*. Bonneville's new journal was the *Bulletin de la bouche de fer*.

tember, and it was published in October, not simply as the work of one man, but as the voice of the Fauchetins.[86]

By August the National Assembly had finally passed a permanent municipal plan for Paris, and elections were called. First came the race for mayor. The Fauchetins and Cordeliers worked to defeat Bailly, who ran for reelection. "My conscience obliges me to vote against him," Brissot wrote in an article entitled "*Des Elections de Paris*," published in his *Patriote français* and reprinted in the Cordeliers' *Révolutions de France et de Brabant*.[87] "M. Bailly is an ambitious man who conceals his real game, and who wants to usurp all power." Nevertheless, the outcome of the mayor's race was devastating for the radicals. Of some 14,000 votes, Bailly obtained 12,550, crushing all other opponents, including Danton, who received only 49.[88]

Bailly's victory was only a taste of things to come. The following week, elections were held for places in a new Communal Assembly, and most of the radicals ran for reelection. The *Cercle Social* urged its readers to vote for democrats, warning that if Bailly received a passive assembly the municipal revolution would be endangered.[89] But at that point no one listened. The Fauchetins were completely routed; Fauchet, Bonneville, Garran-Coulon, and Brissot all lost their elections, as did several Cordeliers. The radicals' bitterness was immediately expressed in their papers. The *Chronique de Paris* wrote:

You have nominated many men who have run away from the revolution, and who, by the ease with which they take arbitrary authority, are inwardly turning towards the Old Regime. You have repudiated many incumbents who had proved their character and their patriotism: the loyal Garran (de Coulon) [*sic*] has not been chosen, and ... you have also rejected the patriot Brissot.[90]

The Cordelier journalist Camille Desmoulins believed that their failure was the result of the new antidemocratic electoral qualifications, which excluded most members of the working class. Desmoulins also did not distinguish between Fauchetin and

[86]Lacroix, *Actes* 4: 346-48, 6: 572, 624, 667.
[87] *Pf*, 30 July 1790, pp. 3-4; *RFB*, 2 August 1790, pp. 593-96.
[88] Hampson, *Danton*, p. 39.
[89] *Bulletin de la bouche de fer*, no. 4, pp. 5-7.
[90] *CdP*, 18 August 1790, pp. 918-19.

Cordeliers losers: "Ungrateful Parisians have forgotten in the elections Danton, the abbé Fauchet, Brissot, Carra, Manuel"; and in another issue Anarchasis Clootz wrote to Desmoulins complaining that "Manuel, Garran, Brissot, Pio, and Pigot" were not elected.[91]

Between August and its last session on 8 October 1790, the Communal Assembly vented its anger on Bailly, delivering the most vicious attacks to date upon his administration.[92] Fauchet was elected president of the Assembly twice during this short period, and he had firm control over its activities. But the Assembly was now a discredited body without any authority. The August elections meant that the Fauchetins would be excluded from the new municipal government, and they were nearly ruined as a political force.

If the Fauchetins were to regain influence, they would have to reconstitute themselves into a new kind of group. There was a precedent. A few months earlier, the Cordeliers had begun the Société des amis des droits de l'homme, and the growing strength of the club served to offset the dismal results of the elections.[93] Fauchet had a similar idea. In the last session of the Communal Assembly, it was announced that its deputies would regroup as the Société fraternelle des anciens représentants de la commune de Paris. This group was composed of the "admirers of Fauchet," and began meeting immediately after the closing of the Communal Assembly.[94] But the group had major disadvantages. First, membership was limited to the small number of persons who had been members of the Communal Assembly; second, the name itself meant that the Fauchetins would continue to be associated with a weak and controversial body; and third, since its members had clearly been rejected by the voters, it was

[91] *RFB*, 16 August 1790, pp. 645-52, 23 August 1790, pp. 409-14, 20 September 1790, p. 190, 27 September 1790, pp. 220-29; 18 October 1790, p. 372. Pio was a Fauchet supporter and a future secretary of the Cercle Social.

[92] See Lacroix's "Introduction" in *Actes* 7.

[93] Alphonse Aulard, "Danton au Club des Cordeliers et au département de Paris," *Rf* 24: 226-46; George M. Robertson, "The Society of the Cordeliers and the French Revolution."

[94] Lacroix, *Actes* 7: 433. The term "admirers of Fauchet" is Lacroix's; see *Actes* 7: 445.

certainly not within the spirit of democracy (and was perhaps illegal) for a legally repudiated political body to reconstitute itself. Thus, while the Société fraternelle might serve as a temporary body, the Fauchetins had to come up with a different kind of organization if their group was to survive.

The Cercle Social was responsible for the new organization. Until October 1790 the Cercle Social was composed of a small and secretive group of Fauchetins. While it had begun two journals and developed some ideas on its own (such as the bouche de fer), it had served primarily as a municipal propaganda center for the Fauchetins. During the second week in October, the Cercle Social began a new journal, the *Bouche de fer*, which announced the establishment of a new club, the Confédération des Amis de la Vérité. Unlike the small and secretive first group, the Confédération was to be very large and public. It was to be led by Fauchet, and its minutes were to be reprinted in the *Bouche de fer*, edited by Bonneville.[95]

The relationship between the Fauchetins and the Confédération des Amis de la Vérité is made clear in the last clash between the Communal Assembly and Mayor Bailly. On 6 October the Communal Assembly, under Fauchet's final presidency, told the National Assembly that Bailly had ordered the arrest of a man who had insulted a traffic officer outside the Opera. This man had now been detained more than twenty-four hours without a hearing, with no formal charges against him. The Communal Assembly claimed that there were at least eighteen other prisoners, "who, for eight days, fifteen days, three weeks, one month, two months and more, have been detained there without any hearing."[96] The Communal Assembly denied that Bailly had any right to arrest innocent citizens in this manner, and accused him of establishing a municipal despotism.

Bailly responded by declaring that he had broken no law and was only carrying out his responsibilities as ultimate chief of the police department. In an open letter to the president of the National Assembly, he wrote:

[95] *Bdf*, no. 1, October 1790, pp. 1-16. See also Lacroix, *Actes* 7: 561-638.
[96] Lacroix, *Actes* 7: 401-404.

I know that the ex-representatives, in their address, challenge my right to imprison, even provisionally. They want this power ... to belong only to the district committees. But they conveniently forget that the decree of the National Assembly for the police of the city of Paris does not give the authority to police to every district committee, but to *the municipal corps*, of which I am chief.[97]

This letter was published on 10 October, two days after the closing of the Communal Assembly. Nevertheless, the Fauche-tins managed to publish a response to the mayor's letter, in the form of a pamphlet by Jacques Godard. "M. the Mayor," Godard began in a typically Fauchetin fashion, "definitely proclaims an absolute independence from all supervision, and is making good use of his arbitrary authority, which is very opposed to principles which constitute national liberty."[98] More specifically, he charged Bailly with violating the law in three ways: first, in ordering the arrest himself; second, in seeking no approval from anyone else; and third, in allowing prisoners to remain so long in jail without a hearing.

The title of this pamphlet makes it clear that Godard was speaking for more than himself:

Réfutation des principes exposés par le maire de Paris, dans sa lettre. ... Par une Société de Citoyens légalement réunis en vue du bien public, au Cirque national, et coalisés a la Confédération générale des Amis de la Vérité.

Refutation of the Principles Explained by the Mayor of Paris. ... By a Society of Citizens Legally Reunited for the Public Good, at the National Circus, and Allied with the General Confederation of the Friends of Truth.

This "Society of Citizens" was nothing other than the Société fraternelle des anciens représentants de la commune de Paris, and the "General Confederation" was obviously the Cercle So-cial's new club. Two points can be drawn from this document: first, that the Fauchetins continued to act as a group after the closing of the Communal Assembly; and second, their activities were absorbed by the Confédération des Amis de la Vérité.

[97] Ibid., 412.
[98] Godard, *Réfutation des principes exposés par le maire de Paris*, p. 11.

Further evidence indicates that the Société fraternelle became part of the Confédération des Amis de la Vérité. The first issue of the *Bouche de fer* described the last session of the Communal Assembly and reprinted Fauchet's farewell address. The *Bouche de fer* also was the only paper that regularly reported the various activities of the Société fraternelle, and in December announced that the group had become a "Committee of the Confédération."[99] This partly explains why virtually all of the Fauchetins (including Brissot, Bancal, Garran-Coulon, Condorcet, and Godard) were active members of the Confédération.

THE CERCLE SOCIAL has usually been described as an apolitical group interested only in utopian ideas, but it is clear that the Fauchetins and the Cercle Social were the same thing and that the Fauchetins were far from apolitical. While it is true that the Cercle Social avoided partisan conflicts for a short period during the fall of 1790, this was only because their foray into municipal politics had temporarily discredited them. But during the spring of 1791, the Cercle Social reasserted itself as a political force in a more organized fashion. The group increasingly gained influence until, by the spring of 1792, its members had become political leaders at the national level. Thus the history of the Cercle Social between October 1790 and June 1793 is understandable only if one appreciates the extent to which its origins lay in the Paris Municpal Revolution of 1789-1790.

[99] *Bdf*, no. 1, October 1790, pp. 10-12; Lacroix, *Actes* 7: 445-53. A letter in the Archives de la Seine 4 AZ 937 shows that in November the Société fraternelle sent a copy of Godard's *Exposé* to the new Communal Assembly.

PART II

The Confédération
des Amis de la Vérité
1790-1791

As it is clearly demonstrated that ignorance, forgetfulness, or scorn of the rights of man are the *only* causes of ... government corruption, one cannot give enough encouragement to writers who combine *ardent* patriotism with the enlightenment that comes from experience.

Bulletin des Amis de la Vérité, 1 January 1793, p. 4.

For what is a merit in the writer may well be a vice in the statesman and the very qualities which go to make great literature can lead to catastrophic revolutions.

Alexis de Tocqueville, *The Old Regime and the French Revolution*, trans. Stuart Gilbert (New York: Anchor Books, 1955), p. 147.

3

Club Politics and
Principles

JACQUES-PIERRE BRISSOT (1754-1793). Elected to the Paris Communal Assembly, Legislative Assembly, and Convention. *Chronique du mois* editor for political affairs. Brissot was too busy with his own political and literary career to become very active in the Confédération des Amis de la Vérité, but he was clearly the most important political leader in the Cercle Social. He was at the center of the Cercle Social's intense network of friendships, and became the most influential leader of the Girondins.
Courtesy of The Newberry Library, Chicago

The most solid movement of your Revolution is philosophy. . . . The patriot par excellence is a philosophe.

Jacques-Pierre Brissot in Aulard, ed., *La Société des Jacobins*, 3: 529.

ON WEDNESDAY afternoon, 13 October 1790, more than 4,000 people gathered in the Palais Royal to attend the first meeting of the Confédération des Amis de la Vérité. Today the Palais Royal is a peaceful garden and park surrounded by small specialty shops. The only sounds heard are those of little children sailing their miniature boats in the park's pond. What a contrast from the eighteenth century! During the early years of the French Revolution the Palais Royal was an important political center, "the meeting place for all the good patriots of Paris," wrote one journalist.[1] Instead of innocent children, the park was filled with demonstrators, speakers, pamphleteers, and politicians. The shops surrounding the park included the most popular bookstores in the capital. Politically interested citizens would go to the Palais Royal to browse through the latest pamphlets and discuss them with their friends. "The Palais Royal," one Cercle Social member noted, "has inundated France with all these brochures which have changed everybody—even the soldier—into philosophers."[2] At the southern end of the park was a fairly large building where the park's owner, the duc d'Orléans, had constructed a circus in 1786. By 1789, the circus was defunct, and the building was rented out to all kinds of political groups for meetings.

As the participants pushed and shoved through the door of the circus building, at least one of them feared "being crushed by the crowd."[3] Included among the well dressed people were deputies of the National Assembly, local politicians, municipal officers, and members of other patriotic societies. They had come

[1] *RdP*, 19-27 September 1789, p. 8. On the 13 October session see *Bdf*, no. 3, October 1790, pp. 17-31. The *Bouche de fer* did not begin dating each issue until 1 January 1791.

[2] Camille Desmoulins, cited in C. A. McClelland, "The Lameths and Lafayette: The Politics of Moderation in the French Revolution, 1789-1791," p. 108; Pierre d'Espezel, *Le Palais Royal*, pp. 156-67.

[3] Halem, *Paris en 1790. Voyage de Halem*, p. 212.

primarily to hear an opening address by the *procureur-général* of the Cercle Social, the abbé Claude Fauchet.

"A magnificent idea brings us together," Fauchet began. "It concerns the beginning of the confederation of men, the coming together of useful truths; tying them into a universal system, getting them accepted into national government; and working in general harmony with the human spirit to compose world happiness." Before 1789, Fauchet maintained, governments had assumed that man was essentially evil, and legislation had the effect of oppressing most people. But the French Revolution had inaugurated an "epoch of regeneration," wherein all states would recognize the essential goodness of men and would exploit potential love among them. France was the vanguard of a "regeneration of the social order," which would soon reach every person in the world.

Clothed in his clerical uniform, this handsome and charismatic priest made quite an impression upon his audience, and he was interrupted several times by applause. A few days later the prestigious *Moniteur* printed a long and favorable article on the meeting, filled with excerpts of Fauchet's speech. The reporter thought Fauchet was "developing the basis for a social union— of a fraternity—where egoism will be rendered chimerical, and patriotism will be reborn." A second meeting was scheduled for Friday, 22 October, and was announced in several of the most important Parisian newspapers.[4]

Bonneville claimed that between eight and nine thousand people attended this second meeting.[5] After opening the session, Fauchet announced that the club must choose a president, and he nominated Guillaume Goupil de Préfeln. A member of the National Assembly, Goupil was becoming a politician of some importance. During the spring of 1790, his speeches for freedom of the press had won him much respect, and the Cercle Social had invited him to join their small group. On this afternoon Goupil made a short speech thanking the Confédération and

[4] *Moniteur* 6: 163-64; *Pf*, 15 October 1789, p. 2, and 19 October 1790, p. 4; *CdP*, 13 October 1790, p. 1144, 14 October 1790, p. 1146, and 20 October 1790, p. 1175; *Courrier de Paris dans les 83 Départements*, 18 October 1790, p. 261.
[5] *Bdf*, no. 7, October 1790, p. 99.

praising the aims of the Cercle Social. He wanted to swear a loyalty oath, but Fauchet would not allow it. "When a citizen such as yourself wants to accept a position, his simple declaration suffices for assuring us that he will fulfill his promise and our hopes." Nevertheless Goupil insisted and proclaimed his fidelity "to the nation, the law, the king, to the Amis de la Vérité, and to all humanity."[6]

The Confédération next chose four secretaries, Bertrand Barère, the Italian diplomat Pio, Jean Lapoype, and Jean-François Michel. Barère was also a deputy to the National Assembly. A skilled attorney, man of letters, and editor of a successful newspaper, he was becoming known as a politician of considerable abilities. Pio had been a chargé d'affaires for the ambassador from Naples. In March 1790 he had been dismissed by his government for expressing ideas favorable to the Revolution. When his Parisian district asked the Communal Assembly to naturalize the Italian, Fauchet proclaimed him a legitimate French citizen in a lavish patriotic ceremony. Since then he had been closely associated with the Fauchetins. Lapoype was drawn from local political circles. A friend of Danton and brother-in-law of the radical journalist Stanislas Fréron, Lapoype was an active member of the Cordeliers club. Michel had been a member of the faculty of medicine at the Université de Montpellier before the Revolution. He moved to Paris and was elected to the Communal Assembly in 1789. He subsequently became a president of that Assembly and one of Fauchet's most important followers.[7]

The highlight of this second meeting was a speech by Fauchet on the aims of the Confédération. If the purpose of the Revolution was ultimately to "banish hate from the earth and allow only love to reign," then the function of the club was to find ways of bringing about this era. But Fauchet explicitly rejected

---

[6] Ibid., p. 102; *Cercle Social*, letter 39 [18 March 1790], p. 209.

[7] Leo Gershoy, *Bertrand Barère, the Reluctant Terrorist*, p. 86. On Pio see Fauchet, *Extrait du Procès-verbal de l'Assemblée générale des Représentants de la Commune de Paris, du jeudi 11 mars 1790*. On Lapoype see Mathiez, *Le Club des Cordeliers pendant la Crise de Varennes, et Le Massacre du Champ de Mars*, p. 121; Censer, *Prelude to Power: The Parisian Radical Press 1789-1791*, p. 32. On Michel, see Etienne Charavey, ed., *L'Assemblée électorale de Paris. 18 novembre 1790-15 juin 1791*, p. 64.

models like the Jacobin club or the Cordeliers club, which closely followed and debated the activities of the National Assembly. He wanted a club of "philosophes," who would limit themselves to speculating upon political principles, leaving the task of developing actual legislation to others. At least one newspaper implicitly understood that such a plan would allow the Fauchetins to maintain a high visibility in revolutionary Paris without becoming embroiled in partisan politics:

... without wanting to follow the progress of the legislative body, which would consequently result in exposing themselves to accusations of raising one podium against another, they will discuss all questions relative to politics, religion, legislation, virtue, sociability, and everything which constitutes the rights and happiness of men.[8]

But could a group like the Fauchetins remain detached and confine themselves to merely speculative thought during an era of such widespread and intense politicization?

Fauchet thought that the best way for the Confédération to proceed was by analyzing the work of some great political theorist, and naturally he turned to the previous generation as the most logical source. "We could submit to the same test the enigmatic Montesquieu, the grave Mably, the eloquent Raynal, and all of the profound political writers." But while any of these writers would do, there was one book that itself had revolutionized political language and summarized all of the important political themes of the new epoch: Jean-Jacques Rousseau's *Social Contract*, which "restated substantially all of the best parts of the greatest authors who have dealt with law."[9] Fauchet announced that each meeting would be devoted to a particular section of the *Social Contract*, which would first be analyzed by himself in a major address and then by various members of the club in discussion.

While French revolutionaries agreed on the value of the *Social Contract*, many questioned the worth of Fauchet's commentaries.

---

[8] *Courrier de Lyon*, 7 November 1790, pp. 42-43; *Bdf*, no. 7, October 1790, p. 110, and no. 8, October 1790, p. 116; Bibliothèque historique de la ville de Paris, Ms. 772, fol. 290.
[9] *Bdf*, no. 8, October 1790, pp. 116-17.

At least one of the most illustrious deans of the Republic of Letters, the literary critic and academician Jean-François de la Harpe, thought that the Cercle Social was little more than organized nonsense. In his journal La Harpe analyzed passages from the *Bouche de fer* and attempted to demonstrate their vagueness or inconsistencies. Fauchet and Bonneville respected the opinion of such a great man and made various attempts to respond. La Harpe would not budge from his first judgment. He simply could not understand how a group of mediocre intellectuals, with such wild-eyed schemes, could ever come down to earth long enough to further the progress of enlightenment.[10]

A different kind of criticism came from some of the Cordelier journalists, who now accused Fauchet and his followers of abandoning the democratic struggle. In two articles published in her radical *Mercure National*, Louise Robert, who had attended the first two meetings, objected to Bonneville's laudatory descriptions of those sessions in the *Bouche de fer*. First, she condemned "the ridiculous mysteries" exploited by the *Bouche de fer*. In her view, a call for a new era based upon love and brotherhood belonged in a journal whose focus was Christian piety, not popular sovereignty. More serious, however, was her objection to the kinds of men chosen to lead the club. For example, Goupil was also a member of the Société de 89, a club led by Sieyès and Lafayette, whom the Cordeliers despised as elitist and aristocratic. Louise Robert wondered why the Cercle Social "welcomed all those whom we call *moderates, ministerials, aristocrats, in short, the enemies of the people?*"[11]

Critics like La Harpe and Robert did not see that many of the failings of the Confédération were due to the fact that it was trying to do something new. At the heart of all Cercle Social projects was a commitment to unite the political and social ideas of the philosophes with the yearnings of the Third Estate. Thus

[10] *Mercure de France*, 18 December 1790, pp. 90-121. Responses by Bonneville and Fauchet in *Mercure de France*, 25 December 1790, pp. 144-54; *Bdf*, 6 January 1791, p. 26; and *Bdf*, 10 January 1791, pp. 49-63.

[11] *Mercure National et Révolutions de l'Europe*, 29 October 1790, pp. 1246-48 and 2 November 1790, pp. 1273-80. See also Pio's vigorous response in 16 November 1790, pp. 1506-1508.

the Confédération des Amis de la Vérité was not merely an academy where men of letters spoke to each other, but rather an attempt by a group of politicians and intellectuals to address themselves to the Third Estate and its concerns. In this sense, the Confédération was halfway between the academies of the Old Regime and popular clubs like the Cordeliers. This was particularly true during the first few months of the Confédération, when the Fauchetins turned away from fighting for a representative democracy and laid plans to democratize French intellectual life.

In the weeks following the second meeting, the Confédération composed a set of rules and regulations, referred to as a "constitution."[12] At the head of the organization was a steering committee called the Directoire du Cercle Social. The directoire was a small group of "patriotic writers" who met every Wednesday evening in one of the meeting rooms of the Palais Royal. Their meetings were only open to those receiving invitations. The directoire was probably the old Cercle Social group that Bonneville had begun in early 1790; at least Bonneville seems to have been the backbone of both groups.

The directoire also established the Imprimerie du Cercle Social, which published the thrice-weekly newspaper, *Bouche de fer*. It continued the work of earlier Cercle Social publications by reprinting letters and memoranda placed into the bouche de fer box, which now hung on the front door of the Imprimerie. The continued use of the box reinforces the hypothesis that the directoire and the older Cercle Social were, in fact, the same group. The newspaper *Bouche de fer* served also as the mouthpiece of the Confédération. The paper was begun about two weeks before the first meeting of the club, and its early articles were actually advertisements for that meeting. Indeed, the popular success of the club was due in large part to the advance work of the *Bouche de fer*. After the club began, the newspaper published its minutes and reprinted speeches of Confédération

<hr />

[12] Unless otherwise noted, the following section is based upon *Bdf*, nos. 1-25, October-November 1790.

members, including Fauchet's commentaries on the *Social Contract*.

The Confédération met every Friday at 5:00 P.M. in the circus building of the Palais Royal. During the first two meetings anyone was welcome, since the Cercle Social was primarily interested in creating a huge event to ensure the success of the club. Soon, though, the directoire decided to restrict membership to those who purchased subscriptions to the *Bouche de fer*. This ingenious plan may have been unique among the multitude of revolutionary clubs and journals, assuring the success of the *Bouche de fer*, and possibly allowing the publishing company to acquire large capital reserves. Moreover, the link between subscription and membership facilitated diffusion of Cercle Social ideas throughout a much greater audience than would have otherwise been possible and thereby raised the organization to national prominence. For example, letters to the editor printed in the paper indicate that the *Bouche de fer* was read in several cities and villages across the country, including Lyon, Bordeaux, Strasbourg, Metz, Besançon, Toulouse, Brest, Nantes, and La Rochelle.

The annual subscription rate for the *Bouche de fer* was twenty-seven livres. Since it took a laborer a month to earn that amount,[13] the journal and organization were clearly aimed at the affluent. Each subscriber received an entrance card that allowed him to attend meetings. Exceptions to this policy were made only for deputies to the National Assembly, for members of the Société de 89, and for the Jacobins. Despite these restrictions, membership seems to have stayed between three and six thousand, an extraordinary number, possibly the largest club in France at that time.[14]

What kinds of people joined the Confédération? Unfortunately no membership or subscription list has ever been found. Nevertheless, an investigation of the *Bouche de fer* and other primary sources has yielded the names of 121 men and women

---

[13] Rudé, *The Crowd in the French Revolution*, p. 21.

[14] *RFB*, no. 54, p. 61, claims 3,000; *Mercure National et Révolutions de l'Europe*, 2 November 1790, pp. 1273-80, claims 4,000-5,000; *Cdm*, November 1792, p. 80 claims 6,000-7,000; *Bdf*, 22 January 1791, p. 132 claims 5,000-6,000.

who attended meetings of the Confédération des Amis de la Vérité (see Appendix A). This is a very small percentage of the total membership, but it may be the most important section; for these people were, in fact, the leaders of the club. The *Bouche de fer* included their names either because they made a speech to the club or because they were honored by other members. There is no way to determine how representative the leadership was of the rank and file. We can only reiterate that the Confédération was but one voluntary association in a sea of such clubs; if a member was unhappy with its leadership, he could freely leave the club—and some did just that.

Of the 121 members listed in Appendix A, 100 can be identified. By and large, they were a group of highly educated publicists, politicians, and writers. They included some of the most important participants in the Revolution, such as Condorcet, Boissy d'Anglas, Jacques-Pierre Brissot, Camille Desmoulins, and the abbé Sieyès. There were also less successful men, such as the mediocre playwright Jean-François Gueroult, who wrote some of Fauchet's speeches. All of these people had at least one thing in common: an appreciation for the ideas of the Enlightenment and, in particular, for the works of Jean-Jacques Rousseau. Whatever the Confédération des Amis de la Vérité later became, it began as a forum where intellectuals and politicians could discuss the application to the Revolution of the ideas of Rousseau and his contemporaries. Thus it is not surprising to find that the club included many disciples of the philosophe. For example, at this time Louis-Sébastien Mercier was putting the final touches on his *De Jean-Jacques Rousseau considéré comme l'un des premiers auteurs de la Révolution*, while Gabriel Brizard was in the midst of editing the complete works of Rousseau. Some of the members had been friends with Jean-Jacques, including Dumesnil and Girardin, who was said to have only "one idea: to put into practice those of his friend the philosophe."[15]

---

[15] Louis-Sébastien Mercier, *De Jean-Jacques Rousseau*; Jean Jacques Rousseau, *Oeuvres complètes*; M¹ˢ de Girardin, *L'Arrestation de dernier ami de Jean-Jacques Rousseau*, p. 61. On Dumesnil see *Cdm*, February 1792, p. 104. On Rousseau's relationship with the Confédération see also Roger Barny, "Jean-Jacques Rousseau dans la Révolution" *Dix-huitième siècle* 6: 59-98; Joan McDonald, *Rousseau and the French Revolution, 1761-1791*, pp. 76-80.

The most striking point concerning the social backgrounds of the known membership is that only two of the identifiable members were involved in occupations requiring manual labor: the carpenter Lanoa and the locksmith Gonnet. Social historians have hypothesized that what defined the ruling elite during that period was no longer noble status, but was the kind of work one engaged in; members of the upper classes did not do manual labor.[16] If this view is correct, then the vast majority of Confédération leaders came from the high plateau of French social life. Most were lawyers, physicians, priests, landlords, professors, journalists, or administrators. An unusually large number were also aspiring intellectuals who wrote plays, essays, and books on topics other than current events.

Our reconstructed membership list does not contain enough names for a sufficient quantitative analysis. Thus it may be helpful to focus on a few typical members to get at least an impressionistic idea of what those active in the club were like. Jean-Baptiste Plaisant, Adrien-Antoine Lamourette, and Camille Desmoulins all exhibit qualities characteristic of the Confédération. During the 1780s Plaisant was a professor of law in his hometown of Tournant (*Seine et Marne*) and a lawyer in the Paris Parlement. He wrote a book on Rousseau, and became so absorbed with the thinker's works that by 1785 he "was already a pronounced Republican."[17] In 1788 Plaisant used his legal skills to advise the Tournant assemblies on the selection of deputies for the Estates General. When the Revolution began he returned to Paris and was elected to its Communal Assembly. He was active in Parisian politics and became an administrator for public works. Yet despite his political activities, Plaisant somehow found the time to write at least six plays on patriotic themes, none of which were published. The Cercle Social offered him an arena in which to integrate his political and intellectual ambitions. During the Terror he was arrested for his moderate political views; he spent several months in prison before the charges against him were dropped.

[16] William Doyle, "Was there an Aristocratic Reaction in Pre-Revolutionary France?" *Past and Present* 57: 97-122.
[17] Archives Nationales, F7 4775⁷⁷, dossier 1, fol. 9 (police dossier of Jean-Baptiste Plaisant); Lacroix, *Actes* 7: 150.

Lamourette had begun a career in a seminary as a professor of theology (where he had been Henri Gregoire's teacher), but had left teaching for a parish in 1775.[18] During the 1780s he wrote a series of books that attempted to reconcile the Enlightenment with French religious life. The anticlerical and anti-Christian aspects of the Enlightenment are well known. By the time Lamourette was writing, the situation had become quite tense. "In general," he wrote, "the philosophes of our century acted too antitheologically, and we theologians perhaps have been a bit too antiphilosophical ourselves."[19] While he admitted that not all philosophes were evil men, he attacked "Boulanger, Voltaire, Diderot, and all the others" for attempting to "destroy all authority, and to obliterate all principles of humane duties." Even the word "philosophe" had become a pejorative term. "One will say of someone: 'he fears neither God nor men. He mistakes and bullies everyone, except when it is to his personal advantage.' And one will naturally respond: 'Here is a *philosophe!*' "[20]

Despite such harsh rhetoric, Lamourette attacked only those philosophes who had crossed the border into the realm of atheism and materialism. He insisted on a fusion of faith and reason, and welcomed all intellectuals who tried to overcome the polarity the radical philosophes had posed. He thought of his own writings as a contribution toward that end. "This work," he wrote in 1788, "is neither a religious book, nor a philosophical production; yet it moves from one character to the other: Enlightenment comes from good Reason, and experience fortifies its consideration of faith. Then does the voice of nature join to that of the Gospel in order to make us accept, adore, and practice

---

[18] Achille Pierre Liébaut, *Lamourette, prêtre et évêque assermenté* is inadequate and must be supplemented with Léon Berthé, "Grégoire, élève de l'abbé Lamourette" *Revue du Nord* 44: 401-46; Norman Ravitch, "Catholicism in Crisis: The Impact of the French Revolution on the Thought of the Abbé Adrien Lamourette" *International Journal of Economic and Social History* no. 9, pp. 354-85; and Daniele Menozzi, *"Philosophes" e "chrétiens éclairés." Politica e religione nella collaborazione de G. H. Mirabeau e A. A. Lamourette (1774-1794)*.

[19] Antoine-Adrien Lamourette, *Pensées sur la philosophie sur la foi*, p. xviij.

[20] Idem, *Les Délices de la religion*, p. lj; *Pensées sur la philosophie de l'incredulité*, pp. 229-34.

[religion]."²¹ He hoped that the word "philosophy" would cease to be used as a party label and would return to its original meaning of searching for truth. Only when Enlightenment and religion were united would thinking men realize that "the morality of the Gospel is the true system of Nature and Reason."²²

Lamourette despised the Roman Catholic Church almost as much as he hated the atheistic philosophes. In its ostentatious wealth and ecclesiastical hierarchies, the Church had turned its back on the poor and had become an oppressive institution. When the Revolution came in 1789, Lamourette embraced it as a sure means of "regenerating" the Church. In 1790, he published a very successful series of sermons called the *Prônes civiques*; no other religious book received the acclaim this one enjoyed in the revolutionary press during 1790 and 1791.²³ Whereas all of his previous writings had been essentially long philosophical or theological works for a limited readership, the *Prônes civiques* was written in a more popular language for rural priests. Lamourette sought to convince the lower clergy that the Revolution would benefit Christianity. He hoped that "the Gospel will be taught and professed in its ancient purity, and in its primitive simplicity and truth." While recognizing that the ideas of the Enlightenment had been partly responsible for the Revolution, he nonetheless insisted that "philosophy, far from turning its strength against religion, employs all its force to the regeneration of Christianity."²⁴

Lamourette became closely associated with Bonneville as early as 1789, when he wrote an article on the French clergy for Bonneville's journal, the *Tribun du peuple*.²⁵ When the Confédération des Amis de la Vérité was established, he was invited to join the Directoire du Cercle Social. He served it faithfully until the spring of 1791, when he left Paris to become archbishop

²¹ Lamourette, *Les Délices*, p. vij.

²² Ibid., p. x; idem, *Pensées . . . l'incredulité*, p. 67.

²³ *Bdf*, no. 24, November 1790, p. 383; *Pf*, 19 October 1790, p. 437; *CdP*, 15 October 1790, p. 1149; *RFB*, no. 63, p. 503; *Mercure de France*, 20 November 1790, pp. 92-94; *Courrier de Lyon*, 1 December 1790, pp. 201-202; *Journal encyclopédique*, 20 June 1791, pp. 63-76.

²⁴ *Prônes civiques ou Le Pasteur patriote*, no. 3, pp. 74-76.

²⁵ *Tribun du peuple*, no. 3, pp. 14-15.

of Lyon. Lamourette saw the Confédération as an arena where patriotism and piety could be fused into an enlightened Christianity. Elected to the Legislative Assembly, he was arrested during the Terror for supposedly aiding the famous Lyon uprising of 1793. He shared a jail cell with Fauchet shortly before being executed under the guillotine in 1794.

Camille Desmoulins, the "cleverist and wittiest of all journalists,"[26] was born the same year as Bonneville and received a good education at the Collège de Louis-le-Grand. At twenty-five he was admitted to the bar, and became a lawyer affiliated with the Paris Parlement. But Desmoulins was bored and unhappy in his new profession. In 1789 he returned to his hometown in the provinces to try to become its deputy to the Estates General. Failing this, he returned to Paris more frustrated than before. He achieved notoriety only after giving a speech at a spontaneous demonstration on 13 July, wherein he urged the crowd to storm the Bastille. During the summer of 1789 he wrote two very popular revolutionary pamphlets, which earned him a place of honor among Parisian publicists. He was one of the few writers who dared at that early date to question the value of monarchy, and his publishers were frightened to print his writings. With his new fame, Desmoulins decided to do what many successful writers did during the Revolution: he started a journal. The *Révolutions de France et de Brabant* appeared every Saturday, though it was more like a fifty-page editorial essay than a newspaper. While its influence is difficult to measure, historians generally agree that within a short time Desmoulins became, in his own words, "one of the most zealous propagandists of the Revolution."[27]

When the Confédération was established this "Voltaire of the streets"[28] joined the club, became its secretary and thus a member of the directoire. A few weeks later he wrote a long article on the club in his journal.[29] Desmoulins had a far too critical and

[26] M.C.M. Simpson, ed., *Reminiscences of a Regicide*, p. 147.

[27] Jacques Janssens, *Camille Desmoulins, le premier républicain de France*, pp. 1-51.

[28] Alphonse de Lamartine, *History of the Girondists* 1: 247.

[29] *RFB*, no. 54, pp. 50-61; *Bdf*, no. 34, December 1790, p. 532.

independent mind merely to heap praise on the Confédération, and he poked fun at the stern and puritanical Fauchet. For all his leadership abilities, Fauchet had been born without a sense of humor, and he was insulted by Desmoulins' friendly gibes. In January, Fauchet told the Confédération that he had approved of Desmoulins' appointment to the directoire only on the advice of friends and, in fact, had never read the publicist's writings. As far as he was concerned, Desmoulins was a false patriot, interested only in ridiculing the Cercle Social.[30] Bonneville and the other leaders of the club, however, saw the article in more objective terms and deemed him a valuable member. Desmoulins continued to attend meetings, and in fact, the Imprimerie du Cercle Social published his *Révolutions de France et de Brabant* during the spring of 1791. Indeed, Desmoulins remained friendly to most leaders of the Cercle Social at least until 1792, when the split between moderate and radical republicans became irreconcilable.

NEARLY all historians who have discussed the Cercle Social have mentioned the group's connection with Freemasonry, and some have even claimed that the Confédération was itself little more than a Masonic lodge.[31] They have seen strong Masonic influences in the Confédération's cosmopolitan schemes and utopian jargon. There is some evidence to support this view. "We invite all Masons," the *Bouche de fer* proclaimed, "to come into the Cercle Social; to address the confessions of the *Bouche de fer*." Fauchet—never a Freemason himself—welcomed all Masons into the Confédération and praised them for spreading subversive ideas before the Revolution. The meeting room of the club was decorated with various kinds of Masonic symbols. For example, on the wall were the insignia of the *Orient universel de France*. The masthead atop every issue of the *Bouche de fer*, showing rays of light shining across the universe, was full of Masonic references. Cercle Social members also often addressed

[30] *Bdf*, 7 January 1791, pp. 36-37.
[31] E.g., McDonald, *Rousseau*, p. 76, and J. M. Thompson, *The French Revolution*, p. 234.

each other with the Masonic title "N" (for Notuma), and the special symbol ∴ was often used in the *Bouche de fer*.[32]

One reason for the appearance of these symbols was that a great many Cercle Social leaders had themselves been Freemasons before the Revolution. Several, for example, had belonged to the progressive Loge des neuf soeurs, whose aims and programs were similar to the Cercle Social. Bonneville not only had belonged to a lodge but had published a two-volume work on the history of Freemasonry and was thus noted as an expert in the field.[33]

Yet despite the strong ties between the Cercle Social and Freemasonry, historians err in calling the club a lodge, or even in suggesting that it developed from a lodge. In order to appreciate the differences between the two organizations, a brief digression on the nature of Freemasonry in the Old Regime is necessary.

French Freemasonry was the creation of the eighteenth-century upper classes. Although the first lodge was begun in 1717, it did not become a significant movement until the middle of the century. By the 1780s, France had over 700 lodges, with some 70,000 adherents. Although Freemasonry preached civic equality, its membership was drawn from the top of the social ladder. "Masonry is a democracy," wrote one historian, "but it is a democracy within an elite."[34]

French Freemasonry had at least two purposes. First it hoped to spread the cosmopolitan values of the Enlightenment throughout the world. "The entire world is only one great republic," said the Grand Master in 1740, "of which each nation is a family and each individual an infant. It is in order to revive and spread these essential maxims found in the nature of man that our

---

[32] *Bdf*, no. 1, October 1790, pp. 9-10, and no. 7, October 1790, pp. 104-107; Halem, *Paris en 1790. Voyage de Halem*, p. 214.

[33] Louis Amiable, *Une Loge maçonnique d'avant 1789*; Nicolas Bonneville, *Les Jésuites chassés de la Maçonnerie*.

[34] Gaston Martin, *La Franc-Maçonnerie française et la préparation de la Révolution*, pp. 8, 36. On eighteenth-century French Freemasonry see Pierre Chevallier, *Histoire de la Franc-Maçonnerie française. Vol 1. La Maçonnerie*, and Daniel Ligou, *Histoire des Franc-Maçons en France*.

society was first established."[35] Second, French Freemasonry offered an alternative for intellectuals and other members of a social elite who were alienated from the Catholic Church and needed a forum in which to share solidarity, fraternity, and love; an arena where they could place their philosophical values within an informal, speculative, and emotional context. While Masonic dogma advocated reason, tolerance, and science, Masonic meetings were filled with superstitious rituals and mystical jargon. This tension appealed to many in the last half of the eighteenth century, and it is in this sense that Masonry partly became a religion of the intellectuals.

Although Freemasonry helped to spead some radical ideas, it was too closely integrated into the Old Regime to survive the events of 1789. One must not forget that Freemasonry was a secret, closed, and elitist organization. The sacred oath required of every Mason included the following words: "I hereby solemnly avow and swear . . . that I will hail and conceal, and never reveal the secrets or secrecy of Masons or Masonry, that shall be revealed to me, unless to a free and worshipful lodge of brothers and fellows well met." Such secrecy and esprit de corps became suspect during the Revolution, and it is no wonder that French Freemasonry fell apart between 1789-1795.[36]

The Confédération praised Freemasonry for its activities before the Revolution. In a despotic society like the Old Regime, truth had to be kept well insulated from the public. The Confédération saw Masons as anti-monks, who had protected the sacred values of liberty, equality, and fraternity during the dark period of the recent past. But since the Revolution had founded a nation upon these very values, there was no longer a need for their secretive organization. This is why, for example, Fauchet lauded Masons for their libertarian ideas, while scolding them for their elitism and their secretive initiation practices. In short, Cercle Social leaders thought that Freemasonry was necessary only in a despotic society, where an elite had to band together

[35] Cited in Martin, *La Franc-Maçonnerie française*, p. 47.
[36] Samuel Prichard, *Masonry Dissected*, p. 16; Chevallier, *Histoire de la Franc-Maçonnerie française*, pp. 342-72.

in secret to protect certain values. But once despotism ceased, Masonry lost its raison d'être.

Thus the Confédération des Amis de la Vérité was not a lodge, but its leaders sought to fill the void left by the demise of Freemasonry by appropriating Masonic language and rituals. This was partly an effort to avoid partisan politics, and partly a means to attract an international following. Within France, the Confédération did not seek any affiliation with Masonic lodges, but rather tried to develop a network of revolutionary clubs. But outside of France, where there were no such clubs, the situation called for a different approach. In "despotic" countries, such as Germany, Masonic lodges still served the same purpose as they had in France before the Revolution. Thus when the Cercle Social wanted to organize a worldwide network, it cultivated Masonic lodges; but it still urged them to drop the elitist pretensions of Freemasonry and affiliate themselves with the Confédération des Amis de la Vérité by transforming themselves into cercles sociaux. The *Bouche de fer* printed several letters by Freemasons asking advice on how to establish their own Cercle Social affiliates. One German lodge was particularly excited about the Confédération's work:

We agree with the advice which you are giving to all Freemasons, to unite themselves in a Cercle Social. ... This had been *our project* for a long time. But we were indecisive about the way to execute it, and often obstructed by obstacles which appeared to us too difficult to surmount.[37]

Masonic Lodges had been social and quasireligious centers for local elites; the transformation to cercles sociaux would make them propaganda and education centers for publicists, philosophers, and all interested citizens.

THE Confédération des Amis de la Vérité was begun during a period when patriotic societies were flourishing throughout the capital. These clubs served many functions. First, in the void left by the demise of court politics, they acted as interest groups for particular causes. For example, the Société des amis des Noirs

---

[37] *Bdf*, no. 14, November 1790, pp. 213-14; see also no. 4, October 1790, p. 34, no. 12, November 1790, p. 288, and 10 April 1791, p. 29.

advocated the abolition of slavery, while the Société des amis de l'union et de l'égalité dans les familles argued for reforms in inheritance laws. Second, in an age when periodicals were manifold and expensive, societies served as reading clubs, allowing their members easy access to the news of the day. More important, clubs provided ways for thinking men to develop personal connections and political constituencies; indeed, virtually every politician, journalist, and intellectual of any importance belonged to some club during this period.[38]

The Confédération did not think of itself as just another club but rather, as the name implied, a federation of all existing clubs. By affiliating with other patriotic societies in France, and with Masonic lodges outside of the nation, the Cercle Social wished to create a worldwide network of Amis de la Vérité. In this sense, the members of the Paris Confédération were thought of as delegates from other organizations and were often addressed in that form. "The Cercle Social is not a club. ... It is an association of citizens spread all over the globe." The Cercle Social hoped that its Paris Confédération would become a "weekly rendezvous of all clubs, societies, and committees."[39]

The Confédération actively pursued contacts with other clubs. It wrote to many provincial societies seeking affiliation and correspondence, and even attempted to begin its own chapters. For example, during the spring of 1791 Henri Bancal, one of the original Fauchetins, offered to begin a Cercle Social branch in England. While on a trip in that country, he wrote to the Confédération of his idea. He hoped that such a group might serve as a forum where French and English intellectuals could meet. Bancal was a good friend of both Bonneville and Fauchet, having been closely associated with them in Parisian politics since the outbreak of the Revolution. Fauchet was excited about the project and eagerly responded to his friend that "the Confederation of the Friends of Truth is entirely animated with the same sentiments and has absolutely the same views. If during your

---

[38] For an excellent contemporary summary of the role of clubs see *Journal des clubs*, Prospectus, pp. 8-9. See also Isabelle Bourdin, *Les Sociétés populaires à Paris pendant la Révolution*, and J. B. Challamel, *Les Clubs contre-révolutionnaires*.

[39] *Qu'est-ce que la bouche de fer*, p. 3; *Bdf*, 19 February 1791, pp. 332-33.

stay in London you can succeed to promote a fraternal connexion betwixt us and some of the English societies which have the same principles and designs as cosmo-political [sic], you will do a great service to the *common interest of men*."[40]

The Confédération also tried to make itself a central federation by inviting members of more prestigious clubs like the Jacobins to attend its meetings without entrance cards. Officials of the Confédération would then write to Jacobin affiliates in the provinces, inviting them to correspond and affiliate with the Cercle Social, implying that some sort of affiliation had been worked out between the two groups.

The attempt at developing a national network of Cercles Sociaux encountered a great deal of hostility from the Jacobins, and the two clubs became bitter rivals. The Amis de la constitution, as the Jacobins were formally called, had begun as a group of deputies in the National Assembly. The organization's goals were more political and less academic than those of the Confédération. The club served primarily as a center where politicians could discuss proposals for national legislation. By the fall of 1790, the Parisian Jacobins had grown to a membership of over 1,000, and had initiated an effort to develop their own national network of affiliated clubs. One requirement for affiliation was that a provincial club could affiliate with no other Parisian organization except the Jacobins.[41]

Since the Confédération already had over four times as many members as the Jacobins and was developing its own contacts among provincial clubs, it is no wonder that many Jacobins suspected the Cercle Social of trying to usurp the Jacobins' authority. A propaganda campaign aimed against the Cercle Social was begun at once. The fight was led by Choderlos de Laclos, editor of the Jacobins' semi-official newspaper. Laclos, who had risen to fame before the Revolution by writing the famous novel,

[40] Bibliothèque Nationale, Nouvelles acquisitions françaises, 9534, fols. 190-95. I have used the English version found in these papers. Brissot probably had a hand in this project. See the letter of 14 April 1791 in E. Bernardin, "Lettres de Lanthenas à Bancal des Issarts" *Annales historiques de la Révolution française* 16: 245.

[41] Michael L. Kennedy, *The Jacobin Clubs in the French Revolution: The First Years*, p. 60; Gérard Walter, *Histoire des Jacobins*, pp. 102-103; Clarence Crane Brinton, *The Jacobins: an Essay in the New History*, p. 36.

Les Liaisons dangereuses, was a questionable character. Historians are generally agreed that Laclos was an agent of the duc d'Orléans, and did everything he could to attain the crown for him. Like one of the characters in his novel, Laclos saw politics only as a way of advancing personal ambitions, and the spirit of 1789 meant little to him. He despised both the political and cosmopolitan views of the Cercle Social.[42] "It seems important that the public become familiar with the true object of the Confédération," Laclos warned a month after the club was established.

> MM. B*** and F***, who are at the head of this society seem to want to establish what the National Assembly is already doing, and overtake it. Their works tend to direct popular opinion towards a constitution which they have founded, not on equality of rights, but on the absurd notion of equality of property. Their system appears to be a mixture of those Martinists, and Rosicrucians. ... If anything was capable of placing us under the yoke of despotism, it would be the attention which the People have given to the insane project of MM. B*** and F***.

Most of this analysis was nonsense. How could a mystical-utopian group usurp the political authority of the National Assembly? Nevertheless, Laclos persuaded enough of his colleagues to pass a decree that was sent to all provincial Jacobin societies, ordering them to avoid contact with the Cercle Social.[43]

The Directoire du Cercle Social reacted angrily to the decree. They accused Laclos of "dishonoring a society of patriots" and protested that the Jacobin club was obstructing the diffusion of patriotic values. More significantly, Cercle Social members argued that its Confédération was better suited to become a center for patriotic clubs. Membership in the Jacobins was by invitation only. Such elitism, it was argued, gave the club an *esprit de corps* that ran counter to the ideals of the Revolution. The Confédération des Amis de la Vérité, on the other hand, had an open admissions policy; whoever subscribed to the *Bouche de fer* was welcomed.[44]

---

[42] Emile Dard, *Le Général Choderlos de Laclos*; Walter, *Jacobins*, p. 85; McClelland, "Lameths and Lafayette," p. 103.

[43] *Journal des amis de la constitution*, 21 November 1790, p. 44, and 21 December 1790, pp. 155-157.

[44] *Bdf*, 19 February 1791, pp. 332-33, and 3 April 1791, p. 27. For a general

Camille Desmoulins was one who saw the rivalry as unnecessary. He pointed out that there were many men who, like
himself, were members of both clubs; indeed, the president of
the Confédération was a member of the Jacobins, and the president of the Jacobins was a member of the Confédération! He
criticized both groups for their territorial behavior and insisted
that no group should be able to monopolize fraternity; since all
clubs supported the promulgation of similar values, they must
all help one another.[45]

The rivalry naturally confused many provincial societies. Several wrote to the Jacobins asking how they should respond to
Cercle Social overtures. Laclos always used the occasion to rid-
icule the group. The Cercle Social, he once responded, "no longer
exists, or at least if it still exists, no one pays attention to it."
When a provincial club told the Cercle Social that their alliance
with the Jacobins precluded any affiliation with the Cercle Social,
Bonneville called them "slaves!"[46]

While the struggle between the two clubs was sometimes
heated, it must be put into perspective. Neither club accused the
other of being counterrevolutionary; there was never a call for
the arrest of leaders, or other such drastic measures. The rivalry
between the Cercle Social and the Jacobins, for example, contrasted markedly with the attack leveled by both groups against
the more aristocratic Club monarchique. That club was begun
by a group of very conservative politicians who wanted to halt
any further extension of the Revolution. The Directoire du Cercle Social denounced it to the Paris Communal Assembly, demanding an end to its "divisive and antirevolutionary maneu-
vers." Thus while the members of the Club monarchique were
considered traitors to the Revolution, the Jacobins and the Cercle
Social saw one another at most as misguided patriots, and more
often as competitors playing the same game.[47]

defense against Laclos' attacks see *Programme du Cercle Social pour la Confédération universelle des Amis de la Vérité* (Paris, ICS, n.d.).

[45] *RFB*, no. 54, pp. 50-61.

[46] *Journal des amis de la constitution*, 1 February 1791, p. 439; *Bdf*, 3 February
1791, pp. 216-17.

[47] *Bdf*, 27 January 1791, p. 178, and 1 June 1791, p. 178; A. Aulard, ed., *La
Société des Jacobins* 1: 437, 448.

4

Regeneration of Culture

ATHANASE AUGER (1734-1792). Professor of Rhetoric, Royal College of Rouen. *Chronique du mois* editor for classical literature. One of the most well-known classicists in Revolutionary France, Auger was a close friend of Jean-Marie Roland and became a kind of intellectual dean of the Cercle Social. His feminist and pedagogical ideas had great influence upon the Confédération des Amis de la Vérité.

Courtesy of The Newberry Library, Chicago

Oh women! It is slavery, which by making you nothing other than degraded pieces of merchandise and objects of jealousy, has banished happiness from the earth.

Bouche de fer, 1 January 1791, p. 4.

WHEN Goupil de Préfeln opened the 10 December 1790 meeting of the Confédération des Amis de la Vérité, he announced that his term as president had expired and that the directoire had chosen Antoine Mailly de Châteaurenard as his successor. Goupil thanked the club for allowing him to serve it and urged members to continue the struggle to transform the French constitution into the "Catechism of Humanity." He assured members that Mailly's "knowledge, talents, and ... virtuous patriotism" made him worthy of their respect and honor.[1]

Mailly, a deputy to the National Assembly and a Freemason (he had belonged to the prestigious Loge des neuf soeurs), delivered an opening address filled with a cosmopolitanism characteristic of the Cercle Social. "I recognize here one of the first temples of a regenerated world," he exclaimed.

I see in it the columns of a Universal Republic. Let us establish here the sanctuary of popular divinity, in harmony with our will and our knowledge. Here we are: all new seeds which will decorate the earth, and procure for it a never-ending stream of the most sacred, virtuous, and sublime truths. This is the way that the entire world will be transformed into one great city by the principal generators of the Fatherland.[2]

Under Mailly's presidency, which ran until May 1791, the Confédération devised schemes designed to implement this idealist cosmology. The club became increasingly convinced that the new regime needed to be strengthened by a more complete regeneration that would transform the customs and manners of the French people. Between October 1790 and May 1791, the club focused on four prominent aspects of that cultural revo-

[1] *Bdf*, no. 34, December 1790, pp. 530-31.
[2] Ibid., p. 532.

lution: civil religion, public education, property, and women's rights.

ONE OF THE primary characteristics of the generation that followed the philosophes was a new interest in religion and religious phenomena. Indeed, the most important contribution that the Cercle Social made to the intellectual history of the Revolution was its exploration of the possibilities for a new relationship between politics and religion. No text was more relevant to this issue than Rousseau's *Social Contract*. In the last chapter entitled "Civil Religion," Rousseau envisioned free nations founded upon a patriotic cult of the Fatherland. Rousseau insisted that the stability of any political system was dependent upon such a social faith.[3] Among Rousseau's disciples, this chapter opened the door to new ways of thinking about politics and religion. Fauchet noted this influence in one of his commentaries on the master: "As the author of the *Social Contract* observes, the Heavens must sanction human laws and the legislator must work according to the divine plan in order to tie the conscience of society into one sacred knot."[4] This idea had already been well developed by Fauchet in his *De la religion nationale* of 1789. Like Rousseau, Fauchet believed that philosophes such as Helvétius and Holbach had been mistaken in thinking that any society could exist without a religion. This was impossible for at least two reasons. First, man "is a religious being by nature," so that a society of atheists is a perversity. Second, and perhaps more important, religion is essential in providing a society with social unity and equality; without it "the bonds of social constitutions would be without strength, and would be easily torn." That both man and society needed religion was not foreign to Enlightenment thought. Most of the philosophes had advocated some sort of "natural" religion, devoid of superstition and mystical rituals. But Fauchet objected even to this view, insisting that religion must be both emotive and rational.

A philosophical religion is not enough. The simple principles of natural law have been accepted only in the smallest of nations; they require

---

[3] Book 4, Chapter 8, of the *Social Contract*.
[4] *Bdf*, 17 January 1791, p. 102.

an essential accessory which gives them power over the imagination, and through it, the feelings. It is necessary to have a Heaven with rewards; a Hell with formidable punishments; a Mediator with thousands of intermediaries between the infinite Being and the mortal creatures; prayers and ritual; the semblance of a religion for both the spiritual and the sensible; one which embraces the diverse faculties of the human mind and heart.[5]

The preoccupation with religious issues was as much a characteristic of the lay members of the Confédération as it was of the priests. Bonneville was busy writing a sociological study of ancient religions during this period. Even Camille Desmoulins was absorbed in the topic. In his first pamphlet, he insisted that atheism was a social disease; without religion a society would crumble. "It is not God who needs religion," he claimed; "it is man. God has no need for incense, professions, and prayers; but we need to have hope, consolation and a rewarder."[6]

The Confédération advocated two kinds of transformations in French religious practice. These were a radical remodeling of ecclesiastical life and the development of a new civil religion. The outbreak of the Revolution was marked by a parallel revolt within the French clergy. During the eighteenth century French priests were beset with glaring inequities. For example, while the archbishop of Strasbourg received some 800,000 livres per year, a country curé living but a few miles away earned 700 livres, and his assistants only 350. By 1789 such exploitive conditions had alienated a good portion of the lower clergy. One priest claimed that the Church had been struck with "a disease at once religious, moral, and political, which cannot be cured by any ordinary remedies such as the modification of the laws."[7]

The Confédération supported the aims of these clergymen.

---

[5] Fauchet, *De la religion nationale*, pp. 41-43.
[6] Camille Desmoulins, *Oeuvres* ... 1: 90.
[7] Cited in Timothy Tackett, *Priest and Parish in Eighteenth Century France: A Social and Political Study of the Curés in a Diocese of Dauphiné, 1750-1791*, p. 263. See also p. 268, where Tackett claims that "perhaps not since the period of the Reformation had such revolutionary transformations been advocated by so large a segment of the Catholic clergy. It was all the more noteworthy in that the impetus was coming from the lower echelons of the ecclesiastical hierarchy." See also William Hayes Williams, "The Priest in History: A Study in Divided Loyalties in the French Lower Clergy from 1776 to 1789."

"Fear the high clergy," Bonneville wrote. "Here are the enemies of the nation."[8] Confédération members agreed that the Church must cease to be an autonomous corporate body; its power and its land must be placed under the state. It should exist only to serve the people. Indeed, Fauchet was one of a number of priests and intellectuals who argued that the parish church should become a kind of propaganda center for rural Frenchmen.[9] They also advocated a democratic and egalitarian clergy, who would serve the people by setting an example for them. Instead of being the wealthiest Frenchmen, they would be the most enlightened. "In a free France," Fauchet wrote, "the clergy will be the elite of the most virtuous men in the nation." Fauchet hoped that the clergy and the intelligentsia would become the same elite, and one newspaper aptly noted that "he himself embodies the double character of priest and philosophe."[10]

More important was the Confédération's insistence that some form of civil religion must be encouraged among the people if the Revolution were to be successful. Confédération members realized that the Revolution was dependent upon the approval of the masses; they knew that aristocrats and reactionary priests could easily persuade large numbers of peasants to turn against the Revolution. They felt that the values of the Revolution had to be immediately inculcated into the hearts of the people and recognized that the most effective way to achieve this was through religion. "Religion," one member wrote, "in inspecting the conscience, exercises its empire where the eye of the law cannot penetrate."[11]

What did these men mean by religion? "Religion," wrote Bonneville, "is literally nothing other than social fraternity."[12]

[8] *Tribun du peuple*, no. 1, p. 7. See also Jacques-Antoine Creuzé-Latouche, *Lettre ... aux municipalités, et aux habitants des campagnes du Département de la Vienne* (Paris: ICS, [1790]), pp. 1-8.

[9] Fauchet, *Encore quatre cris ou Sermon d'un patriote*, Joseph-Marie Lequinio, *Ecole des Laboureurs*, pp. 39-40.

[10] Fauchet, *Oraison funèbre de Charles-Michel de l'Epée*, p. 6; *Journal de la municipalité et des districts*, 1 April 1790, p. 587.

[11] Cressy, *Essai sur les moeurs ou Point de Constitution durable sans moeurs*, p. 148.

[12] *Bdf*, no. 8, October 1790, pp. 115, and no. 32, December 1790, p. 499.

Religion was mankind's most effective unifying principle; only religion could bring people together; it alone could present laws, customs, and philosophy in a coherent worldview for the people. "What are habits and laws without religion?" Cercle Social members repeatedly asked.[13] Club members believed that every free people had developed a civil religion, an idea they may have encountered in Montesquieu's early article on the civil religion of the Romans. The more observant Christian members argued that the new national constitution should be founded upon the Gospel. One priest proclaimed "the marvelous accord between religion and patriotism, between liberty and religion. ... The true Christian will always be the best patriot."[14]

While the members of the Confédération were interested in religion, they did not always agree with each other. Two schools of civil religious thought can be isolated within the Cercle Social. The first was a Christian view developed by Lamourette and Fauchet. Here the patriotic cult of the Fatherland was envisioned to be nothing other than a kind of primitive Christianity. The Church would be stripped of its ostentatious wealth, and Christians would be urged simply to follow the ethical precepts of the Gospel. In this view, Rousseau's civil religion was made explicitly Christian; laws were not created by a legislator, but originated with God. For the other philosophy, Bonneville proposed that Christianity be superseded by a religion better suited to the new epoch, one which would project the values of the Enlightenment onto a supernatural plane. Instead of Christ and his disciples, the philosophes themselves would become the saints of this new church. In the dichotomy between these two approaches we have the embryos for two important institutions that were born later in the Revolution. The Christian school became manifest in the Constitutional Church, in which Fauchet, Lamourette, and other Confédération members became leaders. The other view eventually grew into the Cult of Reason, which attempted to replace the Church with a more philosophical re-

---

[13] E.g., Jean-Baptiste Volfius, *Discours prononcé le 18 mai 1790 à la cérémonie du sermont fédératif*, p. 27; *Pf*, 19 October 1789, pp. 1-2.
[14] Richard Chaix, *De l'influence de la religion sur le patriotisme*, pp. 4-5.

ligion during the Terror.[15] While it is important to note that
the differences between these two groups did not become explicit
until the failure of the Constitutional Church in 1792, tensions
within the club cannot be understood without an awareness of
this schism. Fauchet's attitude toward Voltaire is perhaps the
best illustration of this division.

In his second discourse to the Confédération, Fauchet argued
that, while Voltaire may have been a skillful writer, he did not
deserve the almost divine reverence accorded him by the Republic of Letters. That Voltaire was not an original thinker was
the most favorable thing Fauchet said. He attacked the philosophe for his anti-egalitarian ideas, his connections with members of the aristocracy, and for his personal wealth. Fauchet tried
to establish a connection between social status and religious
outlook by theorizing that Voltaire's wealth and power caused
him to adopt atheism.[16]

Included in the audience on that evening was one of Voltaire's
most loyal disciples, Charles Villette. He and Bonneville were
friends, and he had collaborated on earlier Cercle Social publications. A poet, literary critic, member of the Société de 89 and
the Jacobins, and editor of the influential daily, the *Chronique
de Paris*, Villette was an important figure in the Republic of
Letters. Recently, he had been the first to advocate the deification
of Voltaire in a new civil religion, and wanted the philosophe's
ashes transported to the new Church of Sainte-Geneviève, transforming that building into the Panthéon.[17]

Villette was outraged by Fauchet's speech. Though Bonneville
had offered to make Villette a secretary of the Confédération,
this convinced him to refuse the position. Villette attacked Fauchet
for being a "hypocrite" and a "blasphemer." Far from aiding
the Old Regime, Voltaire "published the courageous truths that
today serve as the basis of our constitution." If he supported the

---

[15] An excellent analysis of the Christian view is Hans Maier, *Revolution and
Church: The Early History of Christian Democracy, 1789-1901*, pp. 68-141; on
the other school see Alphonse Aulard, *Le Culte de la raison et le culte de l'être
suprême, 1793-1794. Essai historique*.

[16] *Bdf*, no. 7, October 1790, pp. 108-11.

[17] *Journal des clubs*, 1: 172-73; *CdP*, 12 November 1790, p. 1262, and 19 March
1791, p. 310.

king, it was only to destroy the despotic power of the Church. Moreover, as leader of the philosophes, Voltaire was at the forefront of those advocating the most progressive changes for France. Indeed, "if it had not been for the philosophes, there would be no Revolution today."[18]

A more penetrating reaction to Fauchet's remarks came from Villette's close friend, Anacharsis Cloots. One of the most colorful figures of the Revolution, and an avowed disciple of the philosophes, Cloots believed that the Revolution was simply the means by which the ideas of the Enlightenment could eventually spread throughout the world. When the Confédération was established, he embraced the organization and was asked to join its directoire.[19] Like Villette, Cloots was put off by Fauchet's attack on "the Father of all modern philosophers, and by consequence, of the Revolution." But what offended Cloots most was the Christian orientation of Fauchet's thought. It was ridiculous for any person who called himself a patriot to stand before the people in clerical dress and preach the Gospel. Christianity, in Cloots' view, had been given over 1,700 years to improve the world; it had only succeeded in creating despotic institutions and absurd doctrines. The Revolution must signal its demise. Cloots insisted that Fauchet had completely misunderstood the concept of French liberty: France would be free only when she was enlightened; reason, not Christianity, was the key to enlightenment.[20] Fauchet did not allow such heresy to go unanswered: "M. Cloots has one capital vice in all of his writings. It is to construct a false morality upon the law, instead of constructing the law upon an eternal morality. He wants no religion at all, because religion to him is only a noose."[21]

Unfortunately, Fauchet overstated his case. While Cloots despised Christianity, he was by no means antireligious. "You are

---

[18] *Courrier de Paris dans les 83 départments*, 28 October 1790, pp. 420-22; *Bdf*, no. 7, October 1790, pp. 148-49.

[19] Anacharsis Cloots, *L'Orateur du genre humain*, p. 28; *Courrier de Paris dans les 83 départements*, 28 October 1790, p. 422; Georges Avenal, *Anacharsis Cloots, l'orateur du genre humain*, pp. 131-83.

[20] This and Cloots' next quote come from a 20 April 1791 letter to Fauchet reprinted in *RFB*, no. 77, p. 574.

[21] *Bdf*, 29 March 1791, p. 581.

too infatuated with the Christian trinity and not enough in love with the civic trinity," Cloots retorted. "The Nation, National Assembly, and King form a much better and more salutary trinity than the Father, Son, and Holy Ghost." What Cloots really wanted was a "natural religion ... a simple religion applicable to all the world."

Thus, what was at the heart of the Voltaire affair was not the value of religion per se, but rather what kind of a faith constituted the best civil religion for a free people. In calmer moments Fauchet himself realized that this was the core of the problem. "You have replaced the Gospels with natural law," he told Cloots, but since the Gospels were already "the perfection of natural law," they need no replacement.[22]

Bonneville tried to find a middle ground between these two positions. Fauchet was technically correct; yes, Voltaire had faults. He was suspicious of the goodness of the people, and often appeared to behave in an aristocratic manner. But Fauchet was nonetheless too severe in his criticism. "His faults," claimed Bonneville, "are great, but THEY ARE THE FAULTS OF HIS CENTURY, of a century which *was not made for the truth*." Criticism of Voltaire must be balanced with a knowledge of the obstacles he faced. While he may have had some of the prejudices of his day, no man of letters ever took more risks in publishing dangerous works, in helping less fortunate writers, or in defending the oppressed and persecuted. "Do not bring to his time ideas, habits, and hopes that were not there," Bonneville warned. While Voltaire would hardly be considered a zealous patriot in 1790, he was certainly one in his own day. "If Voltaire was not a great man, there are no great men in bondage."[23]

[22] Aulard, *Jacobins* 1: 33; *Bdf*, no. 10, October 1790, pp. 156-58. For a different view of Cloots' religious attitudes see Charles A. Gliozzo and James Friguglietti, "The Personal Enemy of Jesus Christ: Anacharsis Cloots, An Irreligious Revolutionary of the Eighteenth Century" *Eighteenth Century Life* 3: 80-84.

[23] *Bdf*, no. 10, October 1790, pp. 150-54. Bonneville's thoughts on Voltaire were taken almost verbatim from his *Histoire de l'Europe* 1: 8. After Fauchet left the Cercle Social, Bonneville praised Villette. The Cercle Social proposed to make Voltaire an honorary member of the Confédération and participated in transferring Voltaire's ashes to the Panthéon. See *Bdf*, 11 [sic] May 1791, pp. 263-66, 24 May 1791, pp. 349-50, and 31 May 1791, p. 13.

Civil religion had the important advantage of bringing the intellectual closer to the people. Before the Revolution, the philosophes had distanced themselves from the uneducated, especially with regard to religion. Freemasonry was open only to the upper classes, while the people's folk rituals were generally shunned. By making the people's interests synonymous with those of the nation, the Revolution refused to tolerate special interest groups that were opposed to the people. The ultimate justification for a group's existence now lay in its service to the people. This placed the intellectual in a vulnerable position, as the attacks upon academies in Marat's *Ami du Peuple* illustrate.[24] Bonneville and his friends attempted to adapt the Republic of Letters to meet the new requirements. The development of a civil religion would go far toward this end. The intelligentsia would retain its elitist composition; it would maintain a distinct identity as a community of thinkers. Yet, since the intelligentsia would also become the new priestly class of a cult of the Fatherland, it would become responsible for promoting rituals, popular symbols, and fetes. Intellectuals would thus become the new cult leaders, assuring their close association with the masses.

RELATED to the development of a civil religion was the Cercle Social's concern for the creation of a national system of public education. As with civil religion, the Cercle Social intended a public educational system to involve a new role for the intellectual. During the Enlightenment, intellectuals had been teachers of only the elite. If the philosophes discussed the general education of the public, it was usually a utopian vision, set far in the future. With the Revolution, patriotic intellectuals like those in the Cercle Social saw a new role for themselves as educators of the masses. "Instruct the people and the people are saved. We must dissipate the prejudices that obscure their reason."[25] This new constituency meant a change in orientation for

---

[24] *Ami du peuple*, 17 August 1790, pp. 4-8.

[25] Jacques Boilleau, "Réflections d'un patriote, et Projet sur la manière d'inspirer au peuple l'amour de la constitution," *Journal des clubs*, 15-21 April 1791, p. 444. On the views of the philosophes, see Harry C. Payne, *The Philosophes and the People*.

the intellectuals. The philosophe taught in order to develop critical thinking. A Diderot essay, for example, was intended to provoke the reader to question in new ways, not to serve as gospel. Cercle Social intellectuals, on the other hand, hoped to feed proper political values to the people, so that they would become patriots. "In the new order of things where we devote ourselves to liberty," proclaimed one Cercle Social prospectus, "every individual can and must serve the Fatherland. It is not enough to develop the faculties of old people, women, and children; their destructive prejudices must be replaced by regenerative virtues."[26]

Confédération members were so concerned with public education that they created a National Educational Committee, which met in the office of the Directoire du Cercle Social every Monday at 5:30 P.M.[27] The Committee believed that any educational system ought to include the basic skills of reading, writing, and arithmetic, culminating in scientific training. The aim of such instruction would be to produce enlightened citizens, capable of making the political decisions required of a free people. Yet this instruction was far from adequate in itself; even if it succeeded, the Revolution might still collapse. A free France needed an educational system that also dealt with "the whole development of their physical and moral faculties."[28] Any successful educational system would teach moral, political, and spiritual values; it would mold a citizenry that was above all loyal to the Revolution and its values. "It will place the constitution on a more solid and immutable basis." Perhaps even more important, Committee members hoped that a centralized, national, democratic educational system would create an egalitarian society. A spokesman for the Committee warned,

If all your schools ... are not uniform, if you introduce into them any differences other than what is necessary for conserving, for all talents,

---

[26] [Etta Palm], *Prospectus pour le Cercle patriotique des Amies de la Vérité* (Paris: ICS, n.d.), p. 1; see also Michel Perrot, *Exposition patriotique des droits de l'homme,* p. 16.

[27] *Bdf,* no. 20, November 1790, p. 320.

[28] "Essai sur l'éducation nationale," *Annales de la Confédération universelle des Amis de la Vérité* (Paris: ICS, 1791), p. 64. The following quotes come from pp. 61, 64, 89.

their distinctive form, I suggest that you will destroy equality in its most basic elements; that you will constitute a rich and a poor, that you will establish the most dangerous and detestable aristocracy.

The National Education Committee recognized that teaching morality presented certain problems. "The dominant philosophy is always in formal opposition to sane morality or to religion itself." Like other members of the Confédération, the Committee urged a reconciliation between Enlightenment and religion. Not only would religion become more enlightened, egalitarian, and fraternal but science would also be reformed. "It is absolutely necessary to regenerate and to class the sciences in such a way that young people can only see a pure and harmonic expression of the universality of beings." Unfortunately the Committee gave no specifics on how this was to be accomplished.

Several members of the Confédération wrote their own discourses calling for a new educational system. Athanase Auger "sensed that there is a new class of citizens who must not be allowed to go without instruction. I am referring to the masses of people in the towns and all of the simple peasants in the country." Auger believed that only one thing could assure the victory of the Third Estate. "It is education that forms culture and prepares a generation of men disposed to cherish and respect the new regime." The government must begin with

elementary schools, where the principle object of teaching will be the principles of the new constitution, the rights and duties of man. There the children would learn, by the most simple and enlightened lessons, to be religious, loyal to the law and king, friends of liberty, enemies of license, attached to the government, and opposed to anarchy.[29]

Other members of the Confédération wrote specifically for less educated readers. The most outstanding examples during 1790-1791 were Joseph-Marie Lequinio, Jean-Louis Reynier, and Joachim Cerutti, who edited journals aimed at the peasantry. Lequinio was an aspiring politician from Brittany, who had spent a large part of his childhood working in the fields. When the Revolution came, he, too, urged all intellectuals to leave their academies and help educate the ignorant bulk of the Third

[29] Athanase Auger, *Cathéchisme du citoyen françois*, p. v; idem, ed. *Organisation des écoles nationales*, pp. 1-2.

Estate. "Every man who is even part philosophe must feel that it is now necessary to write for this class of citizens." The Cercle Social advertised his *Journal des laboureurs*, whose goal was the "political and moral education" of those "living in the country."[30] The journal was actually a series of patriotic essays written in a popular style in order to win the peasants over to the Revolution. Reynier's paper, the *Journal d'agriculture à l'usage des habitants de la campagne*, was also "not aimed at savants, but designed for those who want to learn. It is a means of instruction for all classes."[31] A botanist and academician before the Revolution, Reynier offered advice on more scientific topics, such as methods of keeping insects from destroying turnips. Unfortunately, his articles were too sophisticated for his readers, and the paper was short-lived. Perhaps the best known of these projects was Joachim Cerutti's *Feuille villageoise*, which featured articles by Cercle Social members written for peasants and particularly for rural parish priests. In 1792 the Cercle Social took over publication of the *Feuille villageoise*.[32] These examples demonstrate the effort by Cercle Social intellectuals to go beyond the elitism of the philosophes and establish a closer relationship with the people.

SINCE the Confédération's economic ideas have been seen as belonging to the early development of socialism, they are better known than the group's plans for civil religion and public education. Claude Fauchet had developed radical notions about property even before the Revolution. In his important work, *De la religion nationale*, Fauchet argued that wealth was morally evil. The rich "spread the infection of vice and bring about the ruin of manners and customs." He argued that Christianity was a religion of love and brotherhood, of helping the poor, sick,

---

[30] *Journal des laboureurs*, Prospectus, pp. 1-3; *Bdf*, 12 March 1791, p. 480.

[31] *Journal d'agriculture à l'usage des habitants de la campagne*, Prospectus, p. 1. Reynier also got the Cercle Social to sponsor a project where savants and wealthy people would subsidize elementary agricultural texts for peasants. See the *Projet d'association pour l'encouragement de l'agriculture et des arts agricoles* (Paris: ICS, 1791).

[32] See Chapter 9, below, for a more complete discussion of the *Feuille villageoise*.

and destitute. Charity was therefore the most important commandment that God had given to man. While no society could be without its more successful members, they were obligated to give all that they did not absolutely need to the poor.[33]

Fundamental to Fauchet's ideas was a sincere concern for the impoverished classes. "I am," he proclaimed, "the advocate and friend of the poor." A society that tolerated poverty—much less the social and political oppression of the poor—should not call itself Christian. "What is misery?" he asked. "The deprivation of things essential to living, and [of] the legitimate means to procure them." A person without the means to care for himself was more like a dog, dependent upon greater beings; a society that ignored its poor was, simply, inhumane. Thus Fauchet argued that the first aim of any moral society must be the complete elimination of poverty. He insisted that, while political freedom must accompany the economic amelioration of the poor, it should never replace it. Those who called only for the political enfranchisement of the Third Estate did not understand the meaning of liberty. A man is a slave whenever his lack of means forces him to become dependent upon others; he is free when "he depends only on nature and on his own wisdom."[34]

The major theme of *De la religion nationale* was the regeneration of both government and religion. In the new epoch, government would legislate Christian commandments, while Christianity would support the patriotic values of the state. "Finally a government based upon the Gospel," dreamed Fauchet. "The laws must . . . repress the licentiousness of the rich, their insolent corruption, and all the excesses of this formidable class."[35]

Fauchet advocated three specific laws that would assure self-sufficiency for every citizen. The first was nothing short of an "agrarian law." No person would be allowed to acquire more than 50,000 livres worth of land. Those wealthy landowners who owned more than this limit would be allowed to keep what they already had; but they could neither buy more nor sell parcels

---

[33] Fauchet, *Religion nationale*, pp. 216, 224-25.
[34] *Bdf*, no. 29, December 1790, p. 457; Fauchet, *Discours sur les moeurs rurales*, pp. 18-22.
[35] Fauchet, *Religion nationale*, pp. 216, 224-25.

in excess of the limit. The other two laws derived from the first. One would reform matrimonial law to allow spouses to own land jointly; the third would eliminate primogeniture by providing for the equal division of an estate among all surviving children. Fauchet argued that these laws would have two basic results. First, land and capital would eventually be equally distributed among the population, assuring a self-sufficient and egalitarian nation of small farmers. Second, such an economy would result in higher agricultural production. Huge estates, he reasoned, wasted many acres of land each year; small farmers, on the other hand, used every available acre they could find.[36]

Fauchet's commentaries on Rousseau's *Social Contract* reiterated these theories before the Confédération and in the *Bouche de fer*. During the meeting of 19 November 1790, he specifically discussed the last chapter of Book One, concerning "Real Property." Fauchet found, in a note at the end of this chapter, a justification for his own ideas. It reads, "The social state is advantageous to men only when all have something and none too much." The fact that this sentence was embedded in a footnote did not deter Fauchet from turning it into the central tenet of the chapter. "Sublime Rousseau!" Fauchet exclaimed. "You heard one of the first commands of eternal justice! Yes, every man has a right to the earth and must possess enough land for his existence!"[37]

Fauchet's critics—most notably Choderlos de Laclos—reacted strongly to the speech. They accused him of trying to establish a system based upon "the absurd notion of equality of property." In their view, he was legitimizing the destruction of feudal property by peasants and thus abetting disorder and anarchy. One anonymous foe even denounced Fauchet and the Cercle Social to the National Assembly's Investigations Committee. Such reactions are understandable only after one considers how few politicians and writers tried to find ways of ameliorating the condition of impoverished peasants. "The poor," wrote the pow-

[36] Ibid., pp. 225-28.
[37] *Bdf*, no. 22, November 1790, pp. 342, 346; Jean-Jacques Rousseau, *The Social Contract and Discourses*, p. 22.

erful politician, Isaac Le Chapelier, "are a class not unlike the clergy. . . . They are poor only because they want to be."[38]

Two weeks later Fauchet openly confronted these critics in another speech to the Confédération.

> I could respond that my private thoughts are outside the jurisdiction of the Investigations Committee, and that for these beliefs, I am accountable only to my own reason . . . but I am not timid. I am outspoken and like to be direct. I will therefore . . . affirm that it is impossible to create a viable social constitution without assuring real property to all members of society.

This did not mean, Fauchet maintained, that the peasant should simply take property from his landlord. Fauchet made it clear that he was against all forms of collective violence, no matter what the cause. Any agrarian reform must proceed in a slow and orderly fashion to assure justice for all parties. He advocated nothing more than the passage of his three laws by the National Assembly; the lower classes were presumably expected to be patient until the laws were executed by those who held political power.[39]

In his call for an end to primogeniture, Fauchet's most important supporter was François Lanthenas, the future Girondin member of the Convention. Born at Le Puy in 1754, Lanthenas spent several of his early years in Lyon, where he developed close friendships with Jean-Marie and Manon Roland, later chiefs of the Girondins. During the 1780s, Lanthenas moved to Paris and received a medical degree, but he was too restless to establish a medical practice. Rather, he cast his hopes on becoming a writer, became good friends with Henri Bancal, Jean-Philippe Garran-Coulon, and Jacques-Pierre Brissot, and became a charter member of the liberal antislavery club, the Société des amis des Noirs. While he played no significant role in the Paris Municipal

[38] *Journal des amis de la constitution*, 21 November 1790, p. 44; *Journal des clubs*, 1: 121; *Bdf*, 14 April 1791, pp. 103-107, and no. 29, December 1790, p. 455; Le Chapelier's remark is cited in Richard B. Du Boff, "Economic Thought in Revolutionary France, 1789-1792: The Question of Poverty and Unemployment" *FHS* 4: 446.

[39] *Bdf*, no. 29, December 1790, pp. 451-62, and 29 March 1791, p. 580.

Revolution, he saw Bancal, Brissot, and Garran almost every day.[40]

In 1789 Lanthenas published a long and comprehensive book attacking primogeniture, which was highly praised in both the Fauchetin and Cordelier press.[41] The book's main thesis was that primogeniture led to a growing cleavage between rich and poor, which fueled social inequality. The result was the opposite of what Rousseau had advocated: instead of an egalitarian society in which everyone had moderate assets, primogeniture gave everything to one member of the family and nothing to his siblings. By encouraging inequality, Lanthenas believed that primogeniture had wrecked the economy of the Old Regime and had undermined the stability of the family. "Our inheritance law," he wrote, "was born from the corruption of the feudal system, and it was the nourishment rather than the cure for the anarchy which followed."[42]

Lanthenas' solution was to abolish primogeniture and enact inheritance laws that forced estates to be divided equally among the children upon their parents' death. These notions went back to discussions he had had with his friends during the mid-1780s, several of whom had elder brothers and felt bitter about being excluded from their family fortunes. Garran, for example, had published an article asserting similar views in the *Encyclopédie méthodique*.[43]

At the beginning of 1790, Lanthenas, Bancal, and Brissot all helped to found the Société de 89. But when it became clear that their ideas were too radical for the other members of this club, they deserted it, and in the summer of 1790, Lanthenas created the Société des amis de l'union et de l'égalité dans les

---

[40] *Lettres de Mme Roland* 2: 688-708 (Appendix L); Edith Bernardin, ed., "Lettres de Lanthenas à Bancal des Issarts" *Annales historiques de la Révolution française* 16: 62-68, 152-66, 245-62.

[41] François Lanthenas, *Inconvéniens du droit d'ainesse*. For reviews see *Journal d'Etat et du citoyen*, 17 September 1789, p. 120; *CdP*, 15 October 1789, p. 205; *Pf*, 20 August 1789, p. 4, 18 September 1789, p. 4, and 3 November 1789, p. 4.

[42] Lanthenas, *Inconvéniens*, p. 116.

[43] Ibid., p. 117. Jean-Philippe Garran-Coulon, "Parage," *Encyclopédie méthodique. Jerusprudence*, 10 vols. (Paris: Panckoucke, 1783-1789).

familles, specifically to lobby for more democratic inheritance laws. This club included many members of the Cercle Social, including Bonneville, Brissot, Bancal, Mercier, and Desmoulins. In August 1790, Lanthenas spoke on behalf of the club to the National Assembly. He attacked primogeniture as an example of feudal exploitation of the poor. In its place he asked "that equality of distribution among children be reestablished by a constitutional decree."[44]

After his address to the National Assembly, Lanthenas returned to Lyon for several months, and the Société des amis de l'union et de l'égalité dans les familles was absorbed into the Cercle Social. An early issue of the *Bouche de fer*, for example, included a fascinating article, probably written by Lanthenas' close friend, Madame Roland. She approached the issue of primogeniture in an autobiographical fashion:

> I am a woman and a victim of this arbitrary law. Born into an arrogant system which permitted unequal division ... between children whom nature had given the same rights; a system which facilitated the acquisition of immense wealth in ... a state which rewarded neither virtue nor talent, and in which ignorance and hypocrisy seemed to be given special prerogatives.[45]

She went on to describe how her younger brother, a man with enormous talents and virtues, was forced into a career in the Church, while the eldest sibling allowed his wife to squander the family fortune until they were in debt. Madame Roland reiterated her belief that the Old Regime thus rewarded laziness and discriminated against merit, and she called on the new regime to enact an inheritance law that would give "brothers and sisters equal portions of their father's estate." Even if Madame Roland was not the author of this article, she became one

[44] Claude Perroud, "A Propos de l'abolition du droit d'ainesse" *Rf* 54: 193-202; "Adresse de Lanthenas, Président de la Société des amis de l'union et d'égalité dans les familles," Ph. Sagnac and Pierre Caron, eds., *Recueil de documents sur l'abolition du régime seigneurial*, pp. 643-45. See also André Dejace, *Les Règles de la dévolution successorale sous la Révolution (1789-1794)*.

[45] "Sur les successions," *Bdf*, no. 6, October 1790, pp. 90-92; see also no. 16, November 1790, p. 250. Attribution to Madame Roland is based upon the style of the letter, the postmark "Lyon" at the end, and her close relationship with Lanthenas. See *Lettres de Mme Roland* 2: Appendix L and passim.

of Fauchet's staunchest supporters and "heard him speak many times with extreme pleasure" when she, her husband, and Lanthenas moved back to Paris during the spring of 1791.[46]

Those historians who have studied these ideas have concluded that the Cercle Social was a precursor of nineteenth-century socialism. R. B. Rose, for example, has claimed that the particular significance of the group "lies in the fact that, of the many political clubs and societies founded by the revolutionaries in the early years of the Revolution, [the Cercle Social] was responsible for disseminating the ideas of the philosophes in their most 'socialistic' aspect." Similarly, an historian of socialist thought concluded that the "socialist tendencies" of the Cercle Social are "incontestable." The great twentieth-century historian Alphonse Aulard equated "what we call today socialism" with what "was then called 'the agrarian law,' " and so he was naturally confused by Cercle Social proposals:

Perhaps one might find in this period socialistic demands in the writings of the abbé Fauchet. But ... nothing could be more confusing than the bibliography of the various pamphlets, periodic or otherwise, of Fauchet, Bonneville, and their group.[47]

In fact, the Cercle Social was far from a socialist club. Its proposals for land reform were meant to protect the private property of the small farmer and to redistribute wealth along more democratic lines. Socialism, a term that did not become common until after the French Revolution, means more than compassion for the poor; it "amounts to a belief that all producers ought to share equally in the fruits of combined labor."[48] Fauchet did not see the problem in this light and never questioned the principle of private property; he only objected to its abuse by the wealthy. Luxury, not property, was theft. Indeed, Fauchet and his followers believed that wages and prices should operate according to a free market system. In their view, only an econ-

[46] *Bdf*, no. 6, October 1790, p. 92, and *Lettres de Mme Roland* 2: 259-66.
[47] R. B. Rose, "Socialism and the French Revolution: the Cercle Social and the Enragés" *Bulletin of the John Rylands Library* 141:139-64; Andre Lichtenberger, *Le Socialisme et la Révolution française*, p. 69; Alphonse Aulard, *The French Revolution* 1: 162.
[48] *Dictionary of the History of Ideas*, 4: 284.

omy based upon "the maximum of liberty" and "the minimum of government" could bring about a society in which no one was impoverished.[49]

If the Cercle Social had few socialist tendencies beyond a sincere concern for the poor, neither did it imitate the Physiocrats, the group of eighteenth-century French economic thinkers who advocated an early form of libertarian capitalism. "The Economists," as Fauchet called them, were mistaken "to believe that small landowners were less useful in general, and less productive than the great ones . . . an inconceivable illusion!" Worse, the system proposed by them was irreligious. "The Gospel says: 'unhappiness to the rich'; the Economists say: 'happiness to the rich.' Their doctrine on this point is thus in plain contradiction to that of religion." The Cercle Social believed that libertarian capitalism would result in a corrupt and aristocratic society, similar in its exploitation of the poor to the one destroyed by the Revolution.[50]

At this stage of the Revolution, the Cercle Social was also uninterested in economic growth. For example, one member of the Confédération, the wealthy landowner Alexander de Brie-Serrant, hoped to imitate the British by constructing a canal from the region around Rennes to Pornic, a port on the Atlantic. When he tried to publicize his scheme at Confédération meetings, the club gave him a curt response and refused to grant his speeches much space in the *Bouche de fer*. He was forced to publish them privately.[51]

Thus the Cercle Social was neither a pro-socialist nor a pro-capitalist group; nor did it manifest "socialist tendencies" beyond a humanitarian concern for the laboring classes. In fact, in all of these proposals Cercle Social members were acting more like moralists than like rigorous economic thinkers. Sometimes their arguments were couched in a religious language based upon the Gospels; at other times they were grounded in natural law and

---

[49] *Bdf*, 10 March 1791, p. 494.

[50] Fauchet, *Religion nationale*, pp. 226-29.

[51] Alexandre de Brie-Serrant, *Au Cercle Social des amis de la vérité* (n.p., n.d.); idem, *Mémoires du peuple au peuple, au rapport de huit des comités de l'Assemblée Nationale* (n.p., n.d.).

upon the writings of the philosophes. But whatever the basis, the Cercle Social never called for a peasant revolution (as Laclos charged), but rather for a gradual system of income redistribution in which both poverty and conspicuous consumption would eventually be eliminated.

This interpretation is not meant to diminish the radical nature of these ideas. On the contrary, the Cercle Social went beyond what other groups (such as the Jacobins, or even the Cordeliers) were prepared to advocate.[52] But the radical quality of their proposals had nothing to do with an attack upon private property; rather, the Cercle Social was one of the few groups that, at this early point in the Revolution, recognized that their vision of representative democracy was dependent upon a more fundamental reform of the social structure. It is indeed ironic that in 1792-1793 their ideas would be used against them by the leaders of the urban working classes, the sans-culottes, who became far more militant in their demands for a society based upon social as well as political democracy.

Just as the Cercle Social cannot be described as socialist, one should be careful when referring to the group as a feminist club, as several historians have done.[53] "Feminism" and "feminist" did not come into usage until the end of the nineteenth century, and the feminist movement has become so important in our own time that it is very easy to impose twentieth-century concepts upon men and women who lived two hundred years ago. But the values and goals of eighteenth-century advocates of women's rights were not the same as those of the late twentieth-century feminists. The former believed that women were the "frail" sex and even the most radical accepted the idea that a woman's place was in the home, caring for her children and husband. Their

[52] On the Jacobins see Kennedy, *The Jacobin Clubs in the French Revolution*, pp. 107-27; Mathiez, *The French Revolution*, p. 122. On the Cordeliers see Censer, *Prelude to Power*, pp. 44, 69-72.

[53] Aulard, "Feminisme pendant la Révolution française," *Revue bleue*, 9: 361-66; Jane Abray, "Feminism in the French Revolution" *American Historical Review* 80: 50-51; Lenora Cohen Rosenfield, "The Rights of Women in the French Revolution" *Studies in Eighteenth Century Culture* 7: 121-22; Bourdin, *Les Sociétés populaires*, pp. 139-48.

proposals for the amelioration of women's status were intended to dignify female domesticity, not to undermine the segregation of jobs according to gender. Even those feminists who advocated political equality for women argued that political participation would help women to become better wives and mothers. "And so it is unnecessary to believe that because women could become members of national assemblies," wrote the philosophe Condorcet, "they would immediately abandon their children, their homes, and their needles. They would be only the better fitted to educate their children and to rear men."[54]

Though strikingly different from today's women's liberation movement, a kind of feminism developed during the late Enlightenment that grew into a strong movement during the French Revolution. These eighteenth-century feminists hoped to raise the status of women to the level of men; more specifically, they wanted reforms in matrimonial laws and sought to gain political rights for women. On these points, no revolutionary club was more feminist during the early years of the Revolution than the Cercle Social.

While some writers may glorify the few charming and influential women of the salons and court, the vast majority of women were oppressed, even by the standards of the Old Regime. In matrimonial law, the most important legal arena for women, the husband had the privileges of a despot. He owned all the property and could treat his wife as he wished. Divorce, of course, was illegal in Catholic France. But if the marriage was unsuccessful the couple could live separately if the separation was initiated by the husband. Wifebeating, drunkenness, and abandonment were hazards that women were obliged to tolerate. One modern historian has aptly described the eighteenth-century wife, often trapped in an unhappy situation, as a "half-slave."[55]

[54] Etta Palm, *Appel aux françoises sur la régénération des moeurs et la nécessité de l'influence des femmes dans un gouvernement libre* (Paris: ICS, 1791), p. 39; Condorcet, *Selected Writings*, p. 102.

[55] Leon Abensour, *La Femme et le féminisme avant la Révolution*, pp. 8, 21; Olwen Hufton, "Women in Revolution 1789-1796" *Past and Present* no. 53, 98-121. On the beginnings of a feminist movement see David Williams, "The Politics of Feminism in the French Enlightenment," in Hughes and Williams, eds., *The Varied Pattern: Studies in the Eighteenth Century*, pp. 333-51.

Since its establishment in January 1790, the Cercle Social had devoted itself to improving the lot of women. In an early issue of the journal *Cercle Social*, a woman from Marseilles named Seline wrote that the best way to improve the status of women was by lobbying for the legalization of divorce. She told the Cercle Social about her own marriage. For ten years her relationship with her husband had been loving and fulfilling. But slowly they grew apart. He became cold and distant, and the relationship deteriorated into a formal and unhappy union, without affection. She began to suspect him of having affairs with other women. Legally and financially dependent upon a husband who no longer cared for her, Seline felt trapped and embittered by her situation. A divorce law, she believed, would help her and other women in similar situations to regain "our liberty and our happiness."[56]

The *Cercle Social* published other letters by women reflecting on their plight, and Bonneville wrote strongly worded articles urging the National Assembly to pass a comprehensive divorce bill. "I will prove," he claimed, "that the indissolubility of marriage is contrary to good politics . . . [and that it] is very harmful and even deadly to society." Bonneville's argument focused on the reasons that states legalized conjugal unions in the first place. He claimed that marriage was simply the most practical way that civilized societies made sure that fathers carried out their paternal duties. The identity of a mother is obvious to the community; marriage made the father's identity equally obvious. This was in the state's interest, because "without family ties demarcating clear lines of inheritance as precisely as possible, there would be no way to bind people to each other." For Bonneville, marriage was not a sacrament, but simply a device for holding fathers accountable to their children. But if husband and wife were no longer having sexual relations, Bonneville saw no reason that they should not be permitted to divorce. In Bonneville's view, forcing a couple to remain married after their relationship had deteriorated was in the interests neither of the couple nor the state.[57]

[56] *Cercle Social*, letter 11, pp. 107-12.
[57] Ibid., letter 60, pp. 424-30, and letter 66, pp. 465-77.

For the Cercle Social, then, divorce was the crucial feminist issue. As long as women were forced into a life-long dependence upon their husbands, any plans for developing women into dignified citoyennes would remain utopian. Roderick Phillips has underscored the importance of divorce for women who lived during the French Revolution by investigating those couples who made use of divorce once it became legal in 1792. His findings indicate that women petitioned for divorce more than two-and-a-half times as frequently as men; more important, the most common reason cited for divorce between 1792 and 1801 was wife-beating.[58]

While the legalization of divorce was the primary requirement for ameliorating the condition of women, Cercle Social members developed other important steps as well. In his famous essay "On the Admission of Women to the Rights of Citizenship," Condorcet may have been the first French revolutionary to call for female political equality. While he admitted that "women are superior to men in the gentle and domestic virtues," he argued that this was no reason to exclude them from political participation. Men had political rights because they had been endowed with the capacity "of acquiring moral ideas and of reasoning concerning these ideas." Because women were also endowed with these qualities, "either no individual of the human race has any true rights or all have the same." Since the French Revolution was based upon such enlightened principles, Condorcet urged the National Assembly to rise above their prejudices and grant women the same political rights as men.[59]

These notions reappeared in the Confédération des Amis de la Vérité during the fall of 1790. "Women, be a Citoyenne! Until now you have only been a mother," cried the male feminist, Charles-Louis Rousseau. The pedagogue Athanase Auger hoped that the National Assembly would establish elementary schools for women, which would be "absolutely the same as those for men. We will teach them in the same school and in the same manner." The president of the Confédération, Antoine Mailly,

[58] Roderick Phillips, *Family Breakdown in Late Eighteenth Century France: Divorces in Rouen, 1792-1803*, pp. 108-24.
[59] Condorcet, *Selected Writings*, pp. 97-104.

even found historical evidence for the reaffirmation of women's rights:

We note that the Franks, our ancestors, had great deference for women. They regarded their advice with foreboding and as oracles, convinced that they had something divine in them. This is the source of the proverb still in use today: *ce qu'une femme veut, Dieu le veut.*[60]

More important, the Confédération was the first club to admit women as regular members and the first to establish a separate women's section that "demands equality of rights for all individuals, without discrimination of sex; the laws of a free people must be equal for all beings, like the air and the sun."[61]

The campaign for women's rights in the Cercle Social was led by one of the most radical feminists of the eighteenth century, Etta Palm d'Aelders. Born in 1743 in Groningen, Holland, Palm married into a wealthy family at nineteen, but her husband disappeared on a trip to the Dutch Indies shortly after their marriage. In 1774 she moved to France and later embraced the Revolution by investing money in nationalized land and by translating Mirabeau and Condorcet into Dutch.[62]

In her first speech to the Confédération des Amis de la Vérité on 30 December 1790, Etta Palm was more concerned with ending wifebeating than with attaining political equality for women. "Be just toward us, Messieurs," she began. "Nature created you with superior physical strengths." She argued that the inherent physical weakness of women required laws that protected them against their stronger fathers and husbands. But the oppressive laws of the Old Regime had only exploited their frailty, burdening them with an "inferior existence in society," which "has often forced us into the humiliating situation of

[60] *Bdf*, 29 March 1791, p. 571; see also *Bdf*, no. 20, November 1790, pp. 306-15; and *Bdf*, 6 January 1791, p. 31; Charles-Louis Rousseau, *Essai sur l'éducation et l'existence civile des femmes*; Auger, ed., *Organisation des écoles nationales*, p. 39.

[61] Palm, *Appel aux françoises sur la régénération des moeurs et la nécessité de l'influence des femmes dans un gouvernement libre* (Paris: ICS, 1791), pp. 37-42. This pamphlet is a collection of Palm's most important speeches.

[62] Archives Nationales, T. 1601, fol. 8383 (papers of d'Aelders); W. Koppius, *Etta Palm: Nederland's eerste Feministe*; H. Hardenberg, *Etta Palm: Een Hollandse Parisiene 1743-1799*; Paule-Marie Duhet, *Les Femmes et la Révolution française*; *Moniteur* 11: 60.

being rudely conquered by man's ferocious character." In a pamphlet that appeared a few months later, she was more specific on the female condition during the Old Regime:

Deprived of a civil existence; subjected to the arbitrary will of those closest around them, even up to the secret effusions of the heart; slave at all ages and in all circumstances; daughters subjected to the will of their parents; women subjected to the caprices of a husband, a master; and even when fate seems to have freed them from all despotism, the despotism of mean prejudices, with which their sex has been surrounded, still keeps them bent under its laws; thus from the cradle to the grave women vegetate in a kind of slavery.

Palm scorned some revolutionaries for not working to change the status of women, and she urged the Cercle Social to devote its full attention to this critical problem. "We are your companions and not your slaves," she reminded her audience.[63]

Palm's speech stimulated heated debate, and while the *Bouche de fer* does not reveal the extent of the conflict in the club, an article in Stanislas Fréron's newspaper, the *Orateur du peuple*, claimed that many members of the Confédération were put off by Palm's feminist notions. From other sources we know that several Cercle Social members did not endorse the women's rights movement. In his utopian novel, *2440*, for example, Mercier looked forward to a time when "restored to their proper station, women attended only to those duties to which the Creator has enjoined them: to bear children, and to be the consolation of those who protect them from the evils of life."[64] But such male chauvinist attitudes are hardly surprising. Neither the Jacobins nor the far more puritanical Cordeliers were willing to admit women as regular members or endorse feminist ideas. What is remarkable then, is the extent to which Cercle Social leaders were willing to support Etta Palm, and the reputation the Girondins later attained as spokesmen for the feminist movement.[65]

[63] Palm, *Appel*, pp. 1-9, 41-42.
[64] *L'Orateur du peuple*, no. 46, 3: 359-61; Louis-Sébastien Mercier, *Memoirs of the Year Two Thousand Five Hundred* [sic], pp. 284-97.
[65] Jacqueline Chaumié, "Les Girondins," *Actes du colloque Girondins et Montagnards (Sorbonne, 14 décembre 1975) sous la direction d'Albert Soboul*, pp. 49-51.

In another speech to the Confédération on 18 March 1791, Palm announced plans for a female section, the Confédération des Amies de la Vérité. This group was to have three functions. First, it would devise "a way to prove that they [women] are deserving of justice"; that is, it would lobby for the elimination of primogeniture, protection against wifebeating, a comprehensive divorce bill, and political equality for women. Second, it would "be charged to supervise the establishment of nurseries" for the children of young women from the countryside, who often found themselves pregnant and desperate in Paris. Palm's group hoped to establish affiliate clubs in every section of the capital and in provincial towns to provide care and education for these children. Finally, the female Confédération would also establish free clinics for these indigent women and try to find work for them.[66]

The Cercle Social did more than simply endorse Palm's plan. It permitted the new group to use the headquarters of the Cercle Social as a meeting place and allowed the group to use the *Bouche de fer* for publishing announcements and minutes of meetings. The Directoire du Cercle Social made its sponsorship of Palm's club official on 25 March 1791 by sending a delegation to the first meeting of the Confédération des Amies de la Vérité. President Mailly urged the women "to rectify, by their personal sacrifices, the cruel inequalities that creep into the best governments." After Palm was elected by acclamation to the presidency of the Amies de la Vérité, the group turned its attention to the issue of primogeniture, which had just been officially eliminated by the National Assembly.[67]

The identification of primogeniture as a feminist issue is particularly noteworthy since Lanthenas had said nothing about the status of women in his important treatise on the subject. But women realized that Lanthenas' ideas had special importance for them. Almost immediately after the publication of the treatise

[66] *Bdf*, 23 March 1791, pp. 539-542. See also *Prospectus pour le Cercle patriotique des amies de la vérité* (Paris: ICS, 1791). On the lifestyle of these indigent women see Hufton, "Women in Revolution"; female confédérations were begun in Creil, Alain, and Bordeaux. See *Bdf*, 23 March 1791, p. 539.
[67] *Bdf*, 29 March 1791, pp. 570-75.

in 1789, a reviewer for the *Courrier de Lyon*, almost certainly Madame Roland, made the connection explicit: "One of the most harmful effects of primogeniture," she wrote, "is that it regularly exposes a mother of a family to the contempt and vexations of her husband and the sons preferred by him."[68]

If women were to become independent from men, one place to start was by allowing both male and female children to share their parents' estate equally. It is no wonder, then, that the first meeting of the Amies de la Vérité took on the aura of a celebration. "We express our gratitude for the decree that allows women to an equal share of estates," cried one member. In contrast to the more formal style of the male group, even a twelve-year-old boy (a member's son) was allowed to give a little speech on the National Assembly's new law. "I have always shared with my brothers and sisters," he announced, "and I am glad that the National Assembly has made this so for the whole world!"[69]

After this first meeting, the Confédération des Amies de la Vérité developed an organizational structure and launched a membership drive. Any woman could become a member of the group by contributing dues of three livres per month, a prohibitive sum for all but those women from the most comfortable classes. Throughout the spring of 1791 charter members wrote letters to their friends and acquaintances inviting them to join the club. These letters are further evidence that the women's club was composed of wealthy women who felt a deep sense of noblesse oblige toward their downtrodden sisters. Announcements of their intentions were also sent to several journalists, including Desmoulins, Prudhomme, and Gorsas, but only Brissot consented to publicize the new organization in his newspaper.[70]

Thus during the spring of 1791 the Confédération des Amies de la Vérité was both a charitable organization run by wealthy

[68] *Courrier de Lyon*, 14 October 1789, pp. 313-16, and 15 October 1789, pp. 320-24. At Madame Roland's request, Pétion later made a speech to the National Assembly on the elimination of primogeniture. See *Lettres de Mme Roland* 2: 217, and *Pf*, 17 January 1791, p. 1.

[69] *Bdf*, 29 March 1791, pp. 570-75.

[70] Bibliothèque historique de la ville de Paris, Mss. 777, nos. 72-75; *Pf*, 2 May 1791, p. 477; *Bdf*, 29 March 1791, p. 571.

women to aid their indigent sisters and a political club that lobbied for female equality and liberty. For the first few months political activities were subordinate to the club's charitable functions. But during the summer of 1791 the group was drawn into direct criticism of the National Assembly when the Assembly's Constitutional Committee recommended passage of Article XIII of its new police code:

The charge of adultery can be pursued only by the husband. .... A woman convicted of this offense will be punished, depending on the circumstances, by one year, eighteen months, or two years of imprisonment and by forfeiture of matrimonial arrangements established in her favor. The dowry will not be confiscated; the husband will have control of it no matter what clauses are contained in the marriage ceremony. .... The husband at any time can put an end to the sentence by stating his willingness to take his wife into his home.[71]

In response to this new bill, Etta Palm wrote a highly charged polemic against the bill on behalf of the Cercle Social and all French women. She lashed out at the Constitutional Committee for surpassing "the most unjust thing done in barbarous centuries; this is a refinement of despotism." She warned the National Assembly that the constitution that it was writing would be meaningless unless it assured the freedom and equality of all women.

Will you make slaves those who have zealously contributed to making you free? ... No. No. ... The powers of husband and wife must be equal and separate. The laws cannot establish any difference between these two authorities; they must give equal protection and maintain a perpetual balance between the two married people.[72]

For Etta Palm and the Cercle Social, the French Revolution meant something more than a struggle between nationalism and feudalism, democracy and aristocracy, or republicans and monarchicals; it would remain incomplete without a simultaneous social revolution, a total "regeneration of culture [moeurs],"[73]

[71] Cited in Darline Gay Levy et al., eds., *Women in Revolutionary Paris 1789-1795* (Urbana: University of Illinois Press, 1979), p. 76 n.
[72] Cited in ibid., pp. 75-77; originally printed in Palm, *Appel*, pp. 37-40.
[73] *Bdf*, 23 March 1791, p. 538.

which would finally render to women their just dignity and make them citoyennes. Unfortunately, such a feminist revolution was not even considered by the National Assembly, which at this point was frantically trying to halt any further radicalization of the Revolution. While the inheritance and matrimonial legal reforms achieved during the Revolution may be considered progress, the feminist "regeneration" advocated by the Cercle Social was left largely in the planning stages until finally scrapped altogether by Napoleon.

5

After Fauchet

Jᴇᴀɴ-Aɴᴛᴏɪɴᴇ-Nɪᴄᴏʟᴀs Cᴏɴᴅᴏʀᴄᴇᴛ (1743-1794). Elected to the Paris Communal Assembly, Legislative Assembly, and Convention. Orator of the Confédération des Amis de la Vérité. *Chronique du mois* editor for legislation and national education. The last great Enlightenment philosophe, Condorcet's participation in the Cercle Social gave the group enough clout so that its claim that it was the heir to the great intelligentsia of the Encyclopédie had a germ of truth.
Courtesy of The Newberry Library, Chicago

The fundamental laws have forgotten friendship which connects every-thing, concerning themselves only with discord which divides every-thing. No law has yet taken as a fundamental concept of society, that man is a loving being, and no law has guided public institutions in this conciliatory direction: all have supposed, on the contrary, that man is egotistical and the adversary of his fellow man.

Claude Fauchet, *Bdf*, No. 3, October 1790, p. 19.

DURING the spring of 1791 a feud broke out between Bonneville and Fauchet, and by May Claude Fauchet was no longer a member of the Cercle Social. The dispute was not simply a personality clash, but reflects the extent to which the Cercle Social became involved in efforts to reform the French Catholic Church.

During the 15 April 1791 meeting of the club, Fauchet verbally assaulted Bonneville. He was angry over an epigram Bonneville had taken from Fauchet's first commentary on Rousseau and placed at the head of the recent issue of the *Bouche de fer*. Fauchet believed that the statement made him appear to be an anti-Christian fanatic, ready to discard Christianity for the more pagan ideas of the philosophes. He charged Bonneville with slandering his reputation by taking the phrase out of its context and thereby infusing it with a different meaning.[1]

Fauchet was technically correct. Bonneville did indeed mis-quote him. However, the difference between the two remarks is so small that it is difficult to believe that Fauchet would have risked a scandal over it. In his first commentary on Rousseau, Fauchet had actually said: "It is absolutely necessary that one consider religion as love, and if the Gospel excludes even one man from this religion, the Gospel would have to change in order to include that man."[2] Bonneville's version read, "And if the Gospel moves away from reason, the Gospel would have to change to accommodate it."[3] What bothered Fauchet about the statement was the implication that the Gospel might be imperfect

[1] *Bdf*, 20 April 1791, pp. 181-82.
[2] Ibid., no. 8, October 1790, p. 118.
[3] Ibid., 14 April 1791, p. 101.

and need periodic improvements; yet that notion is the same in both versions. The only substantive difference between the two statements is the substitution of "reason" for "love." Bonneville admitted this much, but insisted that the two statements were fundamentally alike: "Isn't this the same sense, the same thought?" he wrote in the *Bouche de fer*. "Is this really an excusable motive for a public scandal?" Bonneville's point was well taken. In fact, Fauchet's *De la Religion nationale* had explicitly argued that reason, love, and Christian faith were all threads of the same fabric.[4]

The feud had actually been brewing for about two weeks. In the 1 April issue of the *Bouche de fer*, Bonneville had favorably reviewed a new book by Camille Desmoulins that "comprehensively analyzes the thousands of crimes committed by Christianity." Bonneville believed the work "useful to an epoch in which fanatical priests were still active," and he showed support for the book by announcing that copies were available at the Cercle Social headquarters. Two weeks later Fauchet, who had already shown his dislike for Desmoulins, attacked the book and the review. "Where are we, citizens, when patriotic writers welcome irreligion?" He claimed that the Confédération harbored several members who were ready to renounce Christianity at the first opportunity.[5]

Fauchet considered the epigram incident to be the final act of the Cercle Social's impiety and dishonor. He demanded a public apology and retraction. When Bonneville refused, Fauchet resigned from the Cercle Social in a "comically tragic scene."[6] Bonneville protested that the epigram was meant to honor Fauchet. He considered Fauchet's resignation an extreme reaction and expressed surprise at such bizarre behavior. Bonneville suggested that one should draw a distinction between Fauchet the priest and Fauchet the politician: "Concerning the abbé Fauchet: des-

[4] Ibid., 20 April 1791, p. 185; Fauchet, *De la religion nationale*, passim.
[5] Ibid., 1 April 1791, p. 20, and 16 April 1791, pp. 121-29; Camille Desmoulins, *Elôge non-funèbre de Jésus et du Christianisme*. I have not been able to locate this pamphlet, though its first chapter was reprinted in Desmoulins' newspaper, *RFB*, no. 70, pp. 238-40. At this time the newspaper was published by the Cercle Social.
[6] *Bdf*, 14 April 1791, pp. 116-17.

potic priest, deaf by greed and stubbornness; concerning Claude
Fauchet: the greatest orator of the century, the most glorious
speaker."[7] Even if Fauchet's interpretation of Bonneville's action
was justified, his behavior in response seems strange. It was clear
from the Voltaire incident in October 1790 that the Confédération included many members who were hostile toward Christianity. Indeed, during his first speech to the Confédération,
Fauchet welcomed Freemasons and philosophes, promising that
his brand of Christianity would meet their requirements for a
natural and national religion. Could Fauchet have had some
ulterior motive in this affair? His biographer, Jules Charrier,
did not believe so and blamed the scandal on Bonneville.[8] Yet
one wonders why Bonneville would have suddenly turned against
his closest ally. Neither before nor after this incident did Bonneville ever publicly attack an associate; indeed, he rarely mustered
a strong polemic against an enemy! Why would this young man
of rather timid character deliberately offend someone who was
clearly of great importance to him? On the other hand, if Fauchet
suddenly became more orthodox in his religious beliefs, what
caused the change? The answer lies in Fauchet's desire to become
a bishop in the new Constitutional Church.

During the summer of 1790 the National Assembly passed
the Civil Constitution of the Clergy, which nationalized the
French Catholic Church, bringing it under the auspices of the
state. One feature of the Civil Constitution was that priests would
be elected by the same electoral assemblies responsible for choosing political leaders. For example, the episcopacy was reorganized by establishing a bishopric for each department, elected by
the departmental electoral assembly. In this way the National
Assembly hoped that a more democratic and popular clergy
would serve the people in accordance with both Christianity and
the general will of the people. A few months later the National
Assembly strengthened the Civil Constitution by ordering all
priests to sign an oath of loyalty to the nation and to its new
Church. This decree was grudgingly approved by the king in

---

[7] Ibid., 20 April 1791, p. 187, 193-94.
[8] Jules Charrier, *Claude Fauchet: Evêque constitutionnel du Calvados, député
à l'Assemblée legislative et à la Convention 1744-1793*, 1:218-20.

December 1790, and elections were immediately called across
the country to fill the new positions created by the bill.[9]

In several respects the Civil Constitution matched the kind
of civil religion advocated by Fauchet and his Christian followers. By committing the Church to the notion of popular sovereignty through the election of ecclesiastic officers, by dimin-
ishing the influence of Rome, and by subordinating the Church
to the new regime, Fauchet expected the Civil Constitution to
create a democratic, patriotic, and Gospel-oriented Church. While
modern historians have often cited the passage of the Civil Constitution as the moment when "the Revolution 'went wrong,' "[10]
the Cercle Social believed that political stability could not be
attained without this kind of religious reform.

During the early months of 1791, the Cercle Social gathered
all of its resources to lobby for the Civil Constitution. By urging
priests to take the civic oath, and by campaigning for Cercle
Social members who were running in elections for positions in
the new episcopacy, the club hoped to assure the success of the
Civil Constitution. When one of Fauchet's closest followers, the
abbé Richard Chaix, took the civil oath in a church ceremony
on 9 January 1791, Bonneville wrote that Chaix "proved that
there was neither fatherland nor religion for those [priests] who
refused to subscribe to the laws of the general will." Chaix's
speech was meant to serve as an example for other members of
the lower clergy. It was reprinted in the *Bouche de fer* and
published separately by the Cercle Social as a pamphlet. The
abbé Nusse, who "has been useful to many patriotic deputies in
the civil organization of the clergy," told his parishioners that
the Civil Constitution represented a "regeneration of the clergy."
In another pamphlet published by the Cercle Social, Nusse ex-
pounded on that point, emphasizing the priest's new role as a
zealot "for propagating patriotism: the first minister of the Church
must be the friend of his brothers, a man of God, and of the
Fatherland."[11]

⁹ For an overview of these issues see John McManners, *The French Revolution and the Church*.

¹⁰ Ibid., p. 38.

¹¹ *Bdf*, 24 January 1791, p. 148, 27 January 1791, pp. 171-74, 12 March 1791,

Four members of the Cercle Social were elected to the new episcopacy during this period, including Fauchet, Lamourette, Volfius, and Lalande. On several occasions Fauchet praised his three colleagues as "the most eloquent and among the best citizens of France." Their writings were read to the club, and extracts were reprinted in the *Bouche de fer*.[12] In Lamourette's case, there is some evidence that the Rolands helped him attain the bishopric at Lyon. Madame Roland privately urged the editor of the *Courrier de Lyon* to support either Lamourette or Fauchet, and Brissot's *Patriote français* admitted that the Rolands' close friend François Lanthenas had convinced local patriotic clubs to support Lamourette.[13]

As far as Fauchet's own campaign for a bishopric was concerned, it appears that the Cercle Social tried to bring him into the limelight as much as possible during this period. The club sponsored an unusually lavish celebration on 4 February 1791, the first anniversary of the king's official acceptance of national sovereignty. The event was planned by the Cercle Social, under the auspices of the Société fraternelle des anciens représentants de la commune, who now "compose our Surveillance Committee." Fauchet wrote to various governmental bodies, including the National Assembly, asking them to send delegations to the fete. The club hoped it would be the greatest celebration of patriotism since the Federation of the previous 14 July.[14]

---

p. 476, and 15 March 1791, p. 488; Richard Chaix d'Est-Ange, *Serment civique* (Paris: ICS, [1791]); Jean-François Nusse, *Lettre . . . à un curé qui a prêté serment, sur ce que nous attendons de la régénération de l'épiscopat. Lu à l'Assemblée fédérative des Amis de la vérité* (Paris: ICS, 1791). See also François-Bernard Mille, *Serment civique sur la constitution du clergé . . .* (Paris: Grangé, 1791); and Jacques Jallet, *Pourquoi ne jurent-ils pas puisqu'ils savent jurer . . .* (Paris: ICS, [1791]).

[12] *Bdf*, 27 January 1791, p. 442, 23 March 1791, pp. 529, 531, and 20 April 1791, p. 189. See also Luc-François Lalande, *Apologie des décrets de l'Assemblée Nationale sur la constitution civile du clergé*; and Antoine-Adrien Lamourette, *Instruction pastorale . . . au clergé et aux Fidèles de son diocèse* (Lyon: d'Amable Le Roy, 1791).

[13] *Lettres de Mme Roland* 2: 252; *Pf*, 23 March 1791, p. 51.

[14] Archives nationales C54, fol. 535, no. 1 (Fauchet's letter to the National Assembly); *Bdf*, 1 February 1791, pp. 204-209. See also Gabriel-Claude Tanevot-d'Herbault, *Discours prononcé . . . au nom du club fraternel des ci-devant*

The celebration clearly belonged to Fauchet. It was held in the most prestigious site in the city, the Cathedral of Notre Dame. Bonneville reported that 25,000 people were in attendance, and no one disputed that figure. After a few words from various national and local celebrities, Fauchet delivered a major address "on the harmony of Religion and Liberty." The speech was clearly a way for him to further his reputation as a significant political and religious leader. While he said nothing new, he articulated old ideas eloquently. "What is the Catholic Church?" he asked. "Nothing arbitrary, nothing imperial. Always the public voice, always the general will. Birth is nothing, merit is all. Wealth is proscribed ... there are no poor in a truly fraternal society, there are only equals. Everyone works, and all taste the benefits of life in unanimity ... such was Catholicism at the birth of Christianity."[15]

Despite these efforts, Fauchet had a difficult time attaining a bishopric. At first he tried for the position in Nevers, his home region. He made it to the runoff, but was defeated by Guillaume Tollet, a local curé. Fauchet's supporters ran him in ten more departments without success. Bitter and frustrated, he complained that refractory priests and friends of Mayor Bailly had sabotaged his campaign.[16]

A last chance came during the second week in April, when the new bishop of Calvados resigned over a dispute with the National Assembly. Immediately Fauchet's supporters went to work. The Jacobin club in Caen (the Department of Calvados' seat) was contacted, and its leaders assured Fauchet that his chances were good. On 11 April the radical publicist Jean-Louis Carra printed a strong endorsement of Fauchet in his *Annales patriotiques et littéraires*, the most popular newspaper among French patriotic clubs:

---

représentants provisoires de la Commune, invitant à la fête religieuse et civique que ce club se propose de célébrer chaque année, le 4 février ... (Paris, n.p., n.d.).

[15] *Bdf*, 12 February 1791, pp. 258-63, and 19 February 1791, p. 334; Claude Fauchet, *Sermon sur l'accord de la Religion et de la Liberté ... 4 février 1791* (Paris: ICS, 1791), p. 24; *Pf*, 27 February 1791, pp. 211-12.

[16] Charrier, *Claude Fauchet* 1: 211-14.

Cast your vote for a bishop with a great character, a firm and vigorous patriot, one of the heroes of the Revolution, such as, for example, the abbé Fauchet. Aristocrats fear him and constantly attack him because he himself has not stopped defending the rights of the people with energy and frankness. Providence has reserved him for you. Believe me, I know him . . . he has real virtues, an excellent heart, and a sacred burning for liberty which will propagate and refresh among you love for the constitution and principles of order, justice, and humanity. He has been neglected until the present because the cheats and the wicked say above all that no place must be given to the best authors of the Revolution, because they are too hot-headed. . . . Friends, if you are just, if you are wise, you will make the abbé Fauchet your bishop.[17]

The election was scheduled for Sunday, 17 April. Fauchet was naturally nervous about the outcome. It was imperative that he avoid controversy, lest his enemies use it to discredit him. Yet, on Thursday, 14 April—just three days before the Calvados election—Bonneville's epigram appeared in the *Bouche de fer*. From Fauchet's viewpoint, the timing was so bad that he suspected some sort of conspiracy against him. Here was an anti-Christian statement (at least more orthodox Catholics might take it as such) attributed to him on the front page of his club's newspaper. He had to act quickly. The next day, at the club meeting of 15 April, he scolded Bonneville and announced his resignation from the Cercle Social.

It is doubtful whether Fauchet's melodramatic actions had any effect upon his candidacy. What is certain is that he won the election to the bishopric of Calvados, signifying his elevation from a municipal politician to a figure of national prominence. Three weeks later he would leave Paris for Caen, returning in September 1791 as Calvados' deputy to the Legislative Assembly (and still later to the Convention). But just before his departure, he and Bonneville achieved a quick rapprochement. "Claude Fauchet has just been named to the bishopric of Calvados," exclaimed Bonneville in the 22 April issue of the *Bouche de fer*.

---

[17] *Annales patriotiques et littéraires* . . ., 11 April 1791, p. 1279; *Bdf*, 23 March 1791, p. 568. On the popularity of this paper, see Kennedy, *The Jacobin Clubs in the French Revolution*, p. 370.

"This is a double and glorious triumph for the Amis de la Vérité!" He announced to his readers that Fauchet "has not fallen one bit from our many hopes; he has accepted the hand and heart of a friend. This has expunged his injustices, and mine." On Sunday, 24 April, the Cercle Social gave a farewell party for Fauchet, and, on 1 May 1791, Bonneville claimed that 30,000 people met at the Church of Saint-Roch to bid Fauchet goodbye. Claude Fauchet's career with the Cercle Social was over, signaling the beginning of a new period in the club's history.[18]

CLAUDE FAUCHET had stood at the center of the Cercle Social for so long that it was difficult for many to conceive of the club continuing without him. "I have no idea what will become of the Cercle Social," Madame Roland wrote to Henri Bancal on the eve of Fauchet's departure. Since its inception, the club had focused mainly on Fauchet's interests, and each meeting had been highlighted by one of his speeches. His departure naturally signaled changes in the club's membership. Some regulars, such as François Lanthenas, found the meetings dull without Fauchet's fiery orations, and others soon found better ways to spend their Friday evenings.[19]

Contrary to the fears of Madame Roland, however, the Cercle Social survived Fauchet's departure. Under Bonneville's leadership, the club went through some fundamental changes in structure and outlook, but these alterations had far more to do with the political climate of the period than with Fauchet's departure.

The fall and winter of 1790-1791 had been a period of relative calm. The National Assembly was dominated by a group of "Patriots" led by Lafayette, Adrien Duport, and the Lameth brothers, who were writing a constitution that would establish a liberal constitutional monarchy based upon the sovereignty of the nation. In the meantime, local politicians like Bonneville

---

[18] *Bdf*, 22 April 1791, p. 210, 22 [sic] April 1791, pp. 236, 246, and 2 May 1791, pp. 266-67; Gabriel-Claude Tanevot-d'Herbault, *Discours de M. Tanevot, Président de la Société fraternelle des anciens Représentants de la Commune de Paris, à M. L'Evêque du Calvados ...* (Paris: Caisse d'Epargnes, 1791).

[19] *Lettres de Mme Roland* 2: 264, 280.

and Brissot were confident that these national leaders were working on their behalf. But during the spring of 1791, this repose
was broken by a series of events that turned important groups
in Paris, including the Cercle Social and the Cordeliers, against
the National Assembly. Parisian radicals increasingly came to
believe that Lafayette, Duport, and the Lameths were trying to
stop the Revolution before it achieved its democratic goals. Madame Roland "has been to the National Assembly," Lanthenas
wrote about his close friend. "She has now become familiar with
its principal leaders and is convinced that liberty and the constitution will not belong to, and actually do not belong to, the
men who have given the most to the Revolution." Madame
Roland and her friends had realized that their vision of a representative democracy based upon universal suffrage would never
be implemented by the current leaders of the National Assembly.[20]

Even before Fauchet's departure there had been hints that
the Cercle Social was becoming more interested in local political
affairs. On 11 March 1791, President Mailly informed the Confédération that the situation in the capital was growing more
tense. "The commonwealth is endangered," he exclaimed. "We
sense division everywhere. Sincere friends of the constitution are
slandered and persecuted. Egoism and filthy interests isolate the
most zealous defenders and ruin the best plans." What a difference in tone from his universalist pronouncements of the
previous fall and winter! A few weeks later Fauchet placed
blame for the situation specifically on the National Assembly.
Reading from an official decree of the Directoire du Cercle
Social, he told the Confédération that the Assembly was "caught
between the ministers and the nation; between the sovereign
and the prince." The core of the problem lay in the fact that
"three-quarters of the places are occupied by hypocritical aristocrats, unknown persons, and by the most inept creatures in
the world," all of whom were undermining the democratic goals
of the Revolution.[21]

---

[20] Ibid. 2: 240; see also 2: 206.
[21] *Bdf*, no. 34, December 1790, p. 332, and 3 April 1791, pp. 35-36. Another
indication of the Confédération's renewed interest in political affairs was the
Bouche de fer's regular inclusion of news about the National Assembly begin-

The Cercle Social's renewed interest in democratic issues was symbolized by Condorcet's appearance before the Confédération. Condorcet's participation in the Cercle Social dated from the earliest days of the group, when he had used the journal *Cercle Social* to call for a more democratic electoral system. Soon after the establishment of the Confédération, Condorcet had been given the office of "Orator of the Cercle Social," and he had promised that he would speak to the group. By March 1791, however, he had made no appearance, and several club members complained that Condorcet was snubbing them. Bonneville came to his defense, arguing that Condorcet's writing and "a long convalescence are the only causes for his lateness; and far from abandoning the Amis de la Vérité, he has promised to give them an essay for the first meeting in April."[22]

On 1 April Condorcet fulfilled this pledge. In his speech "On National Conventions," he advocated the establishment of a network of regional assemblies that would meet periodically to reform the constitution and review the work of the National Assembly. These conventions would act as a check upon oligarchical tendencies inherent in representative bodies and stimulate debate on fundamental political issues. Moreover, since young people were constantly maturing into citizens (and older citizens dying), periodic conventions were needed to see if the constitution still expressed the will of the people. Conventions, Condorcet reasoned, were an excellent way for each generation to make its contribution to the nation's progress. Consequently, Condorcet called for two kinds of conventions: one to arise spontaneously during crises, and another that would meet about every twenty years.[23]

ning 11 January 1791. Bonneville claimed that he added the new section to the paper after receiving several requests from provincial readers (*Bdf*, 25 March 1791, p. 568).

[22] *Cercle Social*, letter 8, pp. 57-75; *Bdf*, 25 March 1791, p. 567. For Condorcet's activities during this period see Léon Cahen, *Condorcet et la Révolution française*, pp. 250-69.

[23] The speech was reprinted in *Bdf*, 28 April 1791, pp. 237-40, 7 May 1791, pp. 287-91, and 10 May 1791, pp. 311-14, and published separately by the Cercle Social as *De la Convention Nationale* (Paris: ICS, 1791). In August 1791, Condorcet gave a similar speech to the Jacobins, also published by the Cercle Social as *Discours sur les Conventions Nationales ... prononcé le 7 août 1791, à l'assemblée des amis de la constitution* (Paris: ICS, 1791).

Condorcet's speech is typical of the ideology of representative democracy advocated by the Cercle Social. During the Paris Municipal Revolution, Bonneville, Brissot, and Fauchet had proposed periodic meetings of district assemblies to approve or veto the work of the Communal Assembly. Condorcet's conventions projected this same idea onto the national scene. He and the other Cercle Social leaders wanted the National Assembly to exercise real political power, but they also wanted the Assembly's actions to be supervised by all citizens, since sovereignty belonged only to the people. Needless to say, the more conservative leaders of the National Assembly believed that such conventions would be incompatible with maintaining public order.

The Cercle Social's concern for the antidemocratic tendencies of the National Assembly was confirmed on 10 May 1791, when the National Assembly's Constitutional Committee proposed a decree outlawing all collective petitions, that is, petitions submitted by clubs, organizations, parishes, or governmental bodies. Collective petitions had been one of the few ways that inarticulate, powerless, and disfranchised people could influence the debates of the National Assembly. In an age without mass communications, but in which each individual's voice theoretically counted, many citizens viewed collective petitions as an excellent way to understand public opinion. A few radical members of the National Assembly such as Maximilien Robespierre and Henri Grégoire bitterly opposed "the proposed decree as unjust, impolitic, and contrary to the natural rights of man." Despite their objections, the bill was easily passed; only petitions signed by individual "active" citizens would now be received by the Assembly.[24]

This decree particularly infuriated the Cercle Social. A year earlier Condorcet had claimed that collective petitions were a necessary part of the new regime's political process: "Citizens must not only conserve their right to assemble for elections, but they must also conserve their right as men and members of the state to make petitions." Madame Roland saw collective petitions as a way for groups to check the power of the National Assembly

---

[24] *Archives parlementaires de 1787-1860, première série (1787-1799)* 25: 687; *Moniteur* 8: 353-55.

and hold its leaders accountable to their constituents. For women's groups like Etta Palm's Confédération des Amies de la Vérité, collective petitions were one of the only effective ways of publicly expressing their opinions. Bonneville believed that the passage of the bill was evidence of the true desires of Lafayette, Duport, and the Lameths: "the annihilation of the clubs. . . . Men [who have] been isolated, separated from one another, and disunited will be most easy to subjugate." Once this was accomplished, the National Assembly would "chain them in bondage, in order to make them work for its will."[25]

Within hours of the passage of the decree against collective petitions the Directoire du Cercle Social passed a resolution stating that the decree contradicted Article II of the Declaration of the Rights of Man, which guaranteed freedom of thought and freedom of the press. In view of the "aristocratic" nature of the decree, the directoire proposed that the Confédération set aside its next four meetings specifically for debate on the right to petition. More important, the directoire urged the Confédération to invite "not only the members of the club, but even all those who are not members, who want to discuss this issue." Non-members would simply come to the Cercle Social office "where they would be given entrance cards"; all who wished to make a speech could write their names on a sign-up sheet, to be called upon in order.[26]

On 13 May, the directoire presented its resolution to the Confédération, who readily adopted it and authorized the Imprimerie du Cercle Social to publish it as a poster, to be displayed throughout the capital.[27]

The next meeting, on 20 May, was among the most momentous in the Confédération's brief history. After the usual announcements, the president turned the floor over to a deputation from the Cordeliers club, who were to be the first speakers on

[25] Archives de la Seine, VD 12, p. 7; *Lettres de Mme Roland* 2:141-42; *Bdf*, 11 May 1791, pp. 161, 277-78. See also *Pf*, 11 May 1791, pp. 519-20, and 13 May 1791, pp. 531-32.
[26] *Bdf*, 11 May 1791, pp. 250-52.
[27] *Bdf*, 11 May 1791, p. 253. A copy of the poster, beginning "Frères et amis," is in the Bibliothèque Nationale (Fol. Lb 40/3298).

the right to petition. A Cordelier leader began by citing examples of political corruption in the capital. He attacked the National Assembly's decree and read a resolution against it composed by the leaders of the Section du Théâtre-Français. The speech met with great applause, and the Confédération thanked the Cordeliers for attending the meeting.[28]

The dispute over the right to petition also highlighted the agenda of the next Confédération meeting, on 27 May. Another leader of the Cordeliers club, Claude Lebois, delivered a long address against the 10 May decree. A lawyer and municipal politician, Lebois had worked as a barrister for the Parlement of Dijon before moving to Paris in 1787. He claimed that the decree contradicted Article III of the Declaration of the Rights of Man, which stated that the source of all sovereignty "is located in the essence of the nation." The right to petition, Lebois argued, echoing Condorcet's ideas, was necessary to ensure that the will of the people be heard. In a period when electoral participation was limited to a minority of "active" citizens, Lebois viewed the right to petition as a way for "passive" citizens to prevent legislative tyranny. "A legislative assembly without checks would be the worst possible despotism. . . . Each individual would be like a drop of water, such that the first puff of wind would dissipate him into the air." Collective petitions were not in this view a holdover of Old Regime corporatism, as asserted by the National Assembly, but a necessary tool for preserving individual rights and liberties.[29]

A citizen from the Section du Croix-Rouge gave a stirring speech on the same subject at the meeting of 3 June. Like previous speakers he argued that the 10 May decree was a way for the National Assembly to destroy the clubs, isolate citizens, and prepare the way for a new aristocracy. "But it is still necessary to recall, if only to remind those who would forget, that sovereign power essentially resides in the people, and that it is inalienable, indivisible, and incommunicable." On 10 June, the

---

[28] *Bdf*, 24 May 1791, pp. 316-19.

[29] *Bdf*, 1 June 1791, pp. 6-9, and 4 June 1791, pp. 1-9. On Lebois see Etienne Charavay, ed., *L'Assemblée éléctorale de Paris. 26 août 1791 à 12 août 1792*, p. 59.

poet Marie-Emile Duchosal argued the same point. "Today your legislators, by not openly annulling their decree, reverse the reign of the sovereign [people] and plunge it into slavish passivity," he told the Confédération. He claimed that collective petitions were "a way to regenerate the quality of life and to establish true equality among you." At the end of this fourth meeting on collective petitions, the club closed the debate on the issue and passed the following resolution:

The [Confédération] des Amis de la Vérité, after having discussed for four meetings the decree of 10 May 1791 on the right to petition, recognizes and unanimously declares that the decree is contrary to the Declaration of the Rights of Man and Citizen, and that it attacks the sovereignty of the nation. Thus it invites all citizens to demand its revocation.[30]

It is significant that members of the Cordeliers club fully participated in these four meetings. The Cercle Social had been on very friendly terms with the Cordeliers at least since the early months of 1790. When the National Assembly reorganized the Paris municipality from sixty districts into forty-eight sections, the Cordeliers district was eliminated, and Danton organized its leaders into the Cordeliers club. During the summer of 1790, Bonneville joined the club and moved his home and Cercle Social headquarters into its neighborhood. While the Confédération des Amis de la Vérité met in the Circus Arena in the Palais Royal, all other Cercle Social groups including the Confédération des *Amies* de la Vérité and the Directoire du Cercle Social met at the headquarters located at 4, rue du Théâtre-Français, a short walk from the Cordeliers club. Bonneville and his family lived on the second floor, above the offices and presses of the Cercle Social. During the calm months of October 1790 through March 1791, the connections between the two clubs were minimal. But as the Cercle Social became more involved in political issues, its ties with the Cordeliers club became increasingly close. During the days preceding the 20 May meeting, Bonneville had made a special appeal through the *Bouche de fer* for cooperation

[30] *Bdf*, 9 June 1791, pp. 6-12, 19 June 1791, pp. 7-14, 21 June 1791, pp. 1-7, and 13 June 1791, p. 8.

and solidarity between the two clubs. Both groups, he claimed, hoped to "give the voice of the people all its force." He offered to make the presses of the Imprimerie du Cercle Social available to the Cordeliers. The Cordeliers responded favorably to his overtures. During the two-month period between May and July 1791, the two clubs became equal partners in a crusade to impress their democratic principles upon the National Assembly. Members, petitions, meetings, declarations, demonstrations, printing presses—all these things were shared so intimately that it is often difficult to distinguish between the two clubs.[31]

THE CONTROVERSY over the right to petition stimulated two related political movements involving the Cercle Social during this period. These were a renewed campaign against the marc d'argent and the establishment of the Point central des arts et métiers. The marc d'argent (the National Assembly's notorious decree limiting the electorate to those who paid a certain annual percentage of taxes) had never been popular among Cercle Social members, and in March the Cercle Social, reiterating the position it had first taken in February 1790, declared that the marc d'argent "explicitly violates the Declaration of the Rights of Man."[32] But it was not until the National Assembly passed the 10 May decree against collective petitions that a political movement rose in opposition to the marc d'argent. In the minds of the Paris radicals the two issues were intimately connected. Most men and women were excluded from direct participation in the electoral process because of the marc d'argent law; the only way they could voice their will, therefore, was by coming together in voluntary associations, composing petitions expressing their desires, and sending these petitions to the National Assembly. By outlawing this political recourse, the National Assembly was threatening to ignore the vast majority of people who were not

---

[31] *Bdf*, 12 April 1791, p. 91, 22 April 1791, p. 215, and 11 May 1791, pp. 268-71. On Bonneville's residence and office see the memoirs of Madame Bonneville reprinted in Moncure D. Conway, *The Life of Thomas Paine* 2: 433-59. On the Cordeliers club see Albert Mathiez, *Le Club des Cordeliers pendant la crise de Varennes, et le massacre du Champ de Mars*; Robertson, "The Society of the Cordeliers."

[32] *Bdf*, 27 January 1791, p. 184, and 23 March 1791, p. 545.

wealthy enough to become active citizens. The Cercle Social tolerated passive citizenship as long as other ways existed for citizens to express their will. But the 10 May decree convinced Paris radicals that the National Assembly wanted to exclude the majority of French men and women from political life altogether. Reinstatement of the right to petition collectively was no longer enough; the leaders of the Cercle Social and other popular clubs believed that the Revolution would be endangered until the marc d'argent itself was eliminated. Bonneville, for example, proposed that all citizens gather in a national convention during the Bastille holidays of 12-14 July, in order to approve or veto the policies of the National Assembly.[33]

On 7 May, François Robert, the Cordelier journalist and friend of Brissot, founded the Comité central des diverses sociétés fraternelles. A federation of Parisian popular clubs, the Comité became a focal point for political activity aimed at the 10 May decree and the marc d'argent. The Confédération des Amis de la Vérité was one of its first members, and Bonneville was naturally the club's delegate. In a Comité central meeting held at the Cordeliers club on 14 June (which was given extensive coverage in the *Bouche de fer*), the radical activist Lorinet delivered a stinging attack upon the marc d'argent. He believed that the problem revolved around the National Assembly's misunderstanding of the relationship between property and political rights. "The representatives of the nation adhere to this misconceived assertion that it is the property holders who compose the state. From this have come several of our mistakes," he claimed. "It is certainly true that all children of the state have a right to property; but the National Assembly interprets this fact in the opposite sense of the right. Property is never an attribute of man. ... It is only an advantage in which all men should participate." Active citizenship is not an acquired trait, but rather "being born a citizen, I must find the natural right of my liberty consecrated and guaranteed from my birth." Although Lorinet did not cite his sources for this position, it is obvious that he was influenced by Claude Fauchet's argument

[33] *Bdf*, 11 May 1791, p. 288.

on the same topic in his commentary on Rousseau's famous chapter on "Real Property."[34]

The Comité central asked Bonneville to write a petition based upon these views. The petition called for an end to the marc d'argent, the establishment of the kinds of democratic institutions advocated by Condorcet, and the right of all citizens to participate in political life.

Petition to the National Assembly

The undersigned, united in the *Comité central des diverses sociétés fraternelles* of the capital, which seeks the prosperity of the commonwealth, has just been convinced that the day which sees the beginning of the primary assemblies will be the signal of universal reclamation for all those who dream of realizing their hopes.

FATHERS OF THE FATHERLAND,

Those who obey laws that they have not approved or sanctioned are slaves. You have declared that the law can only be the expression of the general will, and that the majority is composed of citizens strangely called inactive.

If you do not fix the sacred time of universal sanction of the law by the absolute totality of citizens; if you do not stop making the cruel demarcation that you produced by your decree of the *marc d'argent* among a fraternal people; if you do not forever eliminate these different degrees of eligibility that so violates your Declaration of the Rights of Man, the Fatherland will be endangered.

On 14 July 1789,

the city of Paris contained 300,000 armed men. The active list, published by the municipality, gives only 80,000 citizens. Compare and judge.

The Comité central passed Bonneville's petition and sent it to the National Assembly, where it was ignored. Nonetheless, its effect was felt in Paris: the Cercle Social published it in the *Bouche de fer* and distributed it as a poster "in all the streets of the capital."[35]

---

[34] *Bdf*, 17 June 1791, p. 2; Mathiez, *Club des Cordeliers*, pp. 30-32.

[35] *Bdf*, 17 June 1791, pp. 9-11. Another petition was drawn up at the same time against the marc d'argent by the Section du Théâtre-Français and re-

The other political movement that paralleled concern over the issues of the right to petition and marc d'argent was the establishment of an organization composed of and protective of the rights of unemployed wage earners. For a brief period during the latter half of 1790, working conditions in Paris had been relatively good; bread was cheap and the rate of unemployment stable. But during the first months of 1791—for reasons that remain unclear—unemployment began to rise sharply and the working class grew increasingly discontented. In January, for example, there were 24,000 workers in the Paris public workshops that had been designed for the unemployed; a few months later the figure had risen to 30,000. Clearly the strain on the municipality's budget was great, and Mayor Bailly moved to relieve that financial drain by announcing on 7 May 1791 that all public workshops in Paris would soon close. His decision, however, precipitated more unrest.[36]

The leaders of the Cercle Social had never liked Bailly, and these new developments only confirmed their suspicions that the aristocratic mayor cared little for the plight of unemployed workers. Five days later, at the next meeting of the Confédération, the club approved B. A. Houard's proposal for the formation of the Point central des arts et métiers, whose purpose was to give the unemployed wage earners a political voice. The new organization was formed as a unit within the Cercle Social. "Its directoire will communicate with ours; it will assemble at the same meeting place (4, rue du Théâtre-Français), and will form for the [Confédération] a new source of enlightenment and support," Houard explained. While the new group was led by the

---

printed by the Cercle Social as "Pétition des citoyens actifs, contre le décret du marc d'argent," *Bdf*, 17 June 1791, pp. 15-16, and 19 June 1791, pp. 1-7. There was some question as to the legality of these petitions in the wake of the 10 May decree. The radicals had two responses: first, they asserted that collective petitions were still legal until the decree was signed by the king; and second, they claimed that these petitions were within the law, representing only individual active citizens.

[36] George Rudé, *The Crowd in the French Revolution*, pp. 82-83; Y. Forado-Cunéo, "Les Ateliers de charité de Paris pendant la Révolution 1789-1791," *Rf* 86(1933): 317-42, 87(1934): 29-61, 103-23. For Bailly's candid views on public workshops see *Mémoires de Bailly* 2: 257.

more bourgeois members of the Cercle Social, it was composed of laborers and artisans.[37]

The Cercle Social hoped that the Point central would not merely prevent the closure of the Paris public workshops, but would work for their expansion until all unemployment had been eliminated. In another address to the Confédération, Houard attacked Bailly's schemes and argued that the National Assembly must create a national system of public workshops for all unemployed workers. In his radical view, a person's natural rights included the right to a job. "His plans embrace the entire kingdom," wrote Bonneville. Houard's speech "was often interrupted by excited applause that made it a memorable experience."[38] The Point central was a natural outgrowth of the Confédération's sympathy for the poor, as exemplified by Fauchet's commentaries on Rousseau. When Fauchet delivered those discourses in November 1790, most members of his audience had believed that the National Assembly would enact his democratic reforms. By May 1791, however, most of the Cercle Social had lost its naïve faith in the National Assembly.

In mid-June the Cercle Social's disillusionment was reconfirmed when the National Assembly supported Bailly's policies by announcing a nationwide closing of all public workshops. The Point central immediately went into action. Determined to help the thousands of workers who were instantly thrown out of work, they composed the following petition at their 28 June meeting in the offices of the Cercle Social:

> Health and Joy to the 22,000 Workers Who Have
> Asked Advice From the Counsels of the
> *bouche de fer*:

Citizens, brothers, friends: with courage and love address yourselves directly to the National Assembly, and offer it the following petition:

[37] *Bdf*, 11 May 1791, p. 258.
[38] *Bdf*, 11 May 1791, p. 330; B. A. Houard, *Moyens et nécessité absolues d'occuper les ouvriers oisifs et ceux des ateliers de charité à des travaux utiles à l'Etat et à eux-mêmes. . . .* (Paris: ICS, [1791]) listed in the British Museum, F. R. 481, 3. I have been unable to locate this rare pamphlet.

We are in poverty, without bread and without work. It is the fault of the bad government that you have destroyed; it is the crime of tyrants whom you have punished. We do not accuse you. We have the right to exist, for all we ask for is work, and we do not stoop to beg from rich aristocrats or hypocritical priests. We could have seized their treasures and their lands for the good of the poor; but this is only for the law to proclaim! Declare that their criminal emigrations exempt them from the law's protection. Let the nation seize their property for itself.

The petition went on to list various kinds of public work projects the state should sponsor: building canals, joining rivers, clearing marshes, and the like. The Cercle Social offered to publish it, and the Cordeliers club offered to have its secretaries sign the petition for any workers who did not know how to write.[39]

Two days later this petition was sent to the National Assembly. The Assembly responded by reducing the number of public jobs to between 4,000 and 5,000, instead of eliminating them altogether; but this compromise did little to satisfy the demands of the Point central. On 4 July the Cercle Social published an open letter from the Point central to Charles Lameth, president of the National Assembly. It informed him of a demonstration by the unemployed, planned for the following day, and warned him of possible violence. The Point central pleaded with him to declare more public jobs to avoid disorder. Lameth promised to look into the matter, thereby deterring the threatened violence.[40]

THE CERCLE Social's campaign for collective petitions, its protests against the marc d'argent, and its activities on behalf of unemployed workers testify to the organization's renewed interest in democratic politics. The 13 May meeting of the Confédération, regarding the right to petition collectively, was the first time

[39] *Bdf*, 29 June 1791, pp. 2-5, 30 June 1791, pp. 5-6, and 27 June 1791, pp. 6-7; Rudé, *The Crowd in the French Revolution*, pp 81-83. Rudé suggests that this is the most moderate petition to come out of the workers' movement during this period, underscoring the fact that the Point central was directed by the non-laboring members of the Cercle Social. Rudé is mistaken, however, when he refers to the Point central as a "Cordeliers club affiliate."

[40] *Bdf*, 4 July 1791, pp. 7-8; Lacroix, *Actes, Second série* 5: 238-40.

that the club had reacted to a specific government decree, and it was also the first time all interested citizens had been invited to participate in its debates. These new activities can be compared to the Confédération's earlier efforts to lobby on behalf of the Civil Constitution of the Clergy. Except for the Bonneville-Fauchet dispute, that earlier campaign was moderate and restrained; Cercle Social members believed that the National Assembly had acted wisely in passing the Civil Constitution and generally expected the nation to support it. In sharp contrast, the May events radicalized and politicized the members of the Confédération des Amis de la Vérité. The Club became increasingly critical of the constitutional monarchists who controlled the National Assembly and suspected, with the Cordeliers club, that the Assembly was no longer acting in the interests of the nation.

6

A Club Transformed:
Toward a Democratic
Republic

THOMAS PAINE (1737-1809). English author of *Common Sense* and *The Rights of Man*. Elected to the Convention. *Chronique du mois* editor. Paine lived in Bonneville's house for several years and published books and pamphlets with the Imprimerie du Cercle Social.
Courtesy of The Newberry Library, Chicago

A patriotic club is a school where one is instructed in the science of free government.

Journal des clubs, October 1790, p. 4.

THE CERCLE SOCIAL'S renewed entry into democratic political affairs altered the club's view of itself. The Cercle Social began as part of a propaganda machine for the Fauchetins during the Paris Municipal Revolution. When that group was discredited by the municipal elections of August 1790, Fauchet and Bonneville established the Confédération des Amis de la Vérité, promising that the club would avoid political participation, limiting itself to speculative concerns. As a result, the club gained a reputation as a haven for intellectuals who enjoyed engaging in abstract discussion. Thus its membership included few workers and comprised members of the bourgeoisie. As long as the club remained chiefly interested in abstract ideas, its organizational structure fit its purpose. But when the club turned to political activities during the spring of 1791, many members began to reevaluate the purpose of the Cercle Social, and indeed, the role of all clubs.

François Lanthenas was the foremost theoretician on clubs within the Cercle Social. Since the publication of his treatise on inheritance law he had been hard at work on a new book analyzing the purposes and functions of revolutionary clubs. A draft was completed during the early months of 1791, and Fauchet read parts of it to the Confédération. In May, Lanthenas loaned the manuscript to Robespierre, who, to the horror of its author, lost it. Nevertheless, some of it was reconstructed and printed in various articles of Brissot's *Patriote français*, and a shortened version appeared later in a Cercle Social journal.[1]

Lanthenas distinguished two types of clubs: patriotic and popular. The former had appeared during the last years of the Old Regime and had flourished during the first years of the Revolution. Patriotic clubs were composed of prominent politicians

[1] *Pf*, 17 May 1791, p. 544; *Bdf*, 20 April 1791, p. 192, *Cdm*, February 1792, pp. 71-89.

and intellectuals who came together to discuss various issues and
sponsor specific reforms. The Jacobin club, composed "of men
from the comfortable class," was the prototype of this genre.
The popular club, on the other hand, was led by the same kind
of men, but its rank-and-file was drawn from workers and
artisans. These clubs—the Cordeliers, for instance—which often
began as local assemblies of interested citizens, had the character
of town-hall meetings, uniting the enlightenment of their leaders
with the democratic spirit of their membership. "The old kind
of club had the audacity to remain isolated, to have special rules,
to be few in numbers and to praise itself as the most enlightened,"
Lanthenas explained. "The new club, strengthened in numbers
and in the rights of the people, would shudder at the stubbornness of its senior to remain separate; it would like all its members
to support the establishment of popular societies."[2]

Lanthenas believed that popular clubs ought to replace the
more elitist patriotic societies. "The first Friends of the Constitution, who came together to defend the rights of an unfortunate
people when the nation was in its lethargy, have been infinitely
useful," he wrote of the Paris Jacobins. "But as for the lovely
role of *protector* that they have played: shouldn't it stop when
the people assembles itself, when the people instructs itself, when
the people wants to care for the Fatherland itself!" This did not
mean that the writers and politicians who staffed Jacobin societies were merely to wither away in the wake of the democratic
movement. On the contrary, Lanthenas envisioned these leaders
beginning "to form a society of tutors for the people" instead
of pretending to be their protectors. Popular clubs were for
Lanthenas more than democratic cadres; they were the perfect
forum where the universal and enlightened ideas of the Cercle
Social could be spread among the masses. In these popular academies the Revolution would give birth to a democratic enlightenment. "We are now working," he wrote to his friend Henri
Bancal, "to bring throughout the empire the popular societies
of which I have often talked with you. Everyone I have talked

[2] *Pf*, 24 December 1791, p. 3, 14 February 1791, P. 178, and 28 February
1791, pp. 214-16.

with about them senses that this is the only way to consolidate the Revolution." For Lanthenas and his friends, the popular club was "the most beautiful institution made since the Revolution."[3]

These views had important implications for the Cercle Social. Its Confédération was established specifically as a federation of the elitist patriotic clubs Lanthenas had described. Lanthenas' comments concerning the Jacobins could just as easily pertain to the Confédération, since its membership dues excluded the lower classes. Yet, by having Lanthenas' views read to the group, and by later publishing his ideas, the Cercle Social demonstrated support for the new kind of club. Lanthenas' colleagues agreed that intellectuals should stop talking only to each other and should become educators of the masses. "It is time to address ourselves to the most numerous class of citizens," Bonneville declared.[4]

During the weeks following the National Assembly's 10 May decree, the Cercle Social showed its commitment to the new type of club. By expanding membership to essentially anyone who wanted to attend club meetings, the Confédération became considerably more democratic; by focusing on issues like the right to petition, it found topics closer to the people's interests. Indeed, during the weeks surrounding the king's flight to Varennes, the Cercle Social transformed itself into a popular club.

DURING the early morning hours of 21 June 1791, King Louis XVI and the royal family secretly boarded a coach and began a ride that dramatically changed the course of the Revolution. They hoped to cross the border into the Austrian Empire, join their Hapsburg relatives, and await the restoration of the Old Regime. Louis had left behind a stinging denunciation of the Revolution, leaving no doubt as to his hatred for the reforms passed by the National Assembly. The king, recognized before reaching his

[3] *Pf*, 28 February 1791, pp. 214-16; Bibliothèque Nationale, Nouvelle acquisitions françaises 9532, fol. 169; Edith Bernardin, "Lettres de Lanthenas à Bancal des Issarts," *Annales historiques de la Révolution française* 16 (1939): 246; See also *Lettres de Mme Roland* 2: 233.
[4] *Bdf*, 23 June 1791, pp. 5-6.

destination, was caught in the village of Varennes and he and his family returned under guard to the capital.[5]

The king's flight to Varennes threw France into a deep political crisis. Until then, only a handful of local politicians had dared to question the monarchy, and their ideas had received no support from any club or governmental body. Neither the Cercle Social nor the Cordeliers had ever called for the elimination of the monarchy. In their view, the French Revolution meant the establishment of a democratic state, something perfectly compatible with constitutional monarchy as long as its constitution was firmly based upon popular sovereignty.

This tolerant attitude toward the monarchy was radically altered by the flight to Varennes. The sophisticated network of overlapping clubs, sectional assemblies, and central federations that had served in previous weeks as mouthpieces for passive citizens were united by the king's actions into a "sort of popular front," which called for the arrest of the king and the establishment of a democratic republic. "The flight of the king," wrote Jean-Marie Roland, "has produced the pleasing result of rallying Patriotism in the wake of a common danger."[6] During the four weeks between the king's flight and the massacre at the Champ de Mars, the Cercle Social and the Cordeliers solidified their partnership and led the other clubs in a popular movement to abolish monarchy in France. Their archenemies in this struggle were the leaders of the National Assembly, who wanted to forgive the king and put the final touches on a constitution that was blatantly antidemocratic. The situation was further complicated by the willingness of some politicians to replace Louis XVI with his cousin, the duc d'Orléans.

Within hours of learning about the king's flight, the Cercle Social decisively endorsed the establishment of a republic. Bonneville made the position clear in a *Bouche de fer* article entitled

---

[5] The best survey of the king's flight to Varennes and the events that followed is Marcel Reinhard, *La Chute de la royauté, 10 août 1792*, pp. 15-156; an older, but still essential source is Alphonse Aulard, *The French Revolution: A Political History*, 1: 260-314.

[6] Reinhard, *Chute de la royauté*, p. 45, uses the term "popular front"; Bibliothèque Nationale, Nouvelle acquisitions françaises, 6241, fols. 83-86.

"No More Kings." He claimed that a free people had no need of monarchs, who were all parasites, living off the blood of their subjects. "No one on this earth needs this kind of monster who devours twenty-five to thirty million people as if they were bread crumbs."[7]

Meanwhile, the Cordeliers wrote a petition declaring that "France is no longer a monarchy; it is a republic, or is at least until all the departments, all the primary assemblies, have spoken their voice on this important question." The Cercle Social published the petition as a poster and reprinted it in the *Bouche de fer*. The following evening, 22 June, the Cordeliers adapted some verses of Voltaire's *Brutus* to fit the current situation:

> Think! On the Champ de Mars, that spot august,
> Did Louis swear faithful to be and just;
> Between himself and people this the tie:
> Our oaths he gives us back, his proved a lie!
> If in all France a traitor linger yet
> Who would a master brook, a king regret,
> Then let the wretch in death a torment find!
> His guilty ashes cast upon the wind,
> Leave but a name here, odious even more
> Than that of Tyrant all free men abhor!

Then followed a declaration in which the Cordeliers swore "individually to stab the tyrants who shall dare to attack our frontiers." Again, the Cercle Social distributed the poem and declaration as a poster and reprinted them in the *Bouche de fer*.[8]

The king's flight to Varennes also had an important impact upon the structure of the Cercle Social, accelerating its transformation into a more political club. Immediately after learning about the incident, Bonneville announced that the directoire was meeting in permanent session. Citizens were urged to inform

[7] *Bdf*, 23 June 1791, pp. 3-6.
[8] *Pétition de la Société des amis des droits de l'Homme et du Citoyen aux Représentants de la Nation* (Paris: ICS, [1791]); *Bdf*, 23 June 1791, pp. 7-8; *Club des Cordeliers . . . Extrait du registre du 22 juin 1791* (Paris: ICS, [1791]), in the Archives Nationales Dxxix^b 365. The translation of the poem is taken from Aulard, *French Revolution* 1: 277; see also Mathiez, *Club des Cordeliers*, pp. 45-47, 50-51; and Reinhard, *Chute de la royauté*, pp. 64-67.

the Cercle Social of political developments by dropping their messages into the bouche de fer that still hung on the door of the headquarters. Moreover, the directoire decided to change the focus and aim of its journal, the *Bouche de fer*. Acting upon the belief that the time had come when intellectuals should speak directly to the people, the directoire transformed the *Bouche de fer* into an eight-page daily, dominated by political commentaries and news of events, rather than by debates on more esoteric subjects. In short, this thrice-weekly academic journal became a popular daily newspaper.[9]

The change was clearly demonstrated in the five issues of 23-29 June, which dealt exclusively with the king's flight and the ensuing political crisis. For example, on 24 June, the *Bouche de fer* labeled Louis XVI "the eternal enemy of equality and liberty," and listed his "crimes." He was charged with sabotaging the Revolution by, among other things, attempting to destroy the patriotic and popular clubs. As for a regency led by the king's cousin, the *Bouche de fer* never ceased to proclaim its militant opposition: "the duc d'Orléans appears to me as an opportunist," wrote Bonneville, "who wants to seize the monarchical scepter of the blind Friends of the Constitution, who serve him as his step-ladder." Bonneville urged citizens to take action and called for a demonstration in front of the Tuileries, where everyone would shout "that only *the law can be the expression of the general will; only the law can reign!*"[10]

Bonneville realized that the term "republic" was unfamiliar to most common people. "The people understand nothing about that word, but without thinking, they repeat their desire for a *republic*." This presented a very dangerous situation because, in Bonneville's view, an ignorant people could never discover their general will. "No situation has ever equaled ours," he wrote. "If we fail the people because of these words, we will all be the first victims of our errors. Let us therefore say to our brothers and friends that one must not simply substitute one obscure term

---

[9] *Bdf*, 21 June 1791, Supplement, p. 3.

[10] *Bdf*, 24 June 1791, pp. 1-8. Bonneville also organized the Point central des arts et métiers into action to bring further pressure upon the National Assembly. See Lacroix, *Actes, Seconde Série* 5: 259.

for another." Instead, he urged the Cercle Social to help the masses understand political concepts by analyzing the language of the debates for them. "Let us begin by defining the terms," Bonneville insisted. For instance, he pointed out, "in defining the word *re-public*, and translating it literally into our language—for it is a Latin word, *res-publica*—all obscurity will vanish." Such logic apparently allowed Bonneville to declare that a republic "is nothing else but literally the commonwealth, the state, the great national community, THE NATIONAL GOVERNMENT"; that is, a government based upon popular sovereignty and universal suffrage.[11] This was no academic word game. Bonneville realized that the large group of unemployed and disfranchised Parisians who might support the Cercle Social's democratic policies did not necessarily share the club's republican sympathies. For many ordinary Parisians, the king remained a popular figure, the victim of aristocratic ministers and reactionary National Assembly deputies. Bonneville hoped to convince them that any democracy was itself a republic and, conversely, that every republic had to be democratic.

The Confédération des Amis de la Vérité generally supported the positions taken by its leaders. The meeting of 1 July, for example, was dominated by speeches calling for a republic based upon universal suffrage. "Today the Cercle Social openly discussed whether or not to keep the monarchy," wrote Madame Roland. "It is the only club in the capital, after the Cordeliers, to discuss the topic so openly. The Jacobins, like the [National] Assembly, go into convulsions at the mention of a republic." Nevertheless, there were also a large number of Cercle Social members who opposed the club's republican activities. This opposition is difficult to detect, for it was easier for a dissident to leave the club than to change its prevailing views, and what dissent did occur was rarely reported in the *Bouche der fer*. But the more conservative members who had helped to found the Confédération, such as Goupil and Chabroud, had probably dropped out of the club some weeks before; others, such as Athanase Auger, were not opposed to a republic per se but did

[11] *Bdf*, 25 June 1791, pp. 1-4. See also *Bdf*, no. 1, October 1790, pp. 6-7.

not see what good could result from the political crisis. "The sciences, letters, and arts, which have produced our glory in the past; can they flourish in the midst of our internecine strife?" Auger rhetorically asked. Perhaps there were also a number of members like author Théophile Mandar, who on 1 July stated his preference for "the pure monarchy of Plato to the republic of the Romans" but who told the club a week later that he had become a committed republican.[12]

AT THIS same time, some Cercle Social leaders also became involved in a new group of republican writers led by Condorcet, which relied upon the Cercle Social for support and publicity. Condorcet "became a convinced republican" immediately after learning of the king's flight, and his decision precipitated a sharp break with his more conservative friends, including Lafayette, whom he now scolded for advocating the reinstatement of the king. Within a few days after the king's flight, Condorcet formed a "Société des républicains," whose purpose was "to enlighten minds about republicanism."[13]

In addition to Condorcet, the Société included Bonneville, Lanthenas, Achille Duchatelet, and Tom Paine. Duchatelet was an army officer who had served in the American War of Independence. His participation in the group resulted from his friendship with Condorcet, and he played a negligible role in the French Revolution. Tom Paine's inclusion is more significant. The celebrated author of *Common Sense* and the *Rights of Man* had been in Paris for a few months, and was actually living in Condorcet's home at the time of the king's flight. Among Paine's other close friends was Bonneville, whose house and wife he later shared (one of Paine's biographers described their lives as "closely interwoven"). Perhaps one of the reasons that Paine

[12] *Lettres de Mme Roland* 2: 320; *Bdf*, 3 July 1791, pp. 1-5, 10 July 1791, p. 5.

[13] *Le Républicain ou le Défenseur du gouvernement représentatif*, 3 July 1791, p. 5; also reprinted in *Pf*, 2 July 1791, pp. 5-6; Etienne Dumont, *Souvenirs de Mirabeau et sur les deux premières assemblées legislatives*, p. 323; Keith Michael Baker, *Condorcet: From Natural Philosophy to Social Mathematics*, pp. 303-306; Léon Cahen, *Condorcet et la Révolution française*, pp. 248-77; Hélène Delsaux, *Condorcet journaliste (1790-1794)*, pp. 49-61.

was drawn into this circle was that Bonneville, Condorcet, and Lanthenas were among the few revolutionaries who knew English; Lanthenas and Bonneville translated several of Paine's works and had them published by the Cercle Social.[14]

The Société des républicains published four issues of the *Républicain ou Le Défenseur du gouvernement représentatif*, a journal composed of polemical, satirical, and theoretical essays all aimed at convincing the literate public of the need for a republic. The leading article of the first issue, probably written by Paine, gave four fundamental reasons that the National Assembly should depose Louis XVI: First, by attempting to desert the nation he had effectively abdicated the throne. Second, the flight had revealed the king's counterrevolutionary character, and the people had forever lost confidence in him as a consequence. Third, the flight itself was illegal, and therefore Louis was a criminal. Finally, the king's actions had at the very least severed the sacred contract that bound nation and king; the people were hence free to choose whatever form of government they wished.[15]

On 8 July Condorcet read one of his articles from the *Républicain* to the Confédération. Shortly before the address, Bonneville reminded the club that Cordorcet's "former ties with Voltaire, d'Alembert, and the works of profound thought, have placed him as the dean at the head of the Republic of Letters ... his glory is an honor for all Friends of Truth." The message was clear: the republican movement was made up not only of the disfranchised mob but of the most illustrious and well-cultivated citizens, who spoke in the name of the great philosophes, the patriarchs of the Revolution. Condorcet's speech wasted no words on the specific characters of Louis XVI or the duc d'Orléans, but waged an attack upon monarchy itself. While admitting that there was no fundamental contradiction between

---

[14] Dumont, *Souvenirs de Mirabeau*, pp. 253-54, 319-21; A. O. Aldridge, "Condorcet et Paine. Leurs rapports intellectuels", *Revue de littérature comparée* 32: 45-65; "closely interwoven" comes from Conway, *Life of Thomas Paine* 1: 307. Conway also believed that Brissot (who also knew some English) was part of the Société (1: 311), a claim supported by Aldridge, *Man of Reason: The Life of Thomas Paine*, pp. 145-46; and David Freeman Hawke, *Paine*, p. 228; and Ellery, *Brissot de Warville*, pp. 170-71.

[15] *Républicain*, 3 July 1791, pp. 3-4. See also, *Lettres de Mme Roland* 2: 319.

democracy and monarchy, Condorcet claimed that monarchy had become a "dangerous and corrupt institution." He called for a democratically elected national convention that would have the authority to transform France into a republic. Monarchy, he argued, "is not at all appropriate for the French nation in the current epoch." The speech was well received and was immediately printed as a pamphlet by the Cercle Social. "Never has a greater cause been placed in more worthy hands," Bonneville declared.[16]

The relationship between the Société des républicains and the Cercle Social was clearly intimate. The Confédération praised the group and distributed 150 free copies of the *Républicain* at one of its meetings. Jean-Marie Roland sent a copy to his friend Champagneux, editor of the *Courrier de Lyon*, urging him to show it to the popular clubs in Lyon. Other Cercle Social members, perhaps influenced by the journal, began to publish republican tracts of their own.[17] While the *Républicain* did not survive the political repression that followed the massacre at the Champ de Mars, all of its members except Duchatelet remained among the most active leaders of the Cercle Social.

ALL OF THESE elements—the democratic movement fueled by an increasingly large group of disfranchised and unemployed people, the republican campaign spearheaded by influential publicists, the reactionary king's inability to lead effectively, and the intransigent group of National Assembly deputies committed to whitewashing the king's crimes against the nation—had combined to create a crisis more serious than anything since the taking of the Bastille. The situation reached its peak toward the middle of July. "The crisis gets deeper and deeper," wrote Madame Roland. "It is possible that within eight days we will be in the midst of a civil war."[18]

[16] *Bdf*, 5 July 1791, p. 3, 10 July 1791, p. 3, 1 July 1791, p. 4; Condorcet, *De la république, ou Un Roi est-il nécessaire à la conservation de la liberté?* (Paris: ICS, [1791]); see also *Pf*, 17 July 1791, p. 72.

[17] *Bdf*, 10 July 1791, pp. 1-2; Bibliothèque Nationale, Nouvelles acquisitions françaises, 6241, fol. 81 (cited in Cahen, *Condorcet*, p. 251). See also Baumier, *De la monarchie française*, and Mège, *Bancal des Issarts*, pp. 36-39.

[18] *Lettres de Mme Roland* 2: 333.

On Friday, 15 July, the Confédération met for what would be its last and most exciting meeting, a session described by Albert Mathiez as a "great republican demonstration." The president of the Confédération, Jean-François Michel, opened the meeting by announcing that "the object of the [Confédération] is boldly to declare that Louis XVI cannot return to the throne, even by a decree of the National Assembly, if he has not received the approval of the communes of the eighty-three departments of the Empire" (a principle to which the Cercle Social returned during the king's trial in 1792). On all sides came shouts and applause: "Hurrah, hurrah, hurrah! To courage, to justice, and to truth!" Numerous speeches and "violent" debate followed. The radical leaders of the popular clubs, most notably François Momoro, a printer and Cordelier officer, dominated the session. They demanded the establishment of a democratic republic, and discussion focused on the most effective way to pressure the National Assembly to depose the king. There was a large minority who were critical of the radical tone of the meeting, but they had difficulty obtaining the floor; even Confédération regulars like Athanase Auger could not make themselves heard. Finally, after hours of turbulent rhetoric, a resolution "definitively adopted by a majority" rebuked the National Assembly for deciding against debating the guilt or innocence of the king.[19]

The adjournment of the meeting did not subdue the crowd's excitement, which had mounted during the evening. A large group of members—one account estimated 4,000—decided to walk to the Jacobin club (which was holding a meeting of its own) to pressure its members to pass a similar resolution. They arrived around 11:00 P.M. The startled Jacobins allowed the leader of this huge delegation to speak to the club. He announced that the delegation intended to go to the Champ de Mars the next

[19] Mathiez, *Club des Cordeliers*, p. 117; *Bdf*, 18 July 1791, pp. 1-5. Born in 1727, Michel taught medicine at the Université de Montpellier before moving to Paris. In 1790 he was elected president of the Paris Communal Assembly. He took over the presidency of the Confédération from Mailly on 13 May 1791. Later he became a professor of rhetoric at the Ecole centrale de Merthe. See Etienne Charavay, *L'Assemblée éléctorale de Paris. 18 novembre 1790-15 juin 1791*, p. 64.

day in order to sign a petition against the reinstatement of the king. He asked that the Jacobins join his group in this drive.[20] It is easy to see why the radicals pressured the Jacobins. A high proportion of their members were deputies to the National Assembly, making the Jacobins the most powerful and well-known patriotic club in France. If the Confédération hoped to influence the National Assembly, the Jacobin club was a natural place to begin. Yet since the king's flight, the club had been unable to decide what to do about the affair. Members were divided into essentially three camps: a small group of men led by Robespierre, Grégoire, Buzot, and Pétion, who sympathized with the Cercle Social position; a sizable number of deputies under the grip of Lafayette and the Lameths, who advocated the reinstatement of the king; and finally, between these positions, Choderlos de Laclos was vigorously campaigning for the replacement of Louis by his mentor, the duc d'Orléans. This division paralyzed the club, and throughout June and July it lost its effectiveness as the leader of Parisian politics.[21]

After heated debate the Jacobins and their visitors agreed to form a committee that would draw up a petition to be approved by the Jacobins the next day before being taken to the demonstration at the Champ de Mars. Brissot, Lanthenas, Danton, Sergent, and Laclos were elected to this committee, which hammered out a petition in the early hours of 16 July. The Jacobins approved it at 11:00 A.M., and it was taken to the Champ de Mars around noon. This petition and the events surrounding it have been the subject of enormous controversy and have continued to generate heated debate among historians. Bonneville provides one account, which previous historians have ignored.[22]

[20] P.J.B. Buchez and P.L. Roux, *Histoire parlementaire de la Révolution française*, 10: 444-45; Reinhard, *Chute de la royauté*, p. 144.

[21] A. Aulard, ed., *La Société des Jacobins. Recueil de documents pour l'histoire du club des Jacobins de Paris* 3: 1-64; on the Orléanist activities during this period see Emile Dard, *Le Général Choderlos de Laclos*, pp. 296-336.

[22] For the historiographical controversy see F. Braesch, "Les Pétitions du Champ de Mars," *Revue historique* 143(1923) (January-April): 192-209 (May-August): 1-37, 181-197; Mathiez, *Club des Cordeliers*, pp. 122-3; "Réponse aux articles de M. Braesch," *Revue historique* 144 (1923), pp. 87-91; and Graham E. Rodmell, "Laclos, Brissot, and the Petitions of the Champ de Mars," *Studies on Voltaire and the Eighteenth Century* 183(1980): 189-222. For the composition

Bonneville arrived at the Champ de Mars on the morning of 16 July to find that 200 people had arrived before him, including a large group from the Cordeliers club. When the deputation from the Jacobins arrived, Danton read the petition, which:

Formally and especially demands that the National Assembly accept on behalf of the nation, the abdication made the 21 June, by Louis XVI himself; of the crown which had been delegated to him, and provide for his replacement by all constitutional means;

The undersigned declaring that they will never recognize Louis XVI for their king, at least until a majority of the nation votes to the contrary.[23]

Bonneville was infuriated by the last phrase of the first paragraph. It was evident that the phrase "provide for his replacement by all constitutional means" was a sort of code language that meant a regency headed by the duc d'Orléans. Bonneville and the other Cercle Social and Cordelier radicals immediately voiced their anger and demanded the removal of the phrase. Many in the crowd blamed the phrase on Brissot, who was already suspected of being an opportunist. But Bonneville thought otherwise: he sensed in this scheme the hand of his archenemy Laclos, who he knew would go to any lengths to get Orléans on the throne. As for Brissot, Bonneville claimed that the committee had accepted Brissot's phrase, "the replacement of *the executive branch* by constitutional means," which meant establishing a republic. He praised Brissot for being an "honest patriot" and claimed that Laclos had somehow changed the phrase after the committee had adjourned its meeting. Sensing the anger of the crowd, Danton agreed to take the petition back to the Jacobins, and told the crowd to return the following day (17 July). Satisfied that he had helped to prevent an Orléanist in-

---

of the Jacobin committee (a subject itself of much dispute) I follow François Sergent's memoirs, *Reminiscences of a Regicide. Edited From the Original Mss. of Sergent-Marceau,* ed. M.C.M. Simpson pp. 122-23. Bonneville's memoir, "Ce qui je sais par moi-même des événements du 16 au Champ de Mars," begins in *Bdf,* 19 July 1791, pp. 3-5, and continues through several issues.

[23] Aulard, *Jacobins* 3: 20; Mathiez, *Club des Cordeliers,* pp. 122-23. Reinhard, *Chute de la royauté,* p. 145, names Danton as the reader and estimates the crowd at 400.

trigue, Bonneville returned to the Cercle Social offices to work on the next edition of the *Bouche de fer*.[24]

That afternoon Bonneville was interrupted by a visit from François Sergent. The Jacobin committee had asked Sergent to see that the petition was published. Sergent had already been to Badouin, the official printer for publications of the National Assembly, but he refused to publish it. Apparently Sergent was unaware of what had just taken place at the Champ de Mars, or perhaps he simply ignored it. At any rate, he left the petition with Bonneville, who agreed to publish it.[25]

Bonneville printed the petition in the *Bouche de fer* and as a broadside for the streets. Sure of his convictions, he altered the end of the original Jacobin petition to read as follows:

Formally and especially demands that the National Assembly accept on behalf of the nation, the abdication made 21 June, by Louis XVI, of the crown which had been delegated to him,

The undersigned declaring that they will never recognize Louis XVI, *nor any other*, for their king, at least until a majority of the nation votes to the contrary.

The petition now had an entirely new meaning. Bonneville republicanized the Jacobin petition by suppressing the "Laclos" phrase and inserting one of his own, "nor any other," which left no doubt where he stood. He told his readers that they could sign this petition at the Cercle Social offices, or the next day (17 July) at the Champ de Mars. "This petition will be sent throughout the empire," he promised.[26]

---

[24] *Bdf*, 20 July 1791, pp. 3-5. There is some evidence that Brissot and the Imprimerie du Cercle Social were coordinating their activities. On 16 or 17 July Jean-Louis Reynier, Bonneville's assistant at the Imprimerie, wrote the following note to Brissot on the margin of the 16 July petition cited above: "J. P. Brissot is asked to repair the note that is in today's issue, according to the enclosed example where there is not 'nor any other,' but 'nor any other until the departments have spoken, etc.,' an essential difference that is essential to correct. L. Reynier." Archives nationales, F⁷ 4622; reprinted in Mathiez, *Club des Cordeliers*, p. 261n. Brissot's activities are also examined in Braesch, "Les Pétitions" (January-April), pp. 203-206; and Ellery, *Brissot de Warville*, pp. 166-80.

[25] *Reminiscences of a Regicide*, pp. 122-23; Mathiez, *Club des Cordeliers*, p. 122n; Braesch, "Les Pétitions," p. 13.

[26] *Bdf*, 17 July 1791, pp. 3-4.

Meanwhile, events moved in quite a different direction in the National Assembly. That body passed two bills that tried to undermine the power of the radicals and to abort any efforts to overthrow the monarchy. The first gave the municipal government extended powers to maintain order, a move aimed at curtailing republican demonstrations. The second decreed that Louis XVI would be completely reinstated when he accepted the constitution; in other words, he simply had to ask forgiveness and all would be forgotten.[27]

That evening, 16 July, Bonneville attended the meeting of the Jacobin club to participate in the debate on the suppression of the Orléanist phrase. But a great change had taken place at the Jacobins. After the morning session, the more conservative wing of the club, led by Lafayette and the Lameths, refused to support the original petition, since they advocated the reinstatement of the king. They split from the group and formed their own Société des amis de la constitution, which met in the convent of the Feuillants. Nevertheless, the remaining Jacobins held a long and excited debate on the petition. Robespierre supported the elimination of the controversial phrase and called for a national convention. Laclos opposed him and urged the club to maintain its original stance. By the end of the evening, however, the club had rejected both alternatives. In the wake of the actions of the National Assembly, the Jacobins realized that the petition in either form was essentially illegal, and, rather than draft a new one, they simply withdrew the petition altogether.[28]

The following day, 17 July, while other radicals went to the Champ de Mars, Bonneville stayed home to write a letter to the tumultuous Jacobins. After describing "the dangers that menace the commonwealth," he proposed that the Jacobins expel the Orléanists and merge with the Cercle Social! He believed that such a union would make the new club the leader, the true federation of all patriotic and popular clubs throughout the nation. "A society where there will be such enlightenment, energy, and effective power, can save liberty by a universal correspondence, at the center of which will be only truth, common

---

[27] Braesch, "Les Pétitions," pp. 11-12; Reinhard, *Chute de la royauté*, p. 145.
[28] *Bdf*, 20 July 1791, pp. 5-6.

to all." Bonneville realized that the crisis offered the Cercle Social opportunities to increase its own influence.[29]

While Bonneville was composing this extraordinary letter, he was interrupted by visitors, who informed him of the massacre that had just taken place at the Champ de Mars. After some five thousand people had signed a petition calling on the National Assembly to rescind its decree reinstating the king and establish a republic, a division of National Guard troops led by Lafayette and Bailly entered the Champ de Mars. Lafayette announced that martial law had been invoked and declared the demonstration illegal. What happened next is far from clear; but within minutes a dozen unarmed demonstrators lay dead, and thirty or forty others had been wounded by the troops' bullets.

This event was the beginning of a repression conducted by the municipal and national authorities that successfully squelched the movement for a democratic republic. The radicals panicked: the Cordeliers club shut down for a number of weeks; Danton fled to England; Desmoulins stopped publishing his journal; Marat went into hiding. As for the Jacobins, on the evening of the massacre, Bonneville's letter was read to the club and quickly discarded; the events of the day had made its republican language too dangerous.[30]

The repression soon reached the Cercle Social. On 19 July Etta Palm, the feminist leader of the Confédération des Amies de la Vérité, was arrested, a move that Bonneville interpreted as an attempt by the government to intimidate the Cercle Social. If this was the intention, the move succeeded. On 21 July, the *Bouche de fer* announced that the Confédération des Amis de la Vérité would no longer meet. "In these times of troubles," wrote Bonneville, "the Cercle Social will immediately close its tribune at the circus arena." A week later, on 28 July, the Directoire du

<hr>

[29] "Aux amis de la constitution, aux Jacobins," *Bdf*, 23 July 1791, pp. 6-7.

[30] Mathiez, *Club des Cordeliers* pp. 128-68; Reinhard, *Chute de la royauté*, pp. 153-55; Aulard, *Jacobins* 3: 23. Shortly after the massacre A.J.P. Belair, military strategist closely associated with the Cercle Social and the Cordeliers, was advised against publishing a series of speeches he had given at the Cordeliers. See his *Extrait du registre des délibérations du Club des Cordeliers ou Adresse aux Françaises sur des objets de la plus grande importance relatifs au salut de la patrie* (Paris: ICS, 1791), p. 1.

Cercle Social announced that the *Bouche de fer* would cease publication. "No, no, I will not abandon you," Bonneville told his readers in the last issue. Nevertheless, the cosmopolitan dreams that had opened the doors of the Confédération were shattered by the guns enforcing martial law.[31]

BETWEEN May and July 1791, the Cercle Social had helped lead the popular movement for a democratic republic in at least four ways: First, it sponsored organizations like the Point central des arts et métiers, which fought for the rights of the disfranchised and unemployed; second, its press, the Imprimerie du Cercle Social, published some of the most important petitions of the period; third, the Cercle Social provided a forum where intellectuals such as Paine, Lanthenas, and Condorcet, could interact with working-class groups, such as the Cordeliers; finally the Cercle Social was the scene of what can only be described as huge republican rallies, obvious in the Confédération's last session on 15 July.

In August martial law was lifted, and the radicals resumed their activities. Marat and Desmoulins openly published their journals, Danton was more popular than ever, and the Cordeliers club reopened its doors. But the Confédération des Amis de la Vérité did not reappear. While the Imprimerie du Cercle Social expanded in several directions, the Cercle Social never reestablished its club. The reasons go deeper than the repression of July 1791. Fauchet and Bonneville had organized the Confédération as a refuge from partisan politics, where local politicians and writers could debate the abstract ideas of political theorists like Rousseau. By the spring of 1791 that conception of a club's role had become obsolete, as Lanthenas' writings on popular clubs make clear. How could Bonneville and Lanthenas criticize other clubs for being elitist when Cercle Social dues remained an exorbitant twenty-seven livres per year? But on the other hand, how could they expect to maintain philosophical discussion if they opened the club to everyone?

The club also no longer served the interests of its founders.

---

[31] *Bdf*, 21 July 1791, p. 8, 25 July 1791, pp. 4-5, and 28 July 1791, pp. 6-8.

Fauchet and Bonneville had created the Confédération to give their discredited political faction an organized form until its members could gain enough public support to re-enter the political scene. The king's flight to Varennes gave them this opportunity. Cercle Social leaders became popular and highly visible in Parisian politics. With elections to the Legislative Assembly to be held in August 1791, Cercle Social leaders looked forward to acquiring offices at the national level.

Finally, while Bonneville's suggestion for a merger between the Cercle Social and the Jacobins was not taken seriously by anyone at the time, that is in fact precisely what occurred during the months following the massacre at the Champ de Mars. The leaders of the Cercle Social, realizing that the split between the Jacobins and the Feuillants had created a void in the Jacobins, became active members of that club (which had shed much of its elitism), and by November 1791, the Imprimerie du Cercle Social had become a mouthpiece for a revived Jacobin club led by Condorcet, Brissot, and their friends. Thus the closing of the Confédération des Amis de la Vérité is evidence not of the demise of the Cercle Social but rather of its ascendance from municipal to national politics.

PART III

The Imprimerie du Cercle Social, 1791-1793

When our legislators finally occupy themselves developing a truly national education, and spread everywhere, including among the less fortunate classes, principles of social happiness and public prosperity ... there is no doubt that the book-trade will become the natural and principal business of a free city. We will faithfully contribute to this development by: our zeal, our enlightened publishing program, and our correspondence on behalf of our authors, in order to merit the confidence of all good citizens, and for the successful expansion of our commerce.

Bulletin des Amis de la Vérité, 1 January 1793, p. 3.

7

Overview of a Girondin Press

MANON ROLAND (1754-1793). In her salon, she played a crucial role
in cementing friendships among leading Girondins.
Courtesy of The Bibliothèque Nationale, Paris

One will find in the office of the Cercle Social various brochures by the same author [Brissot], aptly named *the fearless patriot beyond reproach*. It is good to be able to offer as a response to the slanderers and to a whole group of mediocre, eternally vain, cowardly, and jealous individuals, the first steps of a career which is beginning, and which is already full of courageous patriotic acts and writings. Under a regime of good laws, wherein the sacred qualities of genius in a friend of freedom would be respected, J. P. Brissot would earn an *immense* fortune from his literary works. English bookstores often give a thousand guineas for a single volume which was not worth *la lettre à Barnave*! Legislators, you will no doubt not forget in your wise laws, all that may encourage *agriculture* and *printing*; these useful arts worthy of free men and free cities.

Chronique du mois, February 1792, p. 115.

"M. Bonneville is one of a small number of loyal defenders of liberty," Brissot wrote about his good friend in the *Patriote français*.

It is in order to attain this goal that he established the universal Confédération des Amis de la Vérité. I do not know why he wants to resurrect this idea in the form of a local club with a limited tribune. The great tribune of humanity has been found: it is the press. If all that we did was to convince all men to speak the same language, the press would soon spread the French Revolution everywhere.[1]

Given what we know of Brissot's later activities, this advice seems contradictory; for within a few months, Brissot would hand over the editing of the *Patriote français* to an assistant and lead his friends into the most influential circles of the Paris Jacobin club. Nonetheless, it was sound advice for Bonneville. The Cercle Social's success and national reputation had been in large part due to its press, the Imprimerie du Cercle Social. Confédération meetings, by themselves, reached only a limited number of Parisian intellectuals and politicians. But Cercle Social publications had been able to spread the ideas of the club to a much wider audience and had given the club a national following. Fauchet's commentaries on Rousseau had been debated in

[1] *Pf*, 2 August 1791, p. 135.

public by foes like Laclos and La Harpe only because these men had printed copies of the weekly orations in front of them. Etta Palm had become one of the Revolution's most prominent feminists not solely because of her speeches, but because those speeches had been reprinted and disseminated throughout France by the Imprimerie du Cercle Social. Likewise, by reprinting radical Cercle Social/Cordeliers petitions after the king's flight to Varennes, the Cercle Social had helped to develop a constituency in the provinces for a democratic republic. Without its press, the Cercle Social would have been one of countless clubs in the capital, unknown outside of the most active political circles. Indeed, the ingenious plan of linking newspaper subscriptions to club membership had helped to swell the number of members into the thousands. While a few other clubs, such as the Jacobins and Cordeliers, had published newspapers that printed club minutes and developed club ideas, no other group had collectively owned an entire publishing house, and had planned and executed a full publishing program.

THE IMPORTANCE of the press within the Cercle Social was no accident. Cercle Social members created a mythology around the publisher, who was idolized and revered as a god. For the Cercle Social, politicians, priests, poets, and publicists all had to yield to the publisher's supreme influence and power. Gutenberg's discovery of movable type was seen as the most important event in the history of mankind. They believed it assured the widespread distribution of technology and radical ideas, thereby making human progress a permanent feature of Western society, accelerating the need for a group of philosophes to communicate new ideas to a readership of unprecedented numbers. They also believed the printing press had spelled the end for political systems like the Old Regime, based upon secrecy and arbitrary power. "Blessed be the inventor of the printing press," cried the political theorist Louis Lavicomterie. "It is to him that we owe this wondrous revolution." As early as 1782, Condorcet had been preaching the same message. "Thanks to printing, that preserving art which safeguards human reason," he told the French

Academy, "once a principle useful to public happiness has been discovered it becomes instantly the patrimony of all nations."[2]

Some Cercle Social writers went even further, positing a utopian epoch after the Revolution when the publisher would replace the legislator himself. Instead of a legislature, France's center would contain several bouches de fer, free presses of the people, which would disseminate opinions of an enlightened citizenry. By transforming hitherto private opinions into material for public discourse, the publisher would perform an invaluable service, essential to any free society. "If all men were touched by the feelings coming from you," Brissot wrote to a fellow publicist, "we wouldn't need legislators." His colleague, Joseph Lequinio, one of three Cercle Social authors on the Convention's Committee on Public Instruction, predicted that the new epoch would become the Age of the Publisher, just as the Old Regime had been the Age of the Church. The publisher would not only replace the politician, he would replace the priest as prime spokesman for truth. "It was necessary to have religions before the invention of printing," Lequinio claimed. But today printing "is the most beautiful gift from the heavens, and, without it, the earth would be continually involved in civil and religious wars." One Cercle Social journal echoed these sentiments by calling for a time when "the book-trade will become the natural and principal business of a free city."[3]

The Cercle Social also saw an intimate connection between printing and democracy. Throughout the eighteenth century, political writers, including Montesquieu and Rousseau, had argued that democracies were practical only in small city-states, where all citizens could be quickly assembled. But Cercle Social writers argued that printing offered society a new technology that effectively made the size of a polity irrelevant. Printing created a forum for public debate in which thousands, even

[2] Louis Lavicomterie de Saint-Samson, *La République sans impôts* (Paris: ICS, 1792), pp. 5-6; *BAV*, 8 January 1793, p. 3; M.J.A.N. Condorcet, *Selected Writings*, ed. Keith Michael Baker, p. 7. See also the untitled prospectus probably written by Bonneville in the Bibliothèque historique de la ville de Paris, 604593, p. 1; and the article by Lanthenas in *Pf*, 6 November 1791, p. 531.

[3] Jacques-Pierre Brissot, *Correspondance et papiers*, p. 280; Joseph Lequinio, *Les Préjugés détruits*, 2nd ed. (Paris: ICS, 1793); *BAV*, 1 January 1793, p. 3.

millions, of citizens could participate with one another simultaneously. Condorcet imagined clusters of local assemblies that would coordinate their activities through presses and propose legislative reforms to more centralized conventions.

The knowledge of printing makes it possible for modern constitutions to reach a perfection that they could not otherwise achieve. In this way a sparsely populated people in a large territory can now be as free as the residents of a small city. . . . It is through the printing process alone that discussion among a great people can truly be one.[4]

This reverent attitude toward publishers was best articulated by Jacques Boilleau in an article published in a Cercle Social journal. A barrister in Dijon before the Revolution, Boilleau moved to Paris and became active in the Confédération des Amis de la Vérité. In 1792, he was elected to the Convention where he sat with the Girondins. His article began by echoing his colleagues' admiration for the inventor of the printing press. "Johannes Gutenberg was the first revolutionary, the greatest benefactor to humanity. Without him, you would have had neither Voltaire nor Rousseau." Boilleau claimed that all modern progress, including the Enlightenment and the French Revolution, was due to Gutenberg's invention. He called it "the unique way" to spread knowledge and equality and believed that the importance of the invention was that it substituted writing for speaking as the dominant means of human communication. As long as the mode of enlightenment was oral, progress was retarded. "The orator," he explained, "is more likely to inflame than to enlighten. The writer, on the other hand, has all the time he needs to ponder his ideas, evaluate his style, and place his work in a natural order." The Cercle Social saw in printing the foundation for its hope in a universal, mass enlightenment. "For more than three centuries it has transformed the human species." Boilleau and his colleagues had every expectation that this process would continue until social diseases like tyranny and inequality had been completely eliminated.[5]

---

[4] M.J.A.N. Condorcet, *Des Conventions nationales* (Paris: ICS, 1791), p. 18.
[5] Jacques Boilleau, "De l'imprimerie," *Feuille villageoise*, 4 October 1792, pp.

Behind this idealized view of the publisher was a new and complex relationship that had developed between writer and publisher during the Old Regime. Before the eighteenth century, writers were usually subsidized by either wealthy patrons, the state, or their own family fortunes. During the eighteenth century intellectuals began to earn a living from their writings and began to think of their cultural activities as a profession. This was especially true in England, where writers like Sterne and Swift were envied by contemporaries for the fortunes they made from their writings. But even in France, where primitive copyright laws made writing less lucrative, there were at least the beginnings of a similar movement from patronage and pensions toward professional independence.[6]

This trend clearly made the relations between men of letters and publishers at once intimate and problematic. The writer was usually interested in the dissemination of his ideas and believed that he deserved a just remuneration. The publisher was more often a businessman interested in making as much money as possible from his products. A smart publisher tried to keep his clients happy, but, since all French publishers were at the mercy of an erratic market, this was not an easy task, and tensions between publisher and writer were common. Even the most successful writers of the time, like Voltaire, described publishers as the "hell of writers." Likewise, the so-called Grub Street writers were often angered by the publisher's power to make or break careers, and they complained that only a handful of writers were able to make a living from their books.[7]

Relations between authors and publishers had been formalized in 1789 by Claude Fauchet's Police Committee of the Paris Communal Assembly. Fauchet's committee sponsored legislation that destroyed the archaic privileges in the capital and institu-

---

605-609. Boilleau was one of the few Confédération members who publicly attacked Fauchet for his arrogance. See *Journal des clubs*, 15 April 1791, pp. 433-39.

[6] The best introduction to these issues is Robert Darnton, *The Literary Underground of the Old Regime*.

[7] David I. Kulstein, "The Ideas of Charles-Joseph Pankoucke, Publisher of the *Moniteur universel* in the French Revolution," *FHS* 4(1966): 304-19; the Voltaire quote is cited in John Lough, *An Introduction to Eighteenth Century France*, p. 236; on Grub Street see Darnton, *Literary Underground*, pp. 1-40.

tionalized freedom of the press. Like other Cercle Social members, Fauchet realized the power of publishing. "This beautiful art [contains] the great destiny of the human species." But legislation made clear that it was the publisher who ultimately owned and was therefore responsible for a published work. The author had the right to sell his manuscript freely in the market for a lump sum. But after the work had been sold to the publisher, the author had no more control over it. The legislation specifically stated that the publisher's name had to appear on the work, while the author's name was optional. If a work was found to be libelous or pornographic, the publisher was responsible.[8]

The new legislation was a mixed blessing for writers. On the one hand, the legislation clearly protected the author from legal risks that might arise from his writing. In effect, he was free to write anything he wished, as long as he could find a publisher to print it. But on the other hand, the new laws exacerbated the tension between publishers and writers. Once the author had sold his manuscript, the publisher was legally free to do whatever he wished with it. Publishers often insisted that this gave them the right to edit a manuscript for publication in any fashion. They also controlled distribution, advertisements, and selling price. All of these issues were of anxious concern to authors. Struggles often broke out between editor and publisher over the control of journals. Sometimes the publisher would fire the editor and try to carry on the journal with a new editor. Ultimately the outcome depended upon the fame of the editor. By the summer of 1790, at least one Cordelier journalist, François Robert, was already "tired [of] the despotism of publishers."[9]

It was in this climate, in January 1791, that the Imprimerie du Cercle Social was created. Ironically, however, the newly

[8] Dorimon, "L'Abbé Claude Fauchet, membre de la Commune de Paris," *Revue de la Révolution* 10(1887): 148-70; Henry E. Bourne, "Improvising a Government in Paris in July 1789," *American Historical Review* 10(1904-1905): 306; Claude Fauchet, *Elôge civique de Benjamin Franklin*, p. 5.

[9] *Mercure national et Révolutions de l'Europe*, 9 August 1790, p. 341; Jack Richard Censer, *Prelude to Power: The Parisian Radical Press*, pp. 19-20; W. J. Murry, "The Right-Wing Press in the French Revolution" (Ph.D. Diss., Australian National University, 1971), pp. 143-52.

established freedom of the press meant that few records on the press had to be kept by government officials. Thus practically all records of the Imprimerie, including names of investors, editorial policies, tax returns, inventory lists, and the like have been lost. But at least enough evidence exists to allow for a rough sketch.

The Imprimerie was controlled by "the Directoire of the Imprimerie du Cercle Social," undoubtedly the same body that had founded the Confédération. We do not know the full composition of this group, but at least three intellectuals were included: Bonneville, Lanthenas, and Reynier.[10] Lanthenas, close friend of Brissot and the Rolands, invested 26,000 livres in the Imprimerie in November 1791. Jean-Louis Reynier, a minor scientist and academician before the Revolution, had been one of the earliest members of the Cercle Social, and became Bonneville's assistant at the Imprimerie. If these men are typical of the investors who owned the press, then the Imprimerie du Cercle Social opened the way for a new kind of relationship between writers and publishers, in which writers themselves established their own publishing house. By eliminating the tensions between writer and publisher, they could publish whatever they wished and retain complete editorial control and ownership of their writings. Young or obscure writers could now place their writings in the hands of colleagues, avoiding the demands that a businessman/publisher might make. Enlightenment would replace profit as the book dealer's raison d'être.

The Imprimerie du Cercle Social also served as an interest group that pressured the National Assembly to pass laws favorable to writers. One Cercle Social journal urged the Legislative Assembly "to charge its diverse committees to review new books that could help to enlighten everyone in the Fatherland." More specifically, the Cercle Social urged the government to appoint a "Minister of Public Opinion," who would subsidize works aimed at enlightening the masses. The group also pressed for lower postal rates, always a source of great concern to pub-

[10] Albert Mathiez, "La fortune de Lanthenas," *Annales révolutionnaires* 11(1919): 264-65; Claude Perroud, "Roland et la presse subventionée," *Rf* 62(1912).

lishers. England was often cited as a model of a country in which lower postal rates benefited the entire nation. The Directoire du Cercle Social complained that there was no logical reason why a patriotic writer like Brissot had to worry about money when an Englishman like historian William Robertson could make 25,000 livres per volume. Behind these arguments was the assumption that whatever was good for the publishing industry was good for France.[11]

The Imprimerie du Cercle Social was thus more than a business. "The company of the Directoire of the Imprimerie du Cercle Social, according to its institution, the Confédération des Amis de la Vérité, which has caused great shocks . . . is visibly established on foundations which are much larger than the ordinary bookstore."[12] While most other publishing houses like Panckoucke and Buisson were in business to make a profit, the aim of the Imprimerie du Cercle Social was to further the goals of the directoire and Confédération, that is, to help educate the masses, develop a civil religion, provide a creative center for writers, and serve to develop a discourse for representative democracy.

THE ORIGINS of the Imprimerie are as obscure as those of the Cercle Social itself. The journal *Cercle Social*, begun in early 1790, appeared without any publisher's name, despite the new laws. In June of that year, the Cercle Social ceased publication of *Cercle Social* and began to publish the *Bulletin de la bouche de fer*, the first to carry the Imprimerie's name on it. In fact, there was little difference between these two journals. Both appeared irregularly and were concerned largely with Parisian political affairs. Although the title *Bulletin de la bouche de fer* implied that the journal simply reprinted letters found in the bouche de fer box, both journals were actually conscious imitations of a journalistic style developed in England by radicals

[11] *Cdm*, May 1792, pp. 102-103, June 1793, pp. 62-3, February 1792, p. 115, May 1792, pp. 101-102; *BAV*, 1 January 1793, p. 4; *Créole patriote*, 24 January 1793, p. 1040.
[12] *Constitution françoise, telle qu'elle a été lue à la Convention, le vendredi 15 février 1793* (Paris: ICS, 1793), p. 92.

disillusioned with the Whig establishment; several letters, for example, were attributed to the English muckraker Junius.[13]

It appears that the Imprimerie du Cercle Social was established during the summer of 1790, a date that would also account for Bonneville's move to his new home at 4, rue du Théâtre Français. By that summer other publications appeared bearing the words Imprimerie du Cercle Social on their title pages, including a prospectus for the journal *Bouche de fer*.[14] However, when the first issue of the *Bouche de fer* finally appeared in October 1790, there was no mention of the Imprimerie. Between October and December 1790, the *Bouche de fer* was published by Buisson and sold out of his bookstore in the Palais Royal. In December Buisson informed Bonneville that he was dropping the *Bouche de fer* for Carra's *Annales patriotiques et littéraires*.[15]

On 3 January 1791, when it assumed responsibility for the *Bouche de fer*, the Imprimerie began to print, distribute, and sell its works on a regular basis. Not only was its name on the bottom of the last page of the *Bouche de fer*, but there was also the following advertisement: "The Directors of the Imprimerie du Cercle Social announce that they will be charged, starting 1 February, with the printing and distribution of the *Journal d'agriculture à l'usage des campagnes*, by M. l'abbé Tessier ... and by M. L. Reynier." Given what we know of the ideology of the group, it is understandable that the Imprimerie's first advertised work would be specifically aimed at improving peasant farming and not surprising that one of its editors was himself a leader in the Cercle Social. The advertisement went on to announce that the group was willing to "print in all languages, and to provide at our headquarters a rendezvous for travelers of the Confédération des Amis de la Vérité." The Imprimerie was intended to be linked with the other activities of the Cercle Social.[16]

[13] E.g., *Cercle Social*, pp. 246-304.
[14] *Qu'est-ce que la bouche de fer?* (Paris: ICS, 1790). Bonneville's new address is first mentioned in *Bdf*, 3 January 1791, p. 16.
[15] *Bdf*, no. 32, December 1790, p. 512, no. 20, November 1790, p. 320, 19 February 1791, p. 315.
[16] *Bdf*, 3 January 1791, p. 16. The *Journal d'agriculture*'s title page states, however, that it was printed by another publisher.

When the Imprimerie was begun it was only one among hundreds of presses sprouting up across France. Printing was a booming industry during the Revolution. Louis XVI's decree of 1787, which gave at least a tacit freedom of the press, sparked an explosion in political literature. Over 500 journals were begun between 1789 and 1792, an unprecedented number that reflected a separate revolution in the history of journalism. Such increased demand for printed news caused a rapid inflation in the cost of printing. Arthur Young, for example, noted that the cost of printing more than doubled between 1787 and 1789. Publishing was big business and apparently very profitable as well. While financial records are scarce, scholars have estimated that Brissot's *Patriote français* made a fortune, perhaps more than 30,000 livres per year.[17]

The tremendous increase in the amount of printed news was the result of increased demand, not technological progress. In fact, the printing process was virtually unchanged since Gutenberg's fifteenth-century discovery. The industrial revolution was not to affect the French publishing industry until well into the nineteenth century. During the French Revolution, even the smallest publishing house had to employ at least two workers and a foreman.[18] One worker was in charge of the press itself (*pressier*), while the other was responsible for setting the type (*compositeur*). Usually one of the workers was fairly experienced, while the other served as his apprentice. They worked a twelve-hour day, twenty-four days per month. Wages were based upon the worker's productivity. The publisher Boulard claimed that if a worker were doing his job correctly, one press could turn out 3,000 sheets per day; in this case the worker would be paid six livres daily. The foreman, who was "the chief or director of the press," was to supervise the workers, correct all proofs, and

---

[17] Claude Bellanger et al., *Histoire générale de la presse française* 1: 408-22, 439; Arthur Young, *Travels in France During the Years 1787, 1788, and 1789*, p. 104.

[18] The following details concerning printing are taken from two contemporary handbooks: M. S. Boulard, *Le Manuel de l'imprimeur* (Paris: Boulard, 1791), and Antoine-François Momoro, *Traité élémentaire de l'imprimerie ou Le Manuel de l'imprimeur* (Paris: Momoro, 1793).

keep the accounting books.[19] A good foreman was also expected to know the mechanics of a press and some foreign languages. In small publishing houses, the foreman was probably the publisher himself; but many of the larger publishers hired assistant foremen who specialized in a particular area.

The expense of buying and maintaining a press, the cost of paper, and the long period before making any profit, all made publishing a high-risk, capital-intensive industry. Boulard estimated that it took at least 8,000 livres just to set up a publishing house with one press. Once established, it cost the publisher over 3,000 livres per month to operate the press. This meant that only those with connections to wealthy investors could afford to become publishers. Despite these impediments, the Imprimerie du Cercle Social, which began with only one or two presses, in all likelihood made a substantial profit on subscriptions to their *Bouche de fer*.[20]

Above and beyond these financial considerations, historians agree that the *Bouche de fer* quickly became one of the most important papers on the national scene.[21] It went beyond its nominal function as an organ for the club. By including regular articles on the National Assembly and other political activities, and by devoting much space to letters from the provinces, the paper reflected the views of a politically conscious intelligentsia.

[19] Momoro, *Traité élémentaire*, p. 283.

[20] Boulard, *Le Manuel*, pp. 80-83, calculates printing costs. If his figures are correct, it cost approximately 270 livres to print 6,000 copies of the *Bouche de fer*. The subscription price was nine livres per quarter, or one-fourth livre per issue. At thirty-six issues per year, this would yield an annual gross profit of 44,280 livres. However, it is not clear whether Boulard's figures take into account expenses like overhead costs and interest payments; he himself qualifies the figures by claiming that publishers almost always printed more copies than they sold, and gave away many copies to friends. Moreover, in the case of the Cercle Social, revenues from the press help to pay for the operation of the club. Nevertheless, even if the profit figure were substantially reduced, it still appears that the Cercle Social made a fine return on their investment. For similar methods of calculating printing costs, see Bellanger, *Histoire générale* 1: 439.

[21] Bellanger, *Histoire générale* 1: 449; Alma Söderhjelm, *Le Régime de la presse pendant la Révolution française* 1: 86; Eugène Hatin, *Histoire politique et littéraire de la presse en France* 6: 377-413; Leonard Gallois, *Histoire des journaux et des journalistes de la Révolution française, 1789-1796* 1: 77-96.

Some historians of French Revolutionary journalism have used letters to the editor as a criterion to judge a paper's success; in the case of the *Bouche de fer*, this section was so popular that the Cercle Social sometimes ran out of space and issued club news in a supplement.[22]

The involvement of the Cercle Social in radical affairs during the spring and summer of 1791 affected the Imprimerie as much as the Confédération. Yet while the club and the *Bouche de fer* crumbled in the wake of the massacre at the Champ de Mars, the directoire had no intention of shutting down its presses altogether. "Private correspondence will always be active," it announced. "When our faithful friends and brothers send us important advice, our printers—honest men—will publish them without compromising anyone."[23] Indeed, in the midst of the political repression, the Imprimerie published Bonneville's magnum opus, *De l'esprit des religions*. No Cercle Social publication received more advertising than this one. In the last issue of the *Bouche de fer*, Bonneville urged readers to turn to this abstract study of religions in order to save the nation. "This important work," he boasted, "offers principles preserved in the mysteries of ancient initiations, and whose revelations have been promised from one age to the next, by the Amis de la Vérité to the first free people."[24]

In the months following the massacre at the Champ de Mars, the Imprimerie organized a very large and successful publishing venture, the *Chronique du mois*. With Bonneville in charge, and a staff of sixteen prominent writers and politicians, the *Chronique* included sophisticated essays on a variety of philosophical and social issues. By January 1792, the Imprimerie had begun another paper geared to a similar readership, the *Journal d'histoire naturelle*. A bimonthly series of scientific essays, the *Journal* was the organ of the Paris Société d'histoire naturelle.

The year 1792 saw the greatest expansion of the Imprimerie; many more pamphlets and books were published during that

---

[22] Bellanger, *Histoire générale* 1: 446; *Annales de la Confédération universelle des Amis de la Vérité* (Paris: ICS, 1791).
[23] *Bdf*, 28 July 1791, p. 8.
[24] Ibid.

period than during 1791 and 1793. Sometimes these included
huge projects, such as the thirteen-volume geographical study
of France by Joseph Lavallée and a group of "men of letters."[25]
But as a rule the Imprimerie specialized in the small pamphlet.

After Cercle Social member Jean-Marie Roland became minister of the interior in March 1792, he and the Cercle Social
asked Jean-Baptiste Louvet de Couvray to edit a new publication,
the *Sentinelle*, which defended Roland's policies. Roland gave
smaller subsidies to the *Feuille villageoise*, a very popular and
influential journal written for peasants and rural priests, which
was taken over by the Imprimerie du Cercle Social in September
1792.

Meanwhile the Imprimerie had not forgotten its promise to
export revolutionary ideology across the globe. In February 1792,
for example, the Imprimerie published English and Italian translations of the French constitution and asked for official support
from the Legislative Assembly's Committee of Public Instruction
to distribute them throughout Europe. At the same time, the
Imprimerie was working out a deal with members of the Paris
Société d'agriculture to distribute elementary textbooks to peasants, but this project was dropped when the Roland administration subsidized the dissemination of Cercle Social materials
into the countryside.[26]

As the Imprimerie grew during 1792, its bookstore also expanded, a natural development in an age when most publishers
were also book retailers. The Directors often advertised books
that were on sale at the store and offered to procure any book
that was ordered through it. They even offered credit to regular
customers. A list of about ninety works sold at the Imprimerie
du Cercle Social but published elsewhere reflects a sophisticated
readership who had not forgotten the Enlightenment. One finds
few devotional works or "chap books" that were so important
a part of eighteenth-century popular culture. Nor are there any
pornographic or cheap fictional works typical of most eighteenth-

---

[25] Joseph Lavallée et al., *Voyage dans les départements de la France par une
société d'artistes et gens de lettres* ... , 13 vols. (Paris: ICS, 1792).
[26] *Projet d'association pour l'encouragement de l'agriculture et des arts agricoles*
(Paris: ICS, n.d.); *Cdm*, February 1792, p. 116.

century book dealers. On the contrary, sold at the Imprimerie were the most sophisticated publications of their time, clearly aimed at a very literate readership. The works were fairly evenly split among politics, travel and geography, philosophy, history, fiction, science, and military strategy.[27] Works by Diderot, Rousseau, Montesquieu, Mably, Hume, and Robertson were all available. Not surprisingly, about one-third of the books were by Confédération members or authors who had published other works for the Cercle Social; for example, no fewer than ten works by Brissot were on sale. Many of the advertisements included prices, usually between five and ten livres, clearly out of the range of the sans-culottes.

At the end of 1792 the Imprimerie stopped publishing the *Sentinelle* and started the *Bulletin des Amis de la Vérité*. A four-page, folio daily, the *Bulletin* was the Imprimerie's most expensive project, costing (if Boulard's figures are accurate) perhaps as much as 2,000 livres per week to print. Such an undertaking reflects the success and expansion of the Imprimerie, which, by the spring of 1793, had become one of the nation's most important publishing houses. But a few months later the Imprimerie du Cercle Social was closed by the government, one of the first victims of the Terror. Its sudden and dramatic demise was due to the political behavior of its leading authors and to the press's deep involvement in the partisan struggles for political power.

BETWEEN 1791 and 1793 the Imprimerie became the largest and most important propaganda center for the Girondins. By analyzing the group of Cercle Social authors as a whole, we can see that twelve of the Girondin "Inner Sixty" (those Girondins closest to Brissot) wrote tracts published by the Imprimerie du Cercle Social: Bancal, Barbaroux, Boilleau, Condorcet, Creuzé-Latouche, Dusaulx, Fauchet, Gensonné, Kersaint, Lanthenas,

---

[27] Contemporary politics, 8; travel literature and geography, 11; philosophy and religion, 11; fiction and fine arts, 9; history and political theory, 14; military strategy, 8; science, 14; Enlightenment classics, 11; miscellaneous, 4. For a complete bibliographical listing of these works see Kates, "The Cercle Social: French Intellectuals and the French Revolution," pp. 261-71. On book dealers in general see Darnton, *Literary Underground*, pp. 122-208.

Louvet, and Mercier (see Appendix C). Yet only five members of their rivals, the Montagnards, wrote for the Imprimerie, and even this small number is actually inflated. Camille Desmoulins and Collot d'Herbois published for the group only in 1791, before the split between Brissot and Robespierre. Joseph Lequinio's book was an abstract pedagogical treatise having nothing to do with partisan politics; likewise, Fabre d'Egalantine published a non-ideological play; finally, although Louis Lavicomterie has been classified as a Montagnard on the basis of his voting record, his book on taxation clearly reflects policies espoused by Brissot and Roland. On the other hand, all of the twelve Girondins except Fauchet wrote articles and/or books for the Cercle Social between 1791 and 1793.[28]

But as the early history of the Cercle Social has made clear, the Girondins were not only a political faction but a circle of friends. Thus one must go beyond the narrow criteria of voting behavior to discover Girondins outside the Convention. Eight Cercle Social authors, for example, held posts in the Girondin ministries: Bidermann, Bonnemain, Bonneville, Bosc, Chaussard, Clavière, Roland, and Servan.[29] Three others, Auger, Garran-Coulon, and Paine, can easily be called Girondins on the basis of their close relations with Brissot and Roland.[30] In short,

[28] On classifying political behavior see M. J. Sydenham, *The Girondins*, p. 229; Allison Patrick, *The Men of the First Republic: Political Alignments in the National Convention of 1792*, pp. 317-39; Michel Pertué, "La liste des Girondins de Jean-Paul Marat," *Annales historiques de la Révolution française*, no. 245 (1981): 379-89.

[29] Bosc and Bonnemain worked in the postal division of the Department of the Interior; Bidermann was in charge of purchasing war munitions, Chaussard was a high official in the newly conquered Belgian territories; Bonneville was a commissioner for the Department of the Interior. The most comprehensive study of the Girondin ministry is Edith Bernardin, *Jean-Marie Roland et le ministère de l'intérieur 1792-1793*; on Bonneville see P. Caron, "La Mission de Loyseau et Bonneville à Rouen," *Rf* 86(1933): 236-58, 326-44.

[30] On Auger and Roland see Charles Le Guin, "Roland de la Platière: A Public Servant in the Eighteenth Century", p. 11. Bosc, Bancal, Garran-Coulon, Lanthenas, and Creuzé-Latouche were close friends with each other and the Rolands well before the Revolution. They seem to have had a kind of esprit de corps, perhaps a function of their age, social status, and shared ideals. See the appendixes in *Lettres de Mme Roland*, particularly 2: 736-39. Paines's biographers all agree that he aligned himself closely with the Girondins, and Sydenham gives no reason for his exclusion from the "Inner Sixty."

at least twenty-two Girondins published Cercle Social writings, which constitutes about one-fourth of all Imprimerie authors. What influence did this large minority have upon the Imprimerie? What proportion of Imprimerie books and pamphlets were written by these Girondins (see Appendix B)? They authored fifty-nine of the known books; in other words, one-fourth of Imprimerie authors wrote nearly one-half of the works. Clearly the Girondins had a preponderant influence in the Imprimerie du Cercle Social. What kind of tracts were these? Some of the writings, such as Mercier's plays, were of a fictional, rather than political nature. But the vast majority of Cercle Social publications were direct commentaries on the nature of the Revolution. The list includes some of the most vociferous attacks upon the Montagnards, such as Louvet's *A Maximilien Robespierre et ses royalistes*, and propaganda consciously designed to defend the Girondin ministries, such as the *Lettres et pièces intéressantes pour servir à l'histoire du ministère de Roland, Servan, et Clavière*.[31]

The anonymous writings and journals (containing some of the most blatant examples of political propaganda) also defended the Girondins and attacked the Montagnards. Some pamphlets, such as *Le Générale*, advocated Brissotin war policies, while others tried to develop a moderate republican constituency among the Paris sections. The journals were edited by Girondin leaders, and the three most important of them—the *Chronique du mois*, the *Sentinelle*, and the *Bulletin des Amis de la Vérité*—have long been recognized as Girondin organs.[32] Finally, if we view the whole of the Imprimerie's publications from a different angle, there is not one pamphlet, book, or journal—*not even a page*—that supports the radical policies of the Montagnards where those policies differ from the Girondins.

Thus between 1791 and 1793 the Imprimerie du Cercle Social

[31] Topical and theoretical works on the Revolution, 125; philosophy and religion, 14; science, 4; military strategy, 4; history and political theory, 15; fiction, 10; travel literature, 2.

[32] Bellanger, *Histoire générale* 1: 449-50; Hatin, *Histoire politique* 6: 404; Söderhjelm, *Le Régime de la presse* 1: 224-26; Gallois, *Histoire des journaux* 1: 97-112.

became the preeminent Girondin publishing house. While there were other presses that printed Girondin propaganda, no other press was collectively owned and operated by and for so many Girondin leaders. The Girondins were not only a preponderant influence in the Imprimerie du Cercle Social; the Girondins constituted its core and leadership. This does not mean, of course, that all of the Girondins participated in the Imprimerie or that the Imprimerie served as a kind of party headquarters. The deputies from the Gironde, for example, were almost completely absent from the Imprimerie or club; neither Grangeneuve, Ducos, Lacaze, nor other prominent Girondins like Lanjuinais, Lasource, and Buzot wrote anything for the Imprimerie.

The Imprimerie du Cercle Social was directed by a circle of friends clustered around Bonneville, Brissot, and the Rolands. Most of them had known each other well before the Revolution and had participated together in the Confédération des Amis de la Vérité. They shared a belief in representative democracy, a political vision that changed little between 1789 and 1793. As they ascended to national prominence, they used the Imprimerie du Cercle Social to spread their ideology among their friends and against their rivals. The final chapters of this book explore the degree to which they effectively harnessed the possibilities for propaganda inherent in the Cercle Social presses.

8

An Intellectual Review: The *Chronique du mois*

JOSEPH SERVAN (1741-1808), *top left*. Minister of War (May 1792-June 1792 and October 1792). Along with Clavière and Roland, Servan became one of the heroic "patriot" ministers who were dismissed by the king in June 1792.

ETIENNE CLAVIÈRE (1735-1793), *top right*. Minister of Public Contributions (March 1792-June 1792 and August 1792-June 1793). *Chronique du mois* editor for economic affairs. Financial speculator and economic theorist, Clavière was among Brissot's closest friends.

ARMAND-GUY KERSAINT (1742-1793), *bottom*. Elected to Legislative Assembly and Convention. *Chronique du mois* editor for colonial affairs. His views on colonial trade and slavery were influential among the Girondins. He resigned from the Convention in protest over the trial of Louis XVI.
Courtesy of The Newberry Library, Chicago

The Republic of Letters is one and indivisible.
Chronique du mois, January 1793, p. 63.

THE *Chronique du mois* was the Imprimerie du Cercle Social's longest-running journal, spanning a twenty-month period between the fall of 1791 and the summer of 1793. It was produced by and for French intellectuals who wanted a deeper and more comprehensive analysis of politics and the arts than they could find in the daily newspapers. But the *Chronique* also became the Girondin's leading organ, and this chapter explores that political relationship. In general, the same men who were behind the *Bouche de fer* and the Confédération des Amis de la Vérité began the *Chronique du mois*. The summer of 1791 marked a watershed for these men. It saw the end of their leadership in Paris municipal politics and the beginning of their participation in national political affairs, both as deputies to the Legislative Assembly and as members of a regenerated Jacobin club. By the end of 1791 Brissot and his friends had become among the most powerful politicians in France and had become the leaders of the Jacobins. The *Chronique du mois* both reflected and aided the rise of these men into the national spotlight. The story of its publication begins during the summer of 1791, when its founders emerged from their municipal cocoons.

In August and September 1791, Parisians were obsessed with elections for the Legislative Assembly. The Constituent Assembly had decreed that none of its members could be reelected, so the field was open to new candidates. Until this time the group that had founded the Cercle Social had been composed of largely municipal politicians. The elections for a new national assembly gave these men a great opportunity to attain national office. In June 1791 several Cercle Social leaders had been elected by their districts to the Paris Assembly of Electors, the body responsible for choosing deputies to the Legislative Assembly. The Cercle Social leaders constituted the left wing of the Assembly of Electors, and the events surrounding the king's flight to Varennes helped to enhance their popularity in that body. On 1 September 1791 Garran-Coulon was the first Parisian deputy elected to the

Legislative Assembly; he was soon followed by Brissot, Condorcet, and Godard. Meanwhile, other former Cercle Social leaders who no longer lived in Paris, such as Fauchet and Lamourette, were elected to the Legislative Assembly by their own departmental assemblies. However, not all Cercle Social leaders became national deputies. Nicolas Bonneville, despite a vigorous campaign, secured no more than 143 votes from the more than 700 electors.[1]

Those Cercle Social leaders who won seats in the new national legislature found themselves in a left-wing minority of only 136 deputies, whereas the right wing was represented by 264 Feuillants (360 remaining uncommitted). But if the left wing was a minority, it nonetheless had certain advantages. Most important, its leaders held seats in the legislature, while the leaders of the Feuillants had all previously been members of the Constituent Assembly and were therefore specifically excluded from participation in the new assembly. During the first weeks of the Legislative Assembly, Brissot emerged as the left wing's most powerful leader. He developed close relations between the Paris-based group of ex-municipal politicians like Condorcet and Garran-Coulon and a group of gifted deputies from the department of the Gironde, including Vergniaud, Guadet, and Gensonné. These two groups formed the two main pillars of the political faction that was soon called the Brissotins (or Rolandins), and which historians identify today as the Girondins. Brissot probably brought the two groups together during debates over slavery and the colonial question. The group from the Gironde had known of the Confédération and its abolitionist activities, and was impressed by Brissot's credentials as leader of the Société des amis des Noirs. But the Gironde group was composed of practical politicians, not intellectuals. While they joined hands with the Paris-based Brissotins for a variety of social and political activities, they were not writers and therefore did not become involved in the Imprimerie du Cercle Social.[2]

[1] *L'Assemblée électorale de Paris. 26 août 1791 à 12 août 1792*, passim; Nicolas Bonneville, *Nicolas Bonneville, électeur du département de Paris, aux véritables amis de la liberté* (Paris: ICS, [1791]).

[2] *Bdf*, 11 May 1791, p. 253 (letters by Gensonné and other Bordeaux businessmen on free persons of color); M. J. Sydenham, *The Girondins*, pp. 99-122.

BETWEEN 1789 and 1794 the Paris Jacobin club was used as a springboard for politicians who wanted to acquire status and power in the National Assembly. Unlike the Cercle Social, the Jacobin club was not controlled by any one group throughout its history; rather, as the Convention deputy P.C.F. Daunou observed shortly after the Revolution, the leadership of the Paris Jacobin club itself reflected the stages of the Revolution: "at every turn ... it was abandoned by many of its old members and re-peopled by more zealous innovators."[3] In short, one had to dominate the Jacobins before controlling the National Assembly. The stage beginning with the Legislative Assembly in October 1791 and ending with the September Massacres in 1792 belonged to Brissot. He was elected president of the Jacobins immediately after the opening of the Legislative Assembly. On 16 October he picked Claude Fauchet for his successor, and Condorcet succeeded Fauchet two weeks later. During the following weeks Bancal, Broussonet, Lanthenas, Louvet, and Roland were all elected to Jacobin leadership.[4]

These men used their influence to direct a new propaganda campaign aimed at inculcating revolutionary ideology in all Frenchmen. Calling for "apostolic missions for liberty," the Jacobins hoped to develop a national network of affiliate clubs that would aid the process of national regeneration. Their plan was to become a kind of propaganda center that would distribute important literature to the educated activist as well as the peasant. On 19 September 1791, for example, the Jacobins offered a prize "for the almanac that should be found the best adapted to explain to the people the spirit and principles of the French constitution. ..." A commission composed of Clavière, Condorcet, Lanthenas, Dusaulx, and two others was charged with awarding the prize. One month later they announced that Jean-Marie Collot d'Herbois had won the prize for his *Almanach du Père Gérard*. A series of charming didactic essays, the *Almanach* revolves around the saintly figure of Gérard, a bourgeois savant

---

[3] P.C.F Daunou, "Mémoires pour servir à l'histoire de la Convention Nationale," in M.A.H. Taillandier, ed., *Documents biographiques sur P.C.F. Daunou*, pp. 180-81.

[4] Aulard, ed., *La Société des Jacobins. Recueil de documents pour l'histoire du club des Jacobins de Paris 3: 158-417.*

living in a small village. After Sunday Mass, Gérard would gather the peasants of his town together to instruct them in the political ideas of the Revolution. Liberty, equality, the constitution, and even Louis XVI were warmly praised. The Imprimerie du Cercle Social published an English translation of the *Almanach*, and Collot moved closer to Brissot's circle.[5]

The *Almanach* was a model of Girondin propaganda. In contrast with the Montagnards of 1793-1794, the moderate republicans of 1791-1792 saw the Revolution as an ideological struggle between the forces of Enlightenment, popular sovereignty, and freedom on the one hand, and superstition, corporatism, and Roman Catholicism on the other. They believed that the new regime would win popular support through persuasion, not terror. At least on the domestic scene, they had little faith in the efficacy of violence.

The daily work of this propaganda program was carried out by the Jacobins' Correspondence Committee. Since it was in charge of all contacts between the Paris Jacobins and provincial affiliates, the committee assumed a great importance within the club. The most influential members had ties with the Cercle Social. According to Jean-Baptiste Louvet de Couvray, the future editor of the Cercle Social's *Sentinelle*, most of the committee's work was done by himself and five other men: Duchosal, Bosc, Lanthenas, Bonneville, and Boisguyon. All except Boisguyon had been Confédération members or were Cercle Social authors, and at least two of them, Bonneville and Lanthenas, were also investors in the publishing company.[6]

Thus the relationship between the Jacobins and the Cercle Social became very close during 1791-1792. The Jacobins promoted Cercle Social publications, and the Cercle Social was able to take advantage of the extensive propaganda network that the Jacobins had developed. For example, on 16 November 1791,

[5] J. M. Collot d'Herbois, *Almanach du père Gérard pour l'année 1792*; *The Spirit of the French Constitution or the Almanach of Goodman Gerard for the Year 1792 . . .*, trans. John Oswald (Paris: ICS, 1792); Aulard, *Jacobins* 3: 222-23 and 343; Reinhard, *Chute de la royauté*, pp. 233-35.

[6] Jean-Baptiste Louvet de Couvray, *Mémoires . . . sur la Révolution française* 1: 30-31; Albert Mathiez, "La fortune de Lanthenas," *Rf* 11(1919): 264-65; Aulard, *Jacobins* 3: 331-81.

the Jacobins' Correspondence Committee urged their provincial affiliates to disseminate three patriotic works, all three of which had been published by the Imprimerie du Cercle Social.

The surest way to victory without persecuting aristocrats and priests is to spread good books among all classes of the people; and we especially recommend to you the *Lettre* of Creuzé-Latouche, *L'Esprit des religions* by M. Bonneville, and the *Chronique du mois*.[7]

The "*Lettre* of Creuzé-Latouche" had first been published in 1790 and had gone through two more editions by the end of 1791. Its author, a well-known member of the Constituent Assembly, had been intimate friends with Garran-Coulon, Brissot, Bancal, and Lanthenas since the 1780s. His pamphlet tried to justify the Civil Constitution of the Clergy by explaining why France needed such fundamental reforms in its Gallican Church. Creuzé-Latouche reiterated many of the standard themes of the Enlightenment in arguing that the Church had become a despotic power during the Old Regime. If the Church were not tamed, if it were not brought under the state's control, he believed that it would undermine the three essential goals of the Revolution: "the need to regenerate morality, the security of the constitution, and the expansion of liberty."[8]

De l'esprit des religions was Nicolas Bonneville's magnum opus, the result of twenty years' labor, "written with all my blood."[9] As its title implies, Bonneville hoped to do for religion what Montesquieu had sought to do for politics: to discover the fundamental laws that governed religion throughout the ages. Bonneville's main thesis was that religions were always supernatural manifestations of political values. Through detailed linguistic examination of religious terms in various societies, he

---

[7] Aulard, *Jacobins* 3: 253.

[8] Jacques-Antoine Creuzé-Latouche, *Lettre* ... *à l'Assemblée Nationale aux municipalités, et aux habitants des campagnes du département de la Vienne*, 3rd ed. (Paris: ICS, 1791), p. 10. On Creuzé-Latouche see Jean-Philippe Garran-Coulon, *Notice sur Jacques-Antoine Creuzé-Latouche* ... *lue, le 28 brumaire An 9 au Sénat-Conservateur* ... (n.p., n.d.); Marcel Marion, "Un Révolutionnaire très conservateur: Creuzé-Latouche," *Revue d'histoire moderne* 11(1936): 101-34. For Brissot's favorable reaction to the book see *Pf*, 22 August 1790, p. 4.

[9] *Cdm*, August 1792, pp. 4-6.

argued that in each case religion corresponded to the ideals of the state and constituted a "Cult of the Law." In this atheistic formulation, "man is everything: man is therefore God"; and God, Bonneville discovered, is nothing other than the perfect citizen.[10] Bonneville found that throughout the ages the state had always used religion to "purify" citizens by promoting brotherhood and love through a regeneration of their morals and habits. Bonneville used this kind of argument to place the Revolution's own religious reform within a legitimate sociological context: just as the despotic Old Regime had created a Church with arbitrary powers, so the new regime was obligated to reform the Church along democratic lines. In a free country "the voice of the people is the voice of God."[11]

Much more influential than these two books was the third Cercle Social publication praised in the Jacobins' circular, the *Chronique du mois*, one of the Revolution's most important periodicals.[12] A monthly series of relatively long and sophisticated essays focusing on political theory, political economy, and philosophy, the *Chronique du mois* was aimed at readers who occupied the apex of French society. Yet the fame of the paper did not rest on its articles alone. Indeed, when the Jacobin circular came out, only the prospectus for the *Chronique* had been published. The first full-fledged issue was still two months away. A more important factor in the paper's fame was the group of sixteen editors, led by Bonneville, who produced it and wrote many of its articles. This group included the oldest and most active Cercle Social leaders; they alone authored one-third of all other Cercle Social publications. Each editor was well-

[10] Nicolas Bonneville, *Appendices de la seconde édition de L'esprit des religions; pour servir à l'entretien, à la propagation des bons principes, et à la Confédération universelle des Amis de la vérité* (Paris: ICS, 1792), p. 97.

[11] Nicolas Bonneville, *De l'esprit des religions. Ouvrage promis et nécessaire à la Confédération universelle des Amis de la Vérité* (Paris: ICS, 1791), Part 1, p. 80. According to the usually reliable *Moniteur* (13: 572), the book "sold with a rapidity of which there are few examples in a time of revolution." For a scathing contemporary attack, see Abbé François-Joseph Lefranc, *Conjuration contre la religion catholique et les souverains*, pp. 62-80.

[12] E.g., Reinhard, *Chute de la royauté*, p. 190, refers to it as "among the most important and most enduring" journals.

known in his own right and used the *Chronique* to further his reputation and political career.

The best known of the editors, Brissot, was in charge of political affairs for the journal, but in fact he contributed essays on a variety of topics including a commentary on Helvétius and a discourse on early Christian thought. As we have seen, Brissot was at the zenith of his political career during this period, and his regular participation in the *Chronique* certainly enhanced the paper's prestige.

Brissot's closest associate, Etienne Clavière, was editor for economic matters. The *Chronique*'s first two issues, in fact, consisted exclusively of articles by him. Clavière was a Swiss financier who had been expelled from Geneva in 1783 for his radical political activities. He went to Paris and made a fortune playing the stock market. He also became a ghost writer for Mirabeau and collaborated with Brissot on various projects, including the founding of the Société des amis des Noirs. Like his better-known English contemporary David Ricardo, Clavière's financial successes stimulated a serious interest in political economy, and by the time the first issue of the *Chronique du mois* appeared he was already a well-known expert on monetary affairs. He played an instrumental role in developing the *assignat*, a new type of paper currency.[13] In March 1792, Clavière gave up a seat in the Legislative Assembly to become minister of public contributions (the equivalent of today's minister of finance) in the first Girondin ministry.

There is little need to say anything about Condorcet and every temptation to say too much. As the acknowledged leader of the Republic of Letters and as deputy to the new assembly, Condorcet's name on the title page of a journal was a jewel for any publisher. His contributions to the *Chronique* were regular and important; he was responsible for "observations on legislation and the national education of citizens." But it is a mistake to

---

[13] J. E. Harris, *The Assignats*, p. 9. On Clavière see also Jean Bouchary, *Les Manieurs d'argent à Paris à la fin du xviiie siècle* 1: 1-101; J. Benetruy, *L'Atelier de Mirabeau: Quatre proscrits génévois dans la tourmente révolutionnaire*, passim; and George V. Taylor, "The Paris Bourse on the Eve of the Revolution, 1781-1789" *American Historical Review* 63: 951-77.

suggest, as some historians have, that the *Chronique du mois* was primarily "Condorcet's paper."[14] In fact, he divided his time between many activities and was active in other journals, especially the *Chronique de Paris*.

Louis-Sébastien Mercier was known throughout France as author of a multivolume work on daily life in prerevolutionary Paris, and as an editor of a very popular newspaper, the *Annales patriotiques et littéraires*. A close friend of Bonneville and a member of the Confédération des Amis de la Vérité, Mercier's contribution to the *Chronique* was to record "the details of abuse as in his *Tableau de Paris* and philosophical reflections on the principles of public happiness."[15] In 1792 he was elected to the Convention, where he remained a loyal supporter of Brissot's policies.

Athanase Auger was recruited to write on the relevancy of Greek and Roman political theory to the Revolution. At fifty-seven the eldest member of the group, Auger had for many years been a professor of rhetoric at the Collège royale de Rouen. During the early 1770s one of his closest friends had been the future minister, Jean-Marie Roland. With a few others they had formed a tight-knit study group, where they gave classical nicknames to each other; Roland was called Thales, while Auger was known as Demosthenes. Auger's translations of Demosthenes won him membership into the Académie de Rouen and the more prestigious Académie des inscriptions et belles-lettres. Before the Revolution Auger believed that intellectuals should avoid politics. They had neither the time nor the expertise to pursue such activites outside of academia but required instead the "tranquility necessary for a man of letters." But as soon as the Estates General was called he was repeatedly urged to enter electoral politics.

I have often reproached myself for not participating in my district assemblies. I ask my country to forgive me, and I swear that the only reason that I remain in my study is that already advanced in my career, accustomed to a life of tranquility, and believing myself little prepared

[14] E.g., M. J. Sydenham, *The Girondins*, p. 69; *Cdm*, Prospectus, p. 2; Hélène Delsaux, *Condorcet journaliste*, pp. 71-95.
[15] *Cdm*, Prospectus, p. 2.

for the hubbub of political life, I have thought that I could be more useful to my country by following the ordinary course of my studies.[16]

Auger had spent the early years of the Revolution writing essays on public education and involving himself in several clubs, including the Confédération des Amis de la Vérité.

John Oswald was a Scottish poet whom the *Chronique* described as a "young writer of great talent." Although best known for his poetry, Oswald's prerevolutionary writings were clearly democratic and atheistic, and the *Chronique* classed him among a zealous group of British radicals, including Paine, Makintosh, and Horne-Tooke. Oswald's radicalism even extended to animals: he published a tract against cruelty in 1791. Infused with love for the Revolution, he moved to Paris and became friends with Bonneville. The *Chronique* made him responsible for news of England and "for destroying the popular prejudices" between the two countries.[17]

The *Chronique* chose Antoine Bidermann as their expert on commercial affairs. An ostentatiously wealthy businessman, Bidermann embraced the Revolution in the hope that it would liberate commerce from the arbitrary regulations of the Old Regime. He was a close friend of Clavière; they invested money together in various projects, and Bidermann was an early member of the amis des Noirs. During the time of the Confédération, his home became a center where Brissot and his friends dined and talked. By the time the *Chronique du mois* was established, Bidermann had begun a political career and was a member of the Paris Communal Assembly. After war was declared against Austria in April 1792, Bidermann joined the Roland administration as a director of munitions.[18]

---

[16] Athanase Auger, *Projet d'éducation pour tout le royaume, précédé de quelques réflexions sur l'Assemblée Nationale* (Paris: Didot l'aîné, 1789), pp. 1-4. On Auger and Roland see Bibliothèque Nationale, Nouvelles acquisitions françaises, 6242, fols. 119-21, and Charles A. Le Guin, *Roland de la Platière: A Public Servant in the Eighteenth Century*, pp. 11-12. See also the eulogies for Auger by Hérault-Séchelles and Cubières-Palmézeaux in *Oeuvres posthumes d'Athanase Auger*, 2 vols. (Paris: ICS, 1792), 1: 1-17, 2: 18-22.

[17] *Cdm*, August 1792, p. 112, Prospectus, p. 2. On Oswald see André Lichtenberger, "John Oswald: Écossais, Jacobin et socialiste," *Rf* 22 (1897): 181-95.

[18] On Bidermann see Ch. Poisson, *Les Fournisseurs aux armées sous la Ré-*

Antoine-Jean Broussonet was another writer who had chosen a political career after 1789. Before the Revolution he had been a member of the Académie des sciences and, in 1785, was elected perpetual secretary of the Société royale d'agriculture. In 1790 he began a newspaper designed to improve agricultural techniques among farmers. He soon won a reputation as an ardent patriot and even secured more votes than Brissot in the Paris elections to the Legislative Assembly. A minor figure in the paper, he was in charge of writing about agriculture and rural life.

Another deputy to the Legislative Assembly, Armand-Guy Kersaint was the paper's correspondent for maritime and colonial affairs. Kersaint had been a naval officer for most of his life and embraced the Revolution partly with the hope that it would carry out important reforms in the French Navy. In 1790 he became president of the Paris Assembly of Electors and probably came to know Brissot at that time. He became a follower of Brissot in the Legislative Assembly and continued this association in the Convention.[19]

Garran-Coulon was the *Chronique*'s legal correspondent. In 1791 he was Paris's most popular politician, having won the first seat on Paris's deputation to the Legislative Assembly. Garran, of course, had been involved with the Cercle Social since its earliest days, and he had been close friends with Brissot, Bancal, Lanthenas, and Creuzé-Latouche since well before the Revolution.[20]

Finally, there were three editors whose responsibilities were not specifically delineated; little needs to be said of the first, François Lanthenas, except to recall his important activities in the Confédération des Amis de la Vérité and his intimate friendships with the Rolands and Brissot (he in fact introduced Brissot to the Rolands). Collot d'Herbois joined the group on the basis

volution française . . . J. Bidermann, Cousin, Marx-Berr; Bouchary, *Les manieurs* 1: 25.

[19] On Kersaint see A. Kuscinski, *Dictionnaire des conventionnels*, pp. 355-56; Sydenham, *Girondins*, pp. 69, 105, 229.

[20] On Garran see *Lettres de Mme Roland* 2: 674, 696, and 736. Brissot called Garran "my friend" in *Pf*, 1 January 1791, p. 4.

of his *Almanach du Père Gérard*, which the Jacobins had proclaimed a masterpiece of revolutionary propaganda. The man most responsible for awarding Collot that prize, Jean Dusaulx, was himself an editor. Dusaulx and Bonneville were old friends, having met at d'Alembert's home in the early 1780s. Like so many other Cercle Social authors Dusaulx had been a translator before the Revolution and became a politician in 1789. After a successful term in the Paris Communal Assembly, he became a deputy to the Legislative Assembly and the Convention, where he voted with Brissot.[21]

In addition to the editors, François Bonneville (Nicolas' cousin) was hired to engrave portraits of revolutionaries for the *Chronique du mois*. Each issue featured on its frontispiece one of Bonneville's portraits, usually depicting a leading Girondin. The first seven issues included portraits of Condorcet (January), Fauchet (February), Mercier (March), Auger (April), Garran-Coulon (May), Paine (June), and Brissot (July). François Bonneville became one of the best known portrait engravers of his day, and his works were sold individually at the Imprimerie du Cercle Social. At the same time, his engravings helped to spread the fame of the Girondin leaders, whom he often portrayed in a neoclassical style that emphasized their likeness to the ancient heroes of Greek democracy.[22]

In an era when writers were continually changing papers, it is remarkable that in the twenty turbulent months of the *Chronique du mois*, only one editor left the paper for political reasons: Collot d'Herbois quit in May 1792, probably as a result of the split between Brissot and Robespierre over the war. He was immediately replaced by Tom Paine, an intimate friend of Bonneville and Condorcet. The only other change in the staff came as the result of Athanase Auger's death in February 1792.

---

[21] Kuscinski, *Dictionnaire des conventionnels*, pp. 235-36. On Dusaulx and Bonneville see *Nicolas Bonneville . . . aux véritables amis de la liberté*, p. 10.

[22] The other *Chronique* issues featured portraits of John Horne Tooke, Clavière, Roland, Kersaint, Cerutti, Ankarstrom, Dumouriez, Danton, Le Pelletier St. Fargeau, Custine, Gensonné and Kellermann. On François Bonneville see M.E.T Hamy, "Note sur diverses gravures de Bonneville, réprésentant des Nègres (1794-1803)," *Anthropologie* (1900): 42-46.

He was replaced by M. E. Guadet, one of the outstanding orators of the Legislative Assembly.

The sixteen editors of the *Chronique du mois*, then, were more than a group of journalists. They constituted a tight web of close friends who had been writing, socializing, and politicking together since before the Revolution. All had in common a friendship with Brissot and/or Roland, although the latter was not an editor of the *Chronique*.[23] His absence among the editors is conspicuous but easily explained: the Cercle Social was preparing to begin Roland's own journal, the *Journal des arts utiles*. On 27 February 1792 Roland signed an agreement to edit the journal, but his appointment as minister of the interior forced him to abandon the project. Nevertheless, Roland was one of the six writers, who, while not being editors, contributed articles to the *Chronique du mois*. The other five included two minor writers (Crivelli and Chaussard), two Girondin deputies to the Convention who frequented Roland's salon (Bancal and Gensonné), and an old English friend of Bonneville and Brissot (David Williams).[24]

Historians have recognized that the *Chronique du mois* was one of many journals espousing Girondin ideas. What has been shown here is that the *Chronique du mois* was clearly paramount among them. Of its nine editors who were elected to the Convention during the summer of 1792, all nine were Girondins.[25] While other papers such as the *Annales patriotiques et littéraires*,

[23] Brissot and Roland's own friendship went back to 1788. See Claude Perroud, "Brissot et les Rolands. Collaboration des Rolands au *Patriote français*," *Rf* 34(1918): 404-20. The Rolands were also close to Creuzé-Latouche. When the Rolands were imprisoned, their daughter Eudora went to live with Madame Creuzé-Latouche. See *Lettres de Mme Roland* 2: 484.

[24] On Roland see Claude Perroud, "Roland et la presse subventionée," *Rf* 62(1912): 209; *Lettres de Mme Roland* 2: 408-10. Brissot on Williams: "Of all the English men of letters he seems to me the one who has the most universal philosophy, who is the most free from all national prejudice"; cited in Eloise Ellery, *Brissot de Warville: A Study in the History of the French Revolution*, p. 25. On Bancal and Gensonné see Sydenham, *Girondins*, pp. 227-29.

[25] Sydenham, *Girondins*, p. 229; Patrick, *The Men of the First Republic*, pp. 315-39. The nine were Condorcet, Mercier, Kersaint, Brissot, Garran-Coulon, Lanthenas, Dusaulx, Guadet, and Paine.

the *Chronique de Paris*, and the *Patriote français* have all been recognized as Girondin organs, it is striking that each of their principal editors was also on the staff of the *Chronique du mois*. Indeed, no other revolutionary journal had so many national political leaders employed as regular editors.

TWENTIETH-Century historical writing on the Girondins has emphasized the role they played as apologists for the new commercial bourgeoisie that arose during the eighteenth century. The *Chronique du mois*, as the voice of the Girondins, and particularly as "the mouthpiece for the Girondins in financial matters," may shed some light on this issue and their economic ideas.[26]

There is no doubt that to a great extent the *Chronique du mois* propagated an ideology that was soon adopted by the French bourgeoisie. Even the prospectus of the journal claimed that the *Chronique* was written at least partly with the new class in mind:

These essays will be useful to bankers, financiers, and merchants who must know our internal and external state in order to establish in their transactions commercial relations that assure our national fortune in augmenting their own wealth.[27]

The Girondins who wrote for the *Chronique du mois* called for a completely free domestic commerce, in which the right to acquire property was not to be limited or violated.

The Directors of the Imprimerie du Cercle Social ... have new reasons to be convinced that among a free people individual property is essentially tied to the necessity to serve the interest of the greatest number, and that the nation's prosperity works in accordance with the greatest amount of liberty when properties are better guaranteed, and when social equality is most respected.[28]

---

[26] Marcel Dorigny, "Recherche sur les idées économiques des Girondins," in *Actes du colloque Girondins et Montagnards (Sorbonne, 14 décembre 1975) sous la direction d'Albert Soboul*, pp. 79-102. I owe a great deal to this lucid and important article. See Albert Mathiez, *Girondins et Montagnards*, Chapter 1, for the classic twentieth-century view of the Girondins.

[27] *Cdm*, Prospectus, p. 4.

[28] *BAV*, 1 January 1793, p. 2.

In addition, Creuzé-Latouche warned readers "not to forget for one instant that your subsistence and safety is dependent upon the free commerce of grain and the free circulation of goods," a view supported in articles by Condorcet, Roland and Bidermann.[29]

Cercle Social economic writings were not intended to be only abstract pieces for debates on the nature of political economy, but were usually written on concrete issues and were designed to influence impending legislation. The winter of 1791-1792 was particularly hard for the French economy. Revolt and violence in the colonies had created shortages and inflated prices for sugar and coffee, while an increase in the price of bread was beginning to indicate problems in the supply of that basic commodity. To make matters worse, a lack of confidence in the assignat, the new revolutionary paper money, was creating a monetary crisis. The sans-culottes began to protest these conditions, complaining that wealthy speculators were hoarding scarce commodities and creating a new aristocracy. Their more articulate spokesmen demanded that the government enter the marketplace on the people's behalf, setting a maximum price for certain goods and regulating distribution for the benefit of all.[30]

The Girondins rejected the sans-culottes' position. "These words hoarders and monopolies," cried Creuzé-Latouche, "are only the dangerous visions of foolish women or ignorant persons." The Girondins believed that government regulation of grain would hurt farmers. They claimed that, by investing capital in his crops long before he was certain of his return, the farmer incurred more risks than the consumer. He was therefore entitled to the freedom to sell his product to whomever he pleased, whenever he wished, and for whatever price he could get. If this liberty was not respected, the farmer would have no incen-

[29] Jacques-Antoine Creuzé-Latouche, *Sur les subsistances* (Paris: ICS, 1793), pp. 141-43; Condorcet, "Sur la distribution des assignats et sur l'établissements paiements par registre," *Cdm*, January 1792, pp. 50-52, and "Sur la liberté des subsistances," *Cdm*, March 1792, p. 42; Roland, "Des usuriers et des accapareurs," *Cdm*, April 1792, p. 111; Bidermann, "D'un commerce national," *Cdm*, January 1792, pp. 86-87.

[30] Albert Mathiez, *La Vie chère et le mouvement social sous la Terreur* 1: 29-74.

tive to bring his grain to market, and the entire economy would collapse.[31]

Jean-Marie Roland supported this viewpoint. In a *Chronique du mois* article published in the midst of the economic difficulties and only a few weeks after he became minister of the interior, Roland addressed himself specifically to "hoarders and speculators."[32] He began the essay in a radical mood: "Hoarders are those who have no public consideration"; they desire only to "further the unhappiness of the people" and acquire wealth for themselves. "From this viewpoint," Roland contended, "all speculation is a crime." But here he retreated to safer ground and insisted that, if speculation was a crime, speculators were not the kind of criminals who could be punished. "It is unnecessary to pass a law against the hoarders because one cannot distinguish a monopoly from common business practices, and therefore it would be too easy for the government to harm innocent businessmen." Roland wanted no one to misunderstand him. "I have said it, and I will not cease to repeat it: any man who speculates upon the misery of the people, who tends to procure a particular profit from an unhappy public, is a filthy scoundrel." Nevertheless, Roland also insisted that on the most fundamental level hoarding "is a moral affair," not a legal or even a political one.

Thus the Girondins refused to act against hoarders and speculators even when it was clear that hoarding and speculating might harm national interests. But in external trade the Girondins were not so committed to laissez-faire principles. For the *Chronique*'s April and May 1792 issues, Kersaint wrote a revealing two-part article on trade with India, in which he "demonstrated that commerce with India is destructive to national industry." Kersaint argued that the free importation of Indian textiles and other goods would ruin the French textile industry and put French artisans out of work. However useful free-trade policies might be for the domestic economy, in the international sphere certain French industries needed protection. How could France achieve political stability if its economy was undermined

---

[31] Creuzé-Latouche, *Sur les subsistances*, pp. 30, 41, and 140.

[32] Roland, "Des usuriers et des accapareurs," *Cdm*, April 1792. The following quotes come from pp. 109-11.

by cheap foreign goods? Kersaint urged the Legislative Assembly to outlaw the importation of non-French goods, and he urged his countrymen to buy only French-made products: "Let everyone say to himself: if it's not made with French hands, I don't want it."[33]

Laissez-faire for the domestic economy, protectionism for international commerce: this certainly was not the position of Adam Smith or J. B. Say. But it became, in fact, the position of the French business community throughout the nineteenth century. Historians may hotly contest whether or not the Girondins were consciously appealing to a rising bourgeoisie, but it is clear that they helped to develop an ideology that would dominate French middle-class economic thinking during the next century.[34]

Despite their contributions to this kind of nineteenth-century economic thought, these Girondin economic thinkers sincerely believed that their policies would result in a society where wealth would eventually be equalized and poverty eliminated. "One of the effects of our Revolution," wrote the former speculator Antoine Bidermann, "is above all more equality in wealth." If Bidermann's claim was propaganda, at least it was propaganda in which he and his colleagues themselves believed.[35]

Some Cercle Social writers were worried that in the short run the Revolution's economic policies were indeed benefiting the rich at the expense of the poor. "Many towns," wrote François Lanthenas, near the end of 1791,

still present characteristics that bother the true friends of liberty. The old bourgeoisie is entirely indolent. If equality pleases it, it is for not having any superiors and not for having equals . . . and this vice, which has not been well perceived in the provinces, can one day be reversed. The bourgeois wants to put himself in the place of the noble, and allow the artisan to take his. However, the artisan is the true defender, the sincere friend of the Revolution. He alone forms the National

---

[33] Kersaint, "Sur les établissements et le commerce de l'Inde," *Cdm*, May 1792, p. 56, and April 1792, p. 94. See also, Dorigny, "Recherche," pp. 88-89.
[34] Dorigny, "Recherche," pp. 92-93.
[35] Bidermann, "D'un commerce national," *Cdm*, January 1792, p. 87.

Guard . . . he alone frequents the electoral assemblies. Finally, he alone is worthy of liberty, because he alone has good morals.[36]

Lanthenas' solution was a stringent inheritance tax that would redistribute wealth in an egalitarian fashion. This idea goes back to at least 1790, when it was proposed in the Confédération des Amis de la Vérité and in Lanthenas' Société des amis de l'union et de l'égalité dans les familles. It was reiterated in Bonneville's *De l'esprit des religions*, and, during the spring of 1792, Athanase Auger reformulated the idea in a petition to the Legislative Assembly. Auger's proposal asked the Assembly to pass an inheritance law that would "divide a fertile territory between the most inhabitants possible."[37]

These idealistic views culminated in Louis Lavicomterie's *La République sans impôts*, a fascinating vision of a utopian society based upon Girondin economic ideas, published by the Cercle Social in April 1792. *La République sans impôts* describes a free, tolerant, egalitarian democratic republic without taxes or poverty. How would it evolve? Neither by terror, nor partisan struggles, nor even good laws. Rather, each citizen would be indoctrinated with a pure, virtuous morality, and would be naturally aware of his duties. "Morality will maintain the republic, for which it is the unique base. . . . It must be the only coercive law of a free people; any other which is imposed upon it will be ruinous and abominable."[38] Anything forced upon a people is unjust, including military conscription, economic regulation, and taxes; anything, that is, except morality. Lavicomterie defined morality as "reason put into practice," by which he meant a civil religion emphasizing a Rousseauian spirit of patriotism fostered by a national educational system. If such a civil religion were accepted by the population, then private and public interest would finally be reunited, and "virtue, morality, will be the only

[36] *Pf*, 25 November 1791, pp. 611-12.
[37] Nicholas Bonneville, *Appendices de la seconde édition de l'Esprit des religions; pour servir à l'entretien, à la propagation des bons principes, et à la Confédération universelle des Amis de la Vérité*, 1792, part 1, p. 59; Athanase Auger, "Droits rigoureux du peuple, vrais intérêts du peuple," *Tribut de la Société nationale des neuf soeurs*, 14 November 1791, p. 334; *Cdm*, March 1792, pp. 49-52.
[38] Louis Lavicomterie, *La République sans impôts* (Paris: ICS, 1792), pp. 322-37. The following quotations come from pp. 337, 165, and 225.

interest of man." Families would work hard to produce as much as possible, trying to attain great wealth. But when they heard that a fellow citizen had been the victim of some catastrophe, the compassion and love for their fellow creatures instilled in them by this civil religion would naturally cause them to give generously to their unfortunate brothers. Unlike Fauchet, Lavicomterie did not think that there was anything inherently wrong with wealth, as long as the rich were willing to help the poor. "Wealth does not destroy equality." Thus there would be no need for taxes or any other kind of economic regulation. In Lavicomterie's libertarian vision of an ideal society, the economy was the superstructure, guided by more fundamental shifts in the development of virtue.

Thus Girondin economic thought exhibited a latent tension between two different visions of the French economy: on the one hand, a classical political economy, in which society operates according to certain economic laws that every nation must obey; and on the other hand, an economic language, probably derived from Renaissance ideas of civic virtue, that stressed morality, patriotism, and justice. Writers like Clavière, Bidermann, Kersaint, Condorcet, and Roland tended to view economic problems from the perspective of the laws of political economy, whereas others like Bonneville, Lanthenas, Fauchet, Madame Roland, Auger, and Lavicomterie viewed them as essentially moral problems, the working-out of a struggle between virtue and selfishness. The first group of writers was usually more influential than the second; and many critics would say that the moral writings of the Girondins should be viewed merely as propaganda. But on some important issues, the tension between these two approaches obscured the Girondins' arguments and weakened their political position. The best example of how a language of civic morality obscured a difficult economic dilemma lies in the attitude of the *Chronique du mois* toward the abolition of slavery and the colonial question.

THE FRENCH antislavery movement has been viewed as ineffective and weak, especially when compared to its British counterpart. Daniel Resnick has placed the blame for that weakness on the movement's inability to develop sound economic arguments against slavery and its reliance upon sentimental moral claims. Resnick, like other historians before him, described Brissot's own Imprimerie du Patriote Français as the leading mouthpiece of the abolitionist cause in the French press, ignoring the contributions of the Cercle Social. While few would deny the importance of the Imprimerie du Patriote Français in the antislavery campaign, the Cercle Social also played an important role and drew from a great variety of abolitionist authors.[39]

In 1788 Brissot, Clavière, and a few other like-minded reformers, including Condorcet, had founded the Société des amis des Noirs. Before the Revolution the Société's campaign focused on two specific goals: an immediate end to the slave trade and a more gradual end to slavery itself. The Revolution changed the direction of the movement by raising two essential questions: what did the Declaration of the Rights of Man imply for the political rights of colonial whites, free persons of color, and black slaves; and second, what were its implications for political and commercial relations between France and her West Indian colonies?

Commentators on both sides of the issue focused their attention on France's largest colony, Saint-Domingue. In 1789 its population included 35,440 whites, 26,666 free persons of color, and 509,642 black slaves. Power was in the hands of the small ruling elite of white plantation owners and merchants. As slaves, blacks had no social or political standing whatsoever. But the free persons of color were also completely segregated from the whites and forced to submit to various kinds of social discrimination. Each of these groups interpreted the Revolution in its

[39] Daniel P. Resnick, "The Société des Amis des Noirs and the Abolition of Slavery," *FHS* 7(1972): 558-69. See also Claude Perroud, "La Société française des amis des Noirs," *Rf* 32(1916): 122-47; Léon Cahen, "La Société des amis des Noirs et Condorcet," *Rf* 50(1906): 481-511. The following members of the Confédération des Amis de la Vérité or Cercle Social authors wrote antislavery tracts between 1789-1794: Bonnemain, Brie-Serrant, Brissot, Clavière, Condorcet, Garran-Coulon, Gensonné, Kersaint, Lanthenas, Lavallée, Mandar, Mercier, Milscent, and Raimond. Much of their writing is reviewed in Edward Derbyshire Seeber, *Anti-Slavery Opinion in France During the Second Half of the Eighteenth Century*, pp. 162-72.

own interests. The whites wanted the elimination of certain economic restrictions imposed by the Old Regime and urged the Constituent Assembly to draw the colonial and French economies closer together. They insisted that tampering with the racial situation would bring economic disaster to France and her colonies. The free persons of color claimed that the Declaration of the Rights of Man should apply to them. They demanded to be included in the local colonial assemblies and urged the Constituent Assembly to grant them full civil rights. Although they asked for laws eliminating the slave trade, they said little about the actual abolition of slavery. The main spokesman for the black slaves, Toussaint l'Ouverture, argued that any regime that claimed that its foundations were based upon human rights must immediately abolish slavery.[40]

The Amis des Noirs and the Cercle Social sided with the free persons of color. When the Amis des Noirs led a campaign during the spring of 1791 to induce the Constituent Assembly to grant full civil rights to free persons of color, one of its most important supporters was the Confédération des Amis de la Vérité. The two groups sent letters and notices back and forth, and many people belonged to both clubs. For example, on 1 April 1791 the Confédération's President Mailly read two letters from the Amis des Noirs on the plight of the free persons of color. The Confédération asked Mailly and Fauchet to compose a reply noting that the goals of the Amis des Noirs "have long been recognized by the members of our Confédération as social dogmas."[41]

These efforts were successful insofar as the Legislative Assembly passed a bill in May 1791 that gave full political rights to free people of color. But the struggle was far from over. The white ruling class in Saint-Domingue refused to implement the legislation in their local assemblies. More important still, in Au-

[40] Phillip D. Curtin, "The Declaration of the Rights of Man in Saint-Domingue 1788-1791" *Hispanic American Historical Review* 30: 157-75; Valerie Quinney, "The Problem of Civil Rights for Free Men of Color in the French Revolution" *FHS* 5: 544-58.
[41] *Bdf*, 6 April 1791, pp. 44, 50-51.

gust 1791 a slave insurrection began that destroyed any possibility of the gradual changes envisioned by the Amis des Noirs.

By the summer of 1791, the Confédération des Amis de la Vérité and the Société des amis des Noirs no longer existed as distinct organizations. During the fall of 1791 the Amis des Noirs was absorbed into the Imprimerie du Cercle Social, and the *Chronique du mois* became the primary organ for French abolitionists. No fewer than six of the sixteen original editors had been members of the Amis des Noirs, including Brissot, Clavière, Condorcet, and Lanthenas, who had been among the most vociferous members of that club. In addition, other editors such as Kersaint and Garran-Coulon contributed antislavery articles to the paper.

The Cercle Social also published works by Claude Milscent and Julien Raimond, spokesmen for the cause of Saint-Domingue's free persons of color. Milscent, a close friend of Bonneville, had moved to France and begun his own journal, *Le Créole patriote*. In a series of letters published in the *Bouche de fer*, Milscent argued that the cause of the free persons of color should get top priority in abolitionist circles. After describing the various discriminatory measures imposed on free persons of color, he asked readers to believe that in Saint-Domingue "the condition of the free persons of color is incontestably worse than that of the slaves." In a later Cercle Social pamphlet he suggested that, while slavery is wrong and must be abolished at some point, immediate emancipation would be disastrous. The problem with slaves was not inferiority, but ignorance; slavery had succeeded in robbing them of civilized thought and morals. Milscent concluded that a gradual process of emancipation should begin under the leadership of the free persons of color, who ought to be given their own civil rights without delay.[42]

---

[42] *Bdf*, 19 April 1791, p. 222; Claude Milscent, *Du régime colonial* (Paris: ICS, 1792), passim. In an advertisement for this pamphlet, Bonneville wrote that the Saint-Domingue blacks admired Milscent so much that they called him "the God of good Negroes, the exterminator of the wicked." See *Cdm*, February 1792, pp. 113-14. Milscent later returned the compliment in his own newspaper by urging readers "to read *l'Esprit des religions* and you will see that Bonneville has escaped from the labyrinth of human prejudice and . . . has returned to the source of nature itself. . . . *l'Esprit* des religions will be

Julien Raimond's arguments followed this same line. In fact, when asked about emancipation of slaves, he once candidly replied: "One could hardly suppose that I should want to ruin at one stroke my entire family, which possesses ... seven or eight millions in property at Saint-Domingue."[43] This remark is significant for what it reveals about free persons of color. While they had no political rights and little social standing, free persons of color in Saint-Domingue wielded considerable economic clout and, in fact, cooperated with the whites in controlling slavery. It has been estimated that Saint-Domingue's free persons of color owned one-third of all land and one-fourth of all slaves. This explains why Raimond first courted the pro-slavery Club Massiac after moving to Paris. The Club Massiac had been established by white plantation owners, merchants, and conservative politicians in order to counter the Amis des Noirs. It was only after Raimond failed at the Massiac that he turned to Brissot's group for support.[44]

Cercle Social writers agreed with Milscent and Raimond that an end to slavery should be delayed until free persons of color won their full political rights. "Slavery is in itself a great evil," wrote the future Convention deputy Antoine-Jean Bonnemain. "But it still carries with it an infinite number of abuses and crimes that corrupt morality and annihilate all social virtues." Bonnemain concluded that, while the slave trade should be immediately abolished, the slaves should be emancipated only when "philosophy has undermined their prejudices and crushed their superstition."[45]

While the Imprimerie du Cercle Social was espousing these

---

regarded as the catechism of the mind and heart." See *Créole patriote*, 5 October 1792, p. 107.

[43] Cited in Mercer Cook, "Julien Raimond" *Journal of Negro History* 26: 142-43. See also Luc Nemours, "Julien Raimond, le chef des gens de couleur et sa famille," No. 23, 257-62.

[44] Laura Foner, "The Free People of Color in Louisiana and Saint-Domingue" *Journal of Negro History* 3: 406-30; Gabriel Debien, *Les Colons de Saint-Domingue et la Révolution: Essai sur le Club Massiac. Août 1789-août 1792.*

[45] Antoine-Jean Bonnemain, *Régénération des colonies ou Moyens de restituer graduellement aux hommes leur état politique et d'assurer la prosperité des nations, et moyens pour rétablir ... l'ordre dans les colonies françaises* (Paris: ICS, 1792), pp. 58-66.

moral arguments, their opponents were fighting back with arguments based upon purely economic grounds. Through pages of trade statistics and discussions of colonial commercial activities, the right wing press warned that any change in colonial racial policy would have devastating consequences for the French economy. It reasoned that a strong French economy should be secured to assure the stability of the Revolution before reforms in colonial social structure were initiated. The *Chronique du mois* made no real effort to respond to this kind of argument; it merely reiterated that slavery and the slave trade were evil because they transformed Negroes into beast-like creatures.[46]

Why did the *Chronique du mois* fail to develop strong economic arguments for free persons of color? Since free persons of color were already an economically privileged group, granting them civil rights would have meant neither a change in the economy nor any change in the status of black slaves. But Cercle Social writers had supported free persons of color because they thought that granting them civil rights was the most effective path towards the eventual abolition of slavery, not because it would benefit France's economy. Any change in the Cercle Social's argument would have weakened their position on the abolition of slavery.

A more important question, then, is why the *Chronique du mois* did not develop sound economic arguments against slavery itself? In order to win the propaganda campaign against their opponents, it needed to show that the continuation of racial discrimination would be harmful to the French economy. Evidently Cercle Social writers realized that their opponents were basing their arguments on economic ideas they themselves shared; Kersaint, Clavière, and others had advocated a policy of international commerce that above all favored French economic interests. Unable to show how the abolition of slavery would help the French economy, Cercle Social writers were forced to resort to moral arguments that were less persuasive to the majority of French politicians, who were afraid that even the gradual abolition of slavery would harm French interests.

[46] W. J. Murry, "The Right-Wing Press in the French Revolution, 1789-1792," pp. 210-12.

As THE *Chronique du mois* illustrates, the Girondins were neither strict disciples of the Enlightenment who tried to impose a prefabricated ideology onto the new regime nor demagogic opportunists whose ideas reflected no more than their own self-interest and political ambitions. Girondin ideas emerged from a continual process of compromising between lofty idealism and shrewd Machiavellian behavior. Unfortunately, between 1791 and 1793 the Girondins proved that they were more effective as philosophes than as politicians.

9

Posters for the Sans-Culottes: Louvet and the *Sentinelle*

JEAN-BAPTISTE LOUVET (1760-1797). Elected to the Convention. Editor of the *Sentinelle*. Novelist turned propagandist, Louvet wrote some of the most vociferously anti-Jacobin propaganda published by the Imprimerie du Cercle Social.

Courtesy of The Newberry Library, Chicago

It is not the cause of kings, nor that of one or another individual which sets in movement France and its armies; it is the great cause of all; it is the establishment of a new era which will wipe despotism from the earth and establish, upon immutable principles of peace and of *citizenship*, the great human republic.

Tom Paine, *Lettre ... au peuple françois ... le 25 septembre 1792* (Paris: ICS, [1792]), pp. 2-3.

THE IMPRIMERIE du Cercle Social published the *Sentinelle* between April and November 1792. This period saw a dramatic change in the behavior of the Paris sans-culottes, who now became more active in trying to determine the direction and policies of the Revolution. Three times during this short period (20 June, 10 August, 2-7 September), the sans-culottes waged large, violent demonstrations, including one that toppled the monarchy. The sans-culottes had become a political force to be dealt with. The *Sentinelle* was the Girondins' effort to influence and shape the political behavior of this volatile group.

Usually histories of the French Revolution present the eventual rift between the Girondins and the sans-culottes as inevitable. But the Girondins certainly did not see it that way. They tried hard to secure the support of the sans-culottes, and at least until the September Massacres they thought they had a fair chance of winning their allegiance. If the Girondins failed in this effort, it was because they underestimated the sans-culottes' political power and their ability to articulate their own programs.

In March 1792, six months after the beginning of the Legislative Assembly, the Girondins won a great political victory when the king agreed to dismiss his Feuillant ministers and appoint some Girondins to his cabinet. Particularly gratifying to Brissot were the appointments of two close friends, Etienne Clavière to the ministry of public contributions (i.e., finance) and Jean-Marie Roland to the ministry of the interior (and later Joseph Servan to the ministry of war).[1]

[1] Claude Perroud, "Le Premier Ministre de Roland," *Rf* 42(1902): 511-28; Charles A. Le Guin, *Roland de la Platière: A Public Servant in the Eighteenth Century*, pp. 78-82.

The creation of these first "patriot" ministries was the culmination of a Girondin propaganda campaign to declare war on the Austrian Empire. Since the flight of the king to Varennes, the Girondins had suspected French émigrés of forming a counterrevolutionary army under the auspices of the Austrians. By the beginning of the Legislative Assembly, the Girondins were convinced that the émigrés were ready to attack. They called for severe measures against the émigrés and, more important, a declaration of war against Austria. Speaking to the Jacobin club on 15 December 1791, Brissot offered three essential reasons for war: (1) to purge the eastern frontier of counterrevolutionary aristocrats; (2) to rally the people around a patriotic cause; and (3) to test the loyalty of the king. Brissot might also have mentioned a fourth reason: to strengthen the political position of the Girondins and weaken that of the Feuillants. The call for a declaration of war was a shrewd political tactic. It divided and weakened the Feuillants and the court, while uniting most of the Left and eliciting a great deal of support from uncommitted deputies. Only Robespierre and a few others maintained a pacifist line, and they were ignored for months.[2]

With a majority supporting them in the Legislative Assembly and control of the cabinet, the Girondins dominated national politics, and war was declared on Austria on 20 April 1792. Unfortunately the French forces were not well prepared. The first battles went badly, and a major campaign in Belgium was a disaster. The Girondins had promised a quick and victorious war, and these first setbacks lowered morale. The Feuillant papers, most notably the *Gazette universelle*, seized every opportunity to illustrate the ineptness of the Girondin leadership and the futility of the war. The Girondins viewed the war as a national struggle and considered popular support crucial. They could not allow the right-wing press to control public opinion. Moreover, they were particularly concerned because these right-wing papers were secretly subsidized by the king's private budget,

---

[2] Brissot's speech is reprinted in D. I. Wright, ed., *The French Revolution. Introductory Documents*, pp. 114-22.

the civil list. "We sensed the need," Madame Roland wrote in
her memoirs, "to balance the influence of the aristocracy, of the
civil list and its papers."[3]

Jean-Marie Roland, the new minister of the interior, decided
to counter the right-wing propaganda with a paper of his own,
the *Sentinelle*. It would not be a sophisticated journal like the
Chronique du mois, but rather a paper written in a popular
language aimed for sans-culottes and "pasted on walls in poster
form." But even if he had had the time, Roland could not have
edited such a paper himself. "Having always lived in the provinces," wrote a good friend, "in the retreat of his study, given
up to scholarly works," Roland was an "austere philosophe" and
"laborious savant," not a skillful journalist. Roland and the Girondins needed an editor who was more than simply a political
ally. They required someone with the talent to simplify complex
policies into passionate causes. They needed someone who could
stir the heart. They found their man in Jean-Baptiste Louvet de
Couvray.[4]

Louvet was born in 1760, the son of a Parisian baker whom
Mercier once called "an ignorant and brutal shopkeeper." As a
youth Louvet's heart had been broken in a tumultuous love
affair, and he had turned to Rousseau's writings for solace.
Inspired by the more sentimental writings of the philosophes,
he decided to become an artist himself. In 1787 he published
his first novel, *Une Année de la vie du chevalier Faublas*, which
was immediately successful. The story revolves around the ad-
olescent romances of a young nobleman in prerevolutionary
Paris. In the first part of the novel, Faublas goes to a ball dis-
guised as a girl. An older woman is so impressed with Faublas
that she invites him (her?) to spend the night at her home. When
Faublas tries to tell the woman that he is actually a boy, she
refuses to believe him. Not until they are lying in the same bed
is his true identity pointedly revealed. A tender love scene follows

[3] Madame Roland, *Mémoires* 1: 83.
[4] Jean-Baptiste Louvet de Couvray, *Mémoires . . . sur la Révolution française*
1: 50-51; Bibliothèque Nationale, Nouvelles acquisitions françaises, 9533, fol.
310; Roland, *Mémoires* 1: 225.

in which Faublas loses his virginity, and the story goes on from there.[5]

Today *Faublas* is no longer read, and no literary scholar would rank it with the novels of Rousseau, Laclos, or Stendhal. But in 1787 the book became an overnight bestseller. Before the end of the century *Faublas* went through ten French editions. By 1900 at least twenty more editions had been published, and the novel translated into German, English, Spanish, Italian, and even Russian. The theme of an effeminate boy discovering his masculine sexuality clearly struck a chord among European readers.

When the Revolution began, Louvet was living in the countryside near Paris, writing a sequeal to *Faublas*. He hoped that the royalties from a sequel would make him financially independent. Although the sequel was a success, it did not make its author rich, probably because the public had turned its attention to political events. Louvet himself demonstrated his support for the Revolution by writing a pamphlet in defense of the women who participated in the October Days. The pamphlet won him membership in the Paris Jacobins, but he refused to take any active part in the club. Louvet generally shunned politics and sought to influence the Revolution in a less direct manner. In 1790 he wrote three patriotic plays honoring the Revolution's heroes and mocking its critics, but these efforts were rejected by Parisian theater companies and were never produced.[6]

Louvet's next project was better received. In the spring of 1791 his third novel, *Emile de Varmont*, was published and well reviewed. It was a political novel in which Louvet used a complex web of romantic entanglements to demonstrate the need for legislation pending before the National Assembly on two specific topics: divorce and the marriage of priests. *Varmont* was halfway between *Faublas* and the blatant political propaganda he was soon to write. Here a political pamphlet was woven into a love story.[7]

---

[5] John Rivers, *Louvet: Revolutionist and Romance-Writer*, p. 4; [Jean-Baptiste Louvet de Couvray], *Une Année de la vie du chevalier de Faublas*.

[6] Louvet, *Mémoires* 1: 4-15.

[7] Jean-Baptiste Louvet de Couvray, *Emile de Varmont, ou le divorce nécessaire et les amours du curé Sevin; Moniteur* 9: 15-16; *Logographe*, 18 January 1792, p. 68.

Although *Varmont* was a success, it too failed to bring Louvet the wealth he desired, and he realized that he could no longer afford to sit on the sidelines and write novels and plays. In his memoirs Louvet claims that the Feuillants' whitewashing of the king after the flight to Varennes impelled him to enter the political scene on the side of the radicals. But surely there was more to it than that. Perhaps the success of his political writings gave him confidence in himself as a political commentator. Perhaps his keen sense of his public convinced him that readers were now more interested in politics than fiction.[8]

At any rate, in November 1791 Louvet became more active in the Jacobins and was appointed to its prestigious Correspondence Committee, where he became friendly with Lanthenas, Fauchet, and Brissot. On 25 December he delivered a speech before the National Assembly, warning of an impending invasion by the Austrians and émigrés and calling on the Assembly to declare war immediately. In January he reiterated these sentiments at the Jacobin club, supporting Brissot and sharply denouncing Robespierre's more pacifistic position. The Jacobins rewarded Louvet in February by electing him vice-president and, on 2 March, by giving him the honor of presiding over the club (an occasion marked, not surprisingly, by his refusal to yield the floor to Robespierre).[9]

By the time Roland established the *Sentinelle*, Louvet was well established in successful literary and political careers and was already part of Brissot's circle. He had grown up among Parisian sans-culottes, and his two novels had won him fame among the middle class and established his knowledge of the human heart. Madame Roland thought he was "courageous as a lion, innocent as a child, a common sense person, a good citizen, and a passionate writer," and Brissot's *Patriote français* praised his "rare purity of style, and great strength in his emotions, a vigorous logic, and brilliant eloquence."[10] It is hard to imagine a better choice for the new paper's editor.

There was, of course, no provision in the government's budget for subsidizing journals, particularly those designed to spread

[8] Louvet, *Mémoires* 1: 20-30.
[9] Aulard, *Jacobins* 2: 253, 3: 317-422; *Moniteur* 13: 536.
[10] Roland, *Mémoires* 1: 162; *Pf*, 11 January 1792, p. 42.

the ideology of one specific faction. Party politics were univer-
sally scorned throughout the Revolution, and politicians had to
appear independent, loyal only to the national interest. Thus
Roland could not ask the Assembly for the funds for the *Sentinelle* and had to use money originally appropriated for other
purposes. The arrangments for this laundered money were complex, but essentially the money was funneled through Pétion,
who was the mayor of Paris and a good friend of the Girondins.
Dumouriez, the minister of foreign affairs, would send Pétion
large sums of money for Paris' burgeoning police force. Pétion,
in turn, would send Roland a small portion of this money for
the *Sentinelle* and other "patriotic" publications. Then Roland
or Lanthenas would give the money to the Imprimerie du Cercle
Social. Altogether Roland gave the Imprimerie more than 11,000
livres for the *Sentinelle* alone.[11]

The first issue of the *Sentinelle* was published on 16 May 1792,
and thereafter the new journal appeared irregularly twice or
three times weekly. Usually the Imprimerie du Cercle Social
printed 1,500 copies of each issue, and most of these were pasted
on walls throughout Paris and in a few other large cities. The
quality of paper was poor, often tinged with a pink or grey
color, and the lettering was very large. The subscription price,
three sous per issue, was one-sixth the price of the *Chronique
du mois* and much lower than most other revolutionary journals.
Of course, the Imprimerie du Cercle Social was able to charge
such a price only because of its government subsidy. It hoped
the low price would induce patriots to purchase several copies
and paste them up all over the capital. "The easiest, most prompt,
and least costly way to spread the truth," Louvet declared in
one advertisement, "is with a journal that can be posted."[12]

The *Sentinelle* turned Louvet into an effective political prop-

[11] Claude Perroud, "Roland et la presse subventionnée," *Rf* 62(1912): 207.
This important article is essentially a reprinting of Roland's papers discovered
in the Château de Rosière. They include several letters between the Cercle
Social and Roland or Lanthenas, as well as book lists and receipts.

[12] *Sentinelle*, no. 2, 18 May 1792. (Before 1 July 1792 dates were not printed,
but a list found in the Château de Rosière identifies a date with each issue.
See Perroud, "Roland et la presse subventionnée," p. 209.) The following
quotation also comes from this issue.

agandist. As with most propaganda, the *Sentinelle* had two distinctive purposes: first, it deliberately played upon the emotions
of the reader in order to persuade him to support Girondin
leaders and policies; and second, Louvet used the paper to introduce a number of political symbols (e.g., the "Austrian Committee" and the "Patriotic Ministers"), so that sans-culotte readers could quickly understand and conceptualize Girondin ideology.
Despite its promise to include an "extract of daily news and
reflections," the *Sentinelle* contained very little news and even
less rational debate. Articles were short, simplistic, and repetitive.
Each issue covered only a few topics. No doubt the paper's short
length was a severe constraint for Louvet's bombastic style. But
it allows us to analyze the *Sentinelle*'s content not only for the
purpose of identifying Girondin ideology but also for discovering
what the Girondins thought were the most important issues to
lay before the sans-culottes.

The war with Austria dominated the early issues of the *Sentinelle*. Louvet was determined to harness mass support for the
Girondins and to make the war a truly patriotic cause. Short
anecdotes emphasized the bravery of the common soldier, while
the role of the generals was downplayed. Readers were reminded
that the war was being waged not for any ambitious monarch
nor would-be dictator, but to achieve the Revolution's goals for
the whole nation, and even for the world. By remarking how
foreign peoples "cherish[ed] the French Revolution" and were
gladly welcoming French troops, Louvet portrayed the war as
a liberating crusade.[13]

Once Parisians began discovering that the war was going very
badly, Louvet spent more and more words blaming the Right
for the nation's problems. Central to his propaganda was the
belief that an "Austrian Committee" was directing a conspiracy
to sabotage the war and undermine the Revolution. This Austrian Committee was often invoked but rarely explained. In one
issue Louvet claimed that it was composed of two factions: those
who "want the Revolution to turn against itself. They wish only
that the Counter-Revolution succeed above all else." The other

---

[13] *Sentinelle*, no. 7, 28 May 1792.

faction consisted "of the small number of people who have embraced the Revolution in principle in order to turn it towards their own profit and personal ambition." The first faction was a cover for the court, the second for the Feuillants.[14]

The Austrian Committee was a standard propagandistic tool of several left-wing journalists. But few of them equaled Louvet in his descriptions of the Austrian Committee's intrigues. In one article he accused a major right-wing paper, the *Gazette universelle*, of being the organ of the Committee. The *Gazette* "defended the Ministry when it was Austrian and now attacks it when it is patriotic"; it "portrays the poor as always ready to pillage the rich, so that all property owners rally to the cause of the *nobles*"; and worse, it "exaggerates our losses and the successes of the enemy." A symbol like the Austrian Committee allowed Louvet to convey the image of a virtuous and patriotic regime in danger of being overthrown by a band of mysterious and aristocratic conspirators. At issue was not the actual existence of such a group, but the Girondins' concern for the security of the new regime. The use of an Austrian Committee allowed the Girondins quickly and simply to convey their anxiety to the sans-culottes.[15]

In the cold war between the Girondins and the Feuillants, the latter had the advantage of the king's sympathies. The Girondins' relations with the king deteriorated from cold to hostile during the spring of 1792. In their manners, policies, and pronouncements, the Girondins succeeded in alienating the king to the point where he looked forward to dismissing them. His opportunity came at the beginning of June. The king had refused to sign two bills that the Girondin ministers viewed as essential for the maintenance of order; these were the reorganization of the federal police (a move that would have eliminated the king's own troops), and legal sanctions against priests who refused to swear loyalty to the constitution. Roland sent a bitter letter to the king demanding that he sign the decrees in accordance with the will of the people. Roland frankly and directly criticized the

---

[14] *Sentinelle*, no. 12, 18 June 1792.

[15] *Sentinelle*, no. 12, 18 June 1792; on the Austrian Committee see Sydenham, *The Girondins*, pp. 79, 98, 105, 121.

king for not being a better patriot and warned that if he continued to oppose the desires of the nation people would suspect him of working against the Revolution. When still no response came from Louis, Roland boldly challenged him by making the letter public. This time Louis reacted, dismissing Roland and the other two Girondin ministers, Clavière and Servan.[16]

The Cercle Social quickly organized a propaganda blitz intended to force the king to reappoint the Girondins. The Imprimerie immediately published Roland's letter to the king, and printed the boldest passages in the *Sentinelle*. Within the month appeared the *Lettres et pièces intéressantes pour servir à l'histoire du ministère de Roland, Servan, et Clavière*. A carefully chosen collection of letters and circulars written during their tenure in office, the *Lettres* clearly tried to paint Roland and his colleagues as virtuous patriots fighting on behalf of the people. An editor's introduction refuted charges that the Girondins constituted an insidious party and asked the reader to judge the matter for himself by reading the letters. The reader was not told, however, that Pétion had given the Imprimerie du Cercle Social over 500 livres from government funds for the publication of this pamphlet.[17]

The *Sentinelle* continued to describe the Girondin leaders as popular heroes. Louvet claimed that they had been dismissed just "at the moment when the minister of the interior, Roland, was stimulating departmental activity against fanaticism . . . and terrifying the court in a language worthy of Sparta and Rome." Within only a few months, he claimed, the war with Austria would have been won and the Revolution would have been consolidated.[18]

Girondin writers naturally blamed the fall of their ministers on the intrigues of the Austrian Committee. But they now went further, pointing to Lafayette as the leader of this group and

[16] Charles A. Le Guin, *Roland de la Platière: A Public Servant in the Eighteenth Century*, pp. 85-86.

[17] Jean-Marie Roland, *Lettre écrite au Roi, par le ministère de l'intérieur, le 10 juin 1792* (Paris: ICS; 1792); *Sentinelle*, no. 17, 18 June 1792; Perroud, "Roland et la presse subventionnée," p. 211; *Moniteur* 13: 212.

[18] *Sentinelle*, no. 38, 25 July 1792.

ascribing to him the desire to give the war to the Austrians and establish a dictatorship. Indeed, immediately after the dismissal of the "patriot ministers," the Imprimerie began an assault on Lafayette that became nothing less than character assassination. In practically every issue of the *Sentinelle* until the September Massacres, Louvet blasted Lafayette for being "the court's general, the people's enemy, and the king's friend."[19]

There was some logic to naming Lafayette as the ringleader. A week after the Girondin ministers fell, there was an abortive insurrection by the Parisian masses. For several hours the king and queen were held captive in the Tuileries. When Lafayette got word of this, he issued a proclamation blaming the "Jacobin faction" for the riot and led several divisions of his troops back to Paris to protect the monarchy. It appeared to the Girondins that Lafayette was trying to take advantage of the situation to forward his own ambitions, and for this incident he earned their enduring hatred.[20]

At the end of June the Imprimerie published the *Correspondance du ministère de l'intérieur Roland avec le général Lafayette*, a vicious little pamphlet that sought to discredit Lafayette. The pamphlet focused on an incident that had occurred in May. Two of Lafayette's lieutenants, Lacolombe and Berthier, had met with Roland to discuss the military defense of Paris. According to Roland, one of the men made an offhand remark to the effect that "the soldiers were cowards." The next day Roland wrote a long letter to Lafayette, accusing the officers of counterrevolutionary sentiments and urging Lafayette to dismiss them. Within a week Lacolombe responded, asserting that Roland had misunderstood him; he had been talking about only a particular group of soldiers who were, in fact, the exception to the rule. Lafayette himself wrote Roland a brief response, supporting his officers' interpretation and defending their patriotism. Roland was not satisfied. In two more letters he blasted Lafayette for encouraging the growth of a new aristocracy within the army. The publication of these letters was clearly meant to dem-

[19] *Sentinelle*, no. 24, 1 July 1792, and no. 38, 25 July 1792 for examples.
[20] Reinhard, *Chute de la royauté*, pp. 308-30.

onstrate Roland's view. Yet one wonders if he was making too much of the incident. After all, the entire affair had been over one small remark by an unknown lieutenant, who himself insisted that he had been misunderstood. Considering that Lacolombe and Lafayette had promptly answered the charges, Roland's continued attacks seem unjustified. Moreover, the designation of the pamphlet as letters between Roland and Lafayette was misleading. Lafayette's letter occupied only two pages of the twenty-two page pamphlet. The affair appears to have been a desperate attempt by the ex-ministers to destroy Lafayette and the Feuillants.

Curiously, however, the Girondins did not encourage the Legislative Assembly to impeach Lafayette. While their propaganda was ruthless, they avoided taking direct action. When other left-wing radicals forced an impeachment vote, the Girondins found themselves divided and unsure what to do, and the move failed to gain a majority. The Girondins evidently believed that impeaching Lafayette might further alienate the king; their goal, after all, was not simply to destroy Lafayette, but to pressure the king to take them back into the cabinet.[21]

Throughout June and July the Girondins still hoped that the king could be persuaded to reinstate the "patriotic ministers." Thus, while the *Sentinelle* and other Cercle Social publications attacked Lafayette as an agent of the Austrian Committee, there was no call for the overthrow of the monarchy. But by the beginning of August the Girondins had become thoroughly frustrated with the king and had lost any hope of ruining the Right through propaganda. The *Sentinelle* noted that "the patience of the people is at an end," and the time had come for stronger measures.[22]

On 3 August representatives from the forty-eight Paris sections passed a resolution urging the elimination of the monarchy and the establishment of a republic. Louvet wrote a glowing report of the meeting for the *Sentinelle* and demanded "that Louis XVI be provisionally suspended and that a National Con-

---

[21] For these general developments see ibid., pp. 331-88, and Michael J. Sydenham, *The French Revolution*, pp. 108-109.

[22] *Sentinelle*, no. 44, 5 August 1792.

vention assemble to judge him." He warned readers that the Austrian Committee wanted the enemy to win the war and reestablish absolute monarchy. He urged sans-culottes to resist such treachery by any means possible:

The moment approaches when you will wait no longer. Other enemies will provoke you in other battles: you must not refuse them. They require the full development of *your physical strengths*. The slaves of the kings advance. Prepare your arms, make your strongholds, learn military strategy. Forge! Forge the pikes! And still more pikes! Pikes away! Cover yourself with iron.[23]

Was Louvet encouraging a popular insurrection? Or was he simply warning the people of a military invasion and urging them to prepare to defend themselves? The message is purposely ambiguous. While Louvet realized that the monarchy was endangered, he wanted the Girondins to be in control of the mob, not hostages of a popular panic. He and the other Girondins still hoped to use the imminent threat of a sans-culottes insurrection to pressure the king to take back Roland, Clavière, and Servan. Thus on 9 August he instructed readers to "stay calm," insisting that the overthrow of the monarchy was a matter for the Girondin-led Legislative Assembly; and he warned readers that such momentous political changes would take time. "It is physically impossible that the conduct of Louis XVI be examined, discussed, and judged in the space of twenty-four hours."[24]

While Louvet was trying to harness the power of the sans-culottes for the Girondins, the Paris sections took the issue into their own hands. On 10 August the sections led a new revolution, replacing the municipal government with a new revolutionary Commune, sacking the Tuileries (the home of the royal family), and pressuring the Legislative Assembly to suspend the king and call for elections for a National Convention. Having failed to control the pace of events, the *Sentinelle* now followed them by publishing a generous description of the insurrection. The nation, Louvet wrote, had been under siege by a gang of conspirators, which included "Lafayette with all the courtiers and

[23] *Sentinelle*, no. 44, 5 August 1792, and no. 45, 8 August 1792.
[24] *Sentinelle*, no. 46, 12 August 1792.

Louis XVI with all the kings." The preservation of the Revolution had necessitated the insurrection.[25]

Louvet had his own reasons for supporting the insurrection. The Assembly immediately recalled Roland, Clavière, and Servan, who now formed a cabinet with Monge, Lebrun, and Danton. With its friends back in power, the Imprimerie could look forward to continued prosperity and influence. But there was one immediate difficulty. Until 10 August subsidies for the *Sentinelle* and other Cercle Social publications had been drawn from funds allocated to Pétion, who had now become a victim of the insurrection. It was doubtful whether the new and more radical Commune would give financial assistance to the Imprimerie. Nonetheless, the Girondins did not have to look far for other sources. On 18 August the Assembly voted Roland 100,000 livres for the establishment of a Bureau de l'esprit public. The Assembly intended this new agency "for the printing and distribution, in the departments and the armies, of all writing appropriate for enlightening minds on the criminal plots of the enemies of the state."[26]

The Bureau de l'esprit public was a dream come true for the Imprimerie du Cercle Social. Since the beginning of the Revolution, Bonneville and his friends had urged the government to recognize the necessity for mass education by subsidizing patriotic writing and creating a "Ministry of Public Opinion." Now with many of Cercle Social men in positions of power, the state had sanctioned a propaganda machine for its own use. François Lanthenas was chosen to head the Bureau, which was created within the Division of Public Instruction of the Ministry of the Interior. Immediately Roland and Lanthenas began developing a national network of academics, clergymen, and businessmen, whose task would be to read the pamphlets and journals sent to them by the Bureau to the illiterate citizens around them. By September Roland could report to the Assembly that the program was already on its way toward success. "I have

---

[25] *Sentinelle*, no. 47, 12 August 1792.
[26] Cited in Perroud, "Roland et la presse subventionnée," p. 318. On the Bureau see also Roland, *Mémoires* 1: 92-93, 276-79; and Edith Bernardin, *Jean-Marie Roland et le ministère de l'intérieur*, pp. 513-25.

multiplied the circular letters. I have favored the distribution of writings that seemed to me the most appropriate for enlightening citizens on the state of things, and on their true interests. Perhaps I have had some success."[27]

The greatest beneficiary of the new Bureau was naturally the Imprimerie du Cercle Social. Between May and August subsidies had supported an average printing of only 1,500 copies of the *Sentinelle*. After the creation of the Bureau the increase in subsidies allowed for a much greater circulation, often exceeding 10,000 copies per issue. Nor was the *Sentinelle* alone in partaking of the good fortune. The government subsidized many other Cercle Social publications, including the *Chronique du mois* and some of Lanthenas' own works. Moreover, when Roland's assistants would travel to the provinces, they often took along a set of Cercle Social publications for free distribution.[28]

One of the most important ingredients in this expanded propaganda program was the acquisition by the Imprimerie of the *Feuille villageoise*. In many ways the *Sentinelle* and the *Feuille villageoise* were two sides of the same coin; the former was aimed at urban sans-culottes; the latter particularly designed to encourage patriotism among the peasantry. Its editors insisted that the paper "is not really a journal at all; rather, it is a course of popular instruction, where principles take precedence over facts." In this endeavor the *Feuille villageoise* appears to have succeeded better than any other journal.[29]

The *Feuille villageoise* had been founded in 1790 by Joachim Cerutti, a former priest and Paris politician who had also belonged to the Confédération des Amis de la Vérité. By preaching a Rousseauian civil religion and by appealing to radical parish

[27] Bernardin, *Jean-Marie Roland*, pp. 210-11, 510-12; Jean-Marie Roland, *Convention Nationale. Lettre du ministère de l'intérieur à la Convention Nationale, du 30 septembre 1792 . . .* (Paris: ICS, [1792]), p. 6. According to Perroud, "Roland et la presse subventionnée," p. 407, on 27 October Roland gave the Cercle Social 1,174 livres to print 50,000 copies of this pamphlet.

[28] Perroud, "Roland et la presse subventionnée," pp. 322-23, 404-409.

[29] *Feuille villageoise*, 13 December 1792, pp. 242-43; Michael L. Kennedy, *The Jacobin Clubs in the French Revolution*, p. 370. On the *Feuille villageoise* see Melvin Edelstein, *La Feuille villageoise: Communication et modernisation dans les régions rurales pendant la révolution*.

priests, the paper became an instant success and may have reached a circulation as high as 11,000. The Confédération had recognized that its own aims and spirit were akin to those of the *Feuille villageoise*. On 11 March 1791 one member "made a worthy speech concerning a work entitled the *Feuille villageoise*." Even at that early date, the speaker had urged the National Assembly to subsidize the paper so that it could be freely distributed across the nation. The Imprimerie du Cercle Social had admired Cerutti's work so much that it had commissioned Bonneville's cousin, François Bonneville, to engrave Cerutti's portrait for an issue of the *Chronique du mois*. In February 1792, Cerutti died and the paper was carried on by two other Parisian intellectuals, Philippe Grouvelle and Pierre-Louis Ginguené. At first the *Feuille villageoise* was non-ideological and almost apolitical in its instruction. But as the revolutionary factions became more sharply defined in 1792, the editors began to side with the Girondins. By the summer of 1792, they were clearly preaching the Girondin line: praising Roland, attacking Lafayette, and printing articles by men like Lanthenas and Boilleau.[30]

Desenne, the publisher of the *Feuille villageoise*, became increasingly concerned about the paper's direction. He was worried that the journal's political involvement would inhibit its popularity and effectiveness. He believed that a paper that sought to instruct rural folk should be non-ideological. After repeated warnings to Grouvelle and Ginguené, Desenne fired the editors and tried to keep control of the paper for himself. The struggle became a classic battle between editor and publisher. Grouvelle and Ginguené insisted that they should control the paper. The Girondins quickly came to their rescue. The Imprimerie du Cercle Social began publication of a new edition of the paper, and offered readers a two-month free subscription. The move worked; Desenne was forced to give up any plans for continuing his own edition.[31]

[30] *Bdf*, 15 March 1791, p. 481; *Feuille villageoise*, 2 August 1792, pp. 413-14; 26 April 1792, pp. 100-103, 535. There is some evidence that Grouvelle may have been a member of the Confédération. See *Bdf*, 11 May 1791, p. 257.

[31] *Feuille villageoise*, 5 July 1792, p. 337; 19 July 1792, p. 361; *Pf*, 7 July 1792, p. 28; *Sentinelle*, no. 29, 9 July 1792.

AFTER 10 AUGUST Paris became increasingly absorbed with the elections to the National Convention. The *Sentinelle*'s electoral propaganda offers important evidence concerning the Girondins' identity as a political faction on the eve of the elections. On 21 August the *Sentinelle* contained a slate of recommended candidates for the Convention. Of course, the list contained Louvet's closest allies, including Buzot, Pétion, Bonneville, Bancal, Lanthenas—and Louvet himself! But it also contained the names of more radical Jacobins, such as Danton, Collot d'Herbois, François Robert, and even Robespierre. When one recalls that Louvet had built his political career partly on the strength of his reputation as one of Robespierre's principal antagonists, his recommendation of Robespierre and his followers is noteworthy. This was no aberration in Girondin propaganda. Until the fall of 1792, neither the *Sentinelle* nor any other Cercle Social publication attacked Robespierre or any other radical Jacobin, save for Marat. Louvet spent all of his vindictive energy attacking the Feuillants, Lafayette, and the Court. While relations between Montagnards and Girondins were hardly intimate, throughout the summer of 1792 the latter believed that the greatest threat to the Revolution came from the Right. Even after 10 August the Girondins' primary concern was that the Feuillants would win enough seats in the Convention to reinstate the king. On 15 August Louvet warned readers of "a faction whose members [still] fill your podiums, directories, general staff, churches, mansions, and the best streets of your towns; a faction under the name of Feuillants." Thus throughout the spring and summer of 1792 the *Sentinelle* gave the sans-culottes the impression of a unified Jacobin faction working toward a democratic republic.[32]

Between 2 and 7 September 1792, Parisian sans-culottes murdered hundreds of prisoners thought to be engaged in counterrevolutionary activities, an event that came to be known as the September Massacres. The Girondins were horrified by what they saw as a complete breakdown of law and order in the capital. But the Montagnards—Jacobin supporters of Robes-

---

[32] *Sentinelle*, no. 48, 15 August 1792, and no. 52, 21 August 1792. Brissot also tried unsuccessfully to get Bonneville elected to the Convention. See Jean Jaurès, *Histoire socialiste de la Révolution française* 3: 151-53.

pierre and the Commune—saw the Massacres as a manifestation of the people's justice, and therefore justifiable. This attitude made the Montagnards the new objects of Louvet's propaganda. "The aristocracy has changed form," Louvet wrote to his working-class readers. "You no longer have to fight those who have ceased to be powerful, but you must repel those who aspire to become powerful." At the heart of this new power struggle were differing views on the nature of the Revolution. For Robespierre and the Commune, "revolutionary government" was to be established to ensure military and political victory, whereas for Louvet and the Girondins "the French Revolution is finished." The insurrection of 10 August had been necessary to topple the monarchy. But now that the Girondins were leading a republican regime, they wanted Parisians to support the government and maintain law and order. Thus the September Massacres constituted a new kind of threat. "If the insurrection against despotism is sacred," Louvet explained in comparing 10 August with the recent Massacres, "the insurrection against the republic is blasphemous. The first is virtuous, the second is criminal." Louvet went further in placing the blame for the Massacres on the Montagnards. Calculating "their successes upon the innocence of the people," the Montagnards wanted to use the municipal government as a base from which to overthrow the new Convention and rule France. Louvet insisted that such a program could only lead to anarchy and that the power of the Paris Commune had to be proportional with the rest of France. "Equality above all. Equality between men, equality between the departments, between Paris and the rest of France."[33]

Louvet's attacks in the *Sentinelle* were part of a more general campaign by the Imprimerie du Cercle Social to purge the Left of the radical Montagnards. In November the Imprimerie began the *Bulletin des Marseillois*, a short-lived but lively journal edited

---

[33] *Sentinelle*, no. 64, 20 October 1792, no. 61, 29 September 1792; Theodore Di Padova, "The Girondins and the Question of Revolutionary Government," *FHS* 9: 432-50; Marcel Dorigny, "Violence et révolution: Les Girondins et les massacres de septembre," in *Actes du colloque Girondins et Montagnards*, pp. 103-120. See also Bonneville's poem, "Sur les nuits de septembre," in the December 1792 issue of *Cdm*, and reprinted in *Les Poésies de Nicolas Bonneville* (Paris, ICS, 1793) pp. 179-80.

by the well-known Girondin deputy, Charles-Louis Barbaroux. The *Bulletin* viciously attacked Marat, Robespierre, and their followers as "impetuous anarchists who want to replace their government with a tyranny." Barbaroux tried to isolate the Montagnards by reprinting quasi-official provincial addresses that asserted that, however popular Marat and Robespierre were in Paris, they were hated in the provinces. "Legislators," announced one address to the National Convention, purportedly drafted by the executive council of a provincial department, "the Marats, the Robespierres have won our supreme contempt, even more, our horror." Barbaroux urged other provincial bodies and clubs to write the National Convention and "follow our example."[34]

Another component of the Imprimerie's new propaganda against the Montagnards was the attempt to create a moderate, anti-Montagnard constituency among the Paris sections. The Imprimerie du Cercle Social published the minutes and decrees of several friendly sections in poster form and plastered them all over Paris. For instance, on 22 September Roland paid the Imprimerie 288 livres for 6,000 posters of minutes from a recent meeting of the Section des Halles. At this meeting the leaders of the section urged Parisians to remain calm and respect private property. They pleaded that no good could come from escalating the Revolution.[35]

Meanwhile, the fight between Montagnards and Girondins spread to the Jacobin club. Now dominated by Robespierre and his followers, the Jacobins had had enough of the Girondins' attacks and expelled Brissot on 10 October, ostensibly for his anti-Commune views. Brissot responded with a biting pamphlet

[34] *Bulletin des Marseillois*, 13 November 1792, pp. 6-7. See also *Les Députés du département des Bouches-du-Rhône à la Convention Nationale, à Marat* (Paris: ICS, n.d.).

[35] *Section des Halles. Extraits des registres des délibérations de la Section des Halles ... du 17 septembre 1792 ...* (Paris: ICS, [1792]); Perroud, "Roland et la presse subventionnée," p. 405. See also *Section de Marseille. Séance permanente. Extrait des registres des délibérations de la Section du Théâtre-Français et de Marseille, du 19 août 1792 ...* (Paris: ICS, [1792]); *Section de Marseille. Du 24 septembre 1792 ...* (Paris: ICS, [1792]); *Réponse au No. 69 de Marat ... par les citoyens soldats des bataillons nationaux, canonés à Paris ...* (Paris: ICS, [1792]).

in which he promised to destroy "the anarchists who direct and
dishonor" the Jacobins. He then declared war on the Montagnards. "Three revolutions were necessary for saving France:
the first reversed despotism; the second annihilated royalty; the
third must crush anarchy. And it is to this last revolution that
. . . I have consecrated my pen and all my efforts." What followed
was a frank and bitter account of these "anarchists" and "dis-
organizers," culminating with the charge that it was "Marat . . .
Chabot, Robespierre, Collot d'Herbois, etc., . . . who, while
preaching theoretically an equality of departments, in fact elevate
Paris above all of them; who thus elevate it only to elevate
themselves, who wish the unity of the republic only that they
may consolidate the entire republic about their little center of
intrigue, and from that center dominate all the departments."
Roland gave the Imprimerie du Cercle Social more than 1,500
livres for over 7,500 copies, and it was published both in the
Chronique du mois and as a separate pamphlet.[36]

Brissot's expulsion from the Jacobins only intensified the power
struggle between Girondins and Montagnards, a struggle that
came to dominate the National Convention during the fall of
1792. On 29 October Roland delivered a report to the Convention
on the state of Paris in which he attacked the Commune and
implied that Robespierre was responsible for its mischief. As
one contemporary reported, Robespierre rose to the podium and
accused his enemies of attempting to slander him. It was easy
to invent rumors, "yet who is there among you who dares rise
and accuse me to my face?" "*Moi*," shouted Louvet from across
the hall. A tense, dangerous silence filled the room. "Yes, Robespierre," Louvet finally continued, "it is I who accuse you!"
Louvet was allowed to give a speech, the essence of which was
soon published by the Imprimerie as *A Maximilien Robespierre
et ses royalistes*. It contained all of the points made in Brissot's
pamphlet, charged with Louvet's own romantic style. Roland
partly subsidized this, too, with a gift of 500 livres for 1,000

[36] Jacques-Pierre Brissot, "A tous les républicains de France sur la Société
des Jacobins de Paris," *Cdm*, November 1792, pp. 42-43, 44-46; Perroud, "Roland et la presse subventionnée," p. 408.

copies. The Jacobin club responded a few weeks later by expelling Louvet, Lanthenas, and Roland.[37]

The Girondins were so impressed with Louvet's behavior that they decided to promote him. The publisher Badouin offered him the editorship of the *Journal des débats et décrets*, a well-known national paper that reviewed bills pending before the Convention. The Rolands urged him to accept the post, and sometime in late October or early November he joined the *Journal*. The *Sentinelle* never recovered from his departure. The Imprimerie first hired Publicola Chaussard to take Louvet's place. As a young intellectual who was later to become a professor of classics at the Université de Paris, Chaussard was at this point in his career too inexperienced to fill Louvet's shoes. He was replaced by Joseph Lavallée, who had been in charge of a huge project on French geography for the Imprimerie. But he, too, failed to imitate Louvet's unique combination of political polemic, satire, and gossip, which had made the *Sentinelle* so successful.[38]

The Imprimerie du Cercle Social decided to end the *Sentinelle* and begin a new, different kind of paper, whose editors would include Chaussard, Lavallée, and Bonneville. On 21 November 1792 the last issue of the *Sentinelle* was posted on Paris street corners. It was largely an attack upon Louis XVI and a call for his trial. Roland had commissioned François Bonneville to engrave a picture for the issue. In the center was a large arm with a clenched fist breaking through a brick wall. In the middle was the caption, taken from the Book of Daniel: "God hath numbered thy kingdom and finished it. Thou art weighed in the balance and art found wanting."[39]

[37] John Moore, *A Journal During a Residence in France from the Beginning of August to the Middle of December 1792* 2: 298-99, 305-309; also cited in J. M. Thompson, *Leaders of the French Revolution*, p. 100; Perroud, "Roland et la presse subventionnée," p. 408; A. Aulard, ed., *La Société des Jacobins. Recueil des documents pour l'histoire du club des Jacobins de Paris* 4: 519.

[38] Undated letter from L. Reynier to Roland, reprinted in Buchez and Roux, *Histoire parlementaire de la Révolution française* 28: 104.

[39] *Sentinelle*, no. 72, 21 November 1792; Daniel 5:26-27.

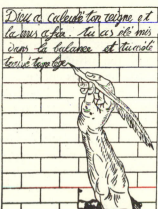

DURING 1792 the Imprimerie du Cercle Social reached the zenith of its development and influence. In the *Sentinelle*, the *Feuille villageoise*, and the *Chronique du mois*, it had control of three important and popular revolutionary journals. Perhaps more significant, each paper was aimed at a different sector of the public (the *Chronique du mois* for intellectuals, the *Sentinelle* for townspeople, and the *Feuille villageoise* for peasants), so the Imprimerie was able to spread its Girondism over a remarkably wide spectrum. Each month the publishing company would bring out a new book or pamphlet by well-known writers like

Mercier, Lanthenas, and Paine. Finally, its chiefs were among the most powerful men in the country, and they were able to obtain secret government subsidies for many of the group's publications.

Louvet's own rise to political power and the great success of his newspaper is the best example of the rise of the Imprimerie du Cercle Social and its intimate relationship with the Girondins. But Louvet's *Sentinelle* also reveals one essential reason why the Girondins ultimately failed to keep the political power they worked so hard to obtain. The Girondins established the *Sentinelle* specifically to develop popular support among the Parisian sans-culottes. While Louvet effectively presented Girondin policies in a language accessible to the people, he became increasingly out of touch with the attitudes of his readers. During the course of 1792, the Parisian sans-culottes came to believe that only a more interventionist, centralized, and "revolutionary" government could win the war with Austria and secure the Revolution.[40] Before the September Massacres, the *Sentinelle* ignored these issues; afterwards, it treated them with hostility and contempt. Louvet tried to shape the opinions of the sans-culottes, but he never seriously attempted to respond to their needs. His rhetorical use of an aristocratic conspiracy and of an imminent Fayettist dictatorship worked well. But his attacks upon the Montagnards and the Commune (who had become popular heroes to the sans-culottes) was a costly mistake. The fact that the Girondins would so readily allow Louvet to leave the *Sentinelle* reveals how diminished the value of a genuine sans-culotte constituency had become to them. Louvet's resignation from the paper confirmed what Brissot had written after his expulsion from the Jacobins: the Revolution would not move forward until the Girondins or their "anarchist" adversaries had been eliminated. Clearly, the next time the sans-culottes rose to action, their object would be the heads of the Girondins.

[40] On the rise of the sans-culottes see Albert Soboul, *Les sans-culottes parisiens en l'an II.*

10

Daily News:
The *Bulletin des Amis*
de la Vérité

JEAN-MARIE ROLAND (1734-1793). Minister of the Interior (March 1792-June 1792 and August 1792-January 1793). Puritanical, austere, and rationalist, Roland was the Girondin's most effective administrator, and one of the important brains behind the Cercle Social.

We often talk about what the Republic owes its citizens; but let us first talk about what citizens owe the Republic.

Bulletin des Amis de la Vérité, 13 April 1793, p. 2.

THE Imprimerie du Cercle Social began the *Bulletin des Amis de la Vérité* as soon as it became clear that the *Sentinelle* could not continue without Louvet. The *Bulletin* was first announced in November 1792, and readers could see that it was a new kind of project for the Imprimerie. Until now all of the Imprimerie's journals had been of a particular genre and directed to a specific readership: the *Bouche de fer* had been a club organ, the *Chronique du Mois* was a series of sophisticated essays for intellectuals, the *Feuille villageoise* was geared to peasants, and the *Sentinelle* was written for sans-culottes in the streets. In contrast, the *Bulletin des Amis de la Vérité* was to be a "review of the work and disposition of the National Convention; of events, plays, announcements of useful books, news, diplomacy, and various stories." The new journal hoped to appeal to a broader readership than its predecessors, including "teachers, heads of families, and legislators of all nations."[1]

From a technical point of view, the *Bulletin* was the Imprimerie's most ambitious project. Not only did the paper appear seven days per week, but it was printed in a large folio format that contained four pages per issue. The *Bulletin* published more material in a single week than the *Chronique, Feuille villageoise*, and *Sentinelle* combined. Yet the price of the paper was no higher than most other Girondin dailies, suggesting that the Imprimerie might have obtained subsidies from some outside source.

To produce this large newspaper, the Imprimerie employed more than thirty contributors. Advertisements promised that the "same men who have worked on our previous publications ... will work on this one," but most of the articles were actually written by more minor authors, such as Gabriel Feydel, Alexandre Belair, Publicola Chaussard, Joseph Lavallée, and François

[1] *Cdm*, November 1792, p. 83; *BAV*, 1 January 1793, p. 4, 9 March 1793, p. 2.

Puthod. One fortunate addition was Bonneville's friend, Claude Milscent, editor of the *Créole patriote*, a Girondin paper that advocated civil rights for free persons of color. In February 1793 the Imprimerie bought the *Créole* and merged it with the *Bulletin*.[2]

The *Bulletin* was begun at a time when the Girondins were in the midst of a political struggle with the Jacobins over control of the Convention, a struggle that would result in May 1793 in the expulsion of the Girondins from the Convention and the collapse of the Imprimerie du Cercle Social. Most modern historians of the French Revolution present the Girondins as moderate republicans supported by the provincial towns, while the Jacobins, or Montagnards, developed a more radical form of republicanism, driven on by the Paris Commune and the sans-culottes.[3] In recent years this simple and rather static view of the political situation has come under criticism. Michael Sydenham has argued that the Girondins were actually indistinguishable from the broad majority of the Convention, and that the notion of a Girondin party was itself a myth developed by the Jacobins. Other historians, while disagreeing with Sydenham's conclusions, have developed other interpretations of the struggle that vary from the orthodox view.[4] The *Bulletin des Amis de la Vérité* offers a unique vantage point from which to examine the Jacobin-Girondin struggle and the more general demise of the Girondins during the spring of 1793.

THE IMPRIMERIE du Cercle Social viewed the *Bulletin des Amis de la Vérité* as a major Girondin organ, devoted to defending the Girondins against the Jacobins. More important, the Imprimerie was now ready to admit that it was not simply a publishing company spreading enlightenment across the planet, but was also the mouthpiece for a group of politicians who were struggling to maintain their leadership of the Convention. This attitude is best illustrated in the very title of the journal. Until

---

[2] *Cdm*, November 1792, p. 85; *Créole patriote*, 5 February 1793, p. 1116; *BAV*, 21 February 1793, p. 2, 23 February 1793, pp. 2-3.

[3] E.g., Albert Mathiez, *Girondins et Montagnards*, Chapter 1.

[4] See Introduction, note 6.

the end of 1792, the term "Amis de la Vérité" had been used to describe the members of the Cercle Social's club, the Confédération des Amis de la Vérité, which had not met since July 1791. Even at that time, the term meant little more than a person who was a lover of truth and enlightenment in some vague sense. But with the start of the *Bulletin*, the term Amis de la Vérité took on a much different meaning: it now referred to the specific group of people who had been with the Cercle Social since its beginning. The *Bulletin* went to great length to convince readers that these men had been working together for a long time: "Where were you," the *Bulletin* rhetorically asked the Jacobins, "In '89 when we not simply talked but acted to reunite the electors and the districts of the whole country?" Where were you, they asked again, "in the first federative assemblies of the *Amis de la Vérité* where we organized a civic education through publicizing and holding our meetings *of 6-7 thousand people?*"[5]

The *Bulletin des Amis de la Vérité* presented itself not simply as the journal of friends of truth, but rather the bulletin of the men of the Cercle Social. "The success of the *Bouche de fer*," they claimed, "prepared the way for the success of the *Chronique du mois*, filled with valuable articles by our most celebrated writers. These works won Europe's attention and will assure the same influence to the *Bulletin des Amis de la Vérité*." The Imprimerie repeatedly made this claim and repeatedly stressed the continuity of the group: "On 28 July 1791, the Amis de la Vérité and their *Bouche de fer* promised to resuscitate their free organization with devotion." The Imprimerie acknowledged that the time had not yet come "to reopen our federated assemblies . . . it suffices to publish a daily bulletin that, by placing men and facts under the true viewpoint, will aid all *Amis de la Vérité*." Thus the *Bulletin* was intended to be the collective voice of the Cercle Social and the "true viewpoint" was undoubtedly Girondin.[6]

The *Bulletin* laid equal stress on the cohesiveness and continuity of the Jacobins, albeit in a negative sense. The paper

---

[5] *Cdm*, November 1792, p. 81.
[6] *BAV*, 1 January 1793, pp. 1-2. See also a much later reiteration of this same theme in *Le Bien informé*, 28 February 1798, Supplement, p. 4.

described a Jacobin club that had always been jealous, exclusive, insincere, and that was constantly trying to ruin the Cercle Social. For example, it discussed how, during the summer of 1791, a group of Jacobins had wanted to use the club as a vehicle for installing the duc d'Orléans on the throne. But fortunately the pure republicanism of the Cercle Social thwarted this plot. "It was the *Bouche de fer* which on that day discovered your intrigues and enlightened you." To support its claim the *Bulletin* reproduced republican petitions published by the Cercle Social after the king had flown to Varennes.[7]

In this fashion the Imprimerie du Cercle Social tried to show that the Jacobins had consistently attempted to steer the Revolution off course. Orléanists, elitists, aristocrats, corporatists, and anarchists—the Jacobins were all of these things, and were therefore the Revolution's main obstacle to the establishment of political stability. "Who are the *monsters* who poison all of the sources of public prosperity?" the *Bulletin* asked in one early issue.

The public accuses Marat, and his pupil Robespierre, and Danton, who each in his turn, fears the public and terrorizes it; and this crowd of dark conspirators that we see agitating each other at the moment of anarchy are like insects in a spoiled liqueur.[8]

Elsewhere the *Bulletin* urged "that the anarchists Marat, his pupil Robespierre, and Danton, and Bazire, and Chabot, etc., be chased out of the Convention; then peace will reign in France."[9]

In painting the Cercle Social as a republican institution existing since the Bastille, and conversely, "Jacobinism" as having always been "an abominable aristocracy,"[10] the *Bulletin* was clearly stretching the truth for its own political purposes. The Cercle Social had not been a purely republican movement since 1789: in 1789 the Cercle Social did not exist. When the Fauchetins created the Confédération des Amis de la Vérité in 1790, its purpose was intellectual rather than political. After the massacre

---

[7] *BAV*, 1 January 1793, p. 3, 3 January 1793, p. 3.
[8] *BAV*, 1 January 1793, p. 4, 2 January 1793, p. 4.
[9] *BAV*, 8 January 1793, p. 1.
[10] *BAV*, 5 March 1793, p. 3.

at the Champ de Mars in July 1791, the members of the Cercle Social joined the Jacobins en masse, and the Imprimerie became little more than a mouthpiece for that club. Moreover, in March 1792, the men who had begun the Cercle Social, and who emerged as part of the Girondins in the Legislative Assembly, dropped their republican rhetoric and accepted ministerial appointments under Louis XVI. Republicanism reentered the Cercle Social only after the 10 August insurrection.

Likewise, the Jacobin Club had never been a group of like-minded men united in action or beliefs; in fact, there never was anything called "Jacobinism." Since its establishment in 1789, the Jacobin club had been a vehicle for various political groups who had used its podium to gain national recognition. At least three periods in the history of the Jacobins can be distinguished. Before the king's flight to Varennes the club had been dominated by constitutional monarchists. While it is true that a small number of them hoped to get the duc d'Orléans to replace his cousin on the throne, the vast majority supported Louis XVI and left the Jacobins on the eve of the massacre of the Champ de Mars to start the Feuillant club. Brissot and his friends then dominated the Jacobins until the summer of 1792, when the Montagnards won control of the club. A few months later the Girondins were expelled from the Jacobins. Thus the history of the Jacobins between 1790 and 1793 is one of tremendous change and almost continuous political struggle. For the *Bulletin* to describe it in terms of a continuous personnel and ideology is a brazen example of propaganda.[11]

The *Bulletin* also misrepresented the relations between Girondins and Jacobins. Between 1789 and 1791 Fauchet, Brissot, and Bonneville had enjoyed a close relationship with Cordelier democrats like Danton. We have already noted the degree to which they cooperated during the Paris Municipal Revolution and the crisis over the king's flight to Varennes. The split within the democratic camp surfaced during the debates over declaring war on Austria, when the Girondins entered the ministry during

[11] Gérard Walter, *Histoire des Jacobins*, passim; Michael Kennedy, *The Jacobin Clubs in the French Revolution*, passim.

the spring of 1792, but did not become significant until the Feuillants were politically liquidated in the summer of 1792. An all-out struggle between Girondins and Jacobins over control of the Convention is not evident until the September Massacres, which the Jacobins accepted as popular justice, but which horrified the Girondins.

Thus the *Bulletin des Amis de la Vérité* projected the Girondin-Jacobin struggle back to the beginning of the Revolution, distorting the real nature of both groups and their relationship to one another in fundamental ways. One obvious effect of this propaganda was to polarize the two groups even further. The political identity of the Girondins was clearly not simply a myth created by the Jacobins. On the contrary, evidence from the *Bulletin* reveals that the Girondin leaders of the Imprimerie du Cercle Social were just as eager to create an unbridgeable gulf between the two groups. "When we publicly proposed the grand idea of a federated pact between nations and began the Cult of the Law—formidable propaganda that aroused friends of liberty everywhere," wrote the Imprimerie's leaders to the Jacobins in the first issue of the *Bulletin*,

you accused us with insolence of not loving the constitution, which today, by your admission, was not a constitution at all, but an arbitrary government. You now propagate all these principles which are ours, and yet you still try to persecute us.[12]

In this passage the *Bulletin* manipulated the pronoun "you." In the first sentence it refers to the Jacobins of 1790; that is, Lafayette, Duport, the Lameths, and others; while in the second sentence, "you" refers to the Jacobins of 1792-1793; that is, Robespierre, Marat, and Danton. Since these two groups were completely different from one another, the charge is meaningless and absurd. Here is an example of the Girondins creating a myth about the continuity of the Jacobins.

If "you" meant the Jacobins, what did the *Bulletin* mean by "we"? No doubt they meant the leaders of the Amis de la Vérité. But who precisely were the Amis de la Vérité? To what extent

---

[12] *BAV*, 1 January 1793, p. 1.

does the Amis de la Vérité correspond with current ideas of the Girondins? The Imprimerie du Cercle Social provided a partial answer in the January 1793 issue of the *Chronique du mois*, published at roughly the same time as the first issues of the *Bulletin*. In another scathing attack upon the Jacobins, the editors drew up a list of the members of the "Parti des Maratistes" and the "Parti National":[13]

Parti des Maratistes	*Parti National*	
Marat	Condorcet	Lanjuinais
Robespierre	Pétion	Dusaulx
Tallien	Brissot	Mercier
Bourdon	Sieyès	Guyton
Bentabole	Rabaud	Manuel
Camille Desmoulins	Buzot	Barère
Panis	Guadet	Lanthenas
Robert	Vergniaud	Fermond
Clootz	Kersaint	Grégoire
Collot d'Herbois	Gensonné	Bancal
Garnier	Louvet	Gorsas
Chabot	Grangeneuve	Dulaure
Bazire	Barbaroux	Carra
Merlin	Garran	Salles
Chales (exchanoine)	Jean-de-Brie	Mailhe, etc.
Pontecoulant (ci-d. marq.)	Creuzé-la-touche	
Lepelletier de St.-Fargeau		
Duhem		

The Maratistes included virtually all of the Jacobin leaders. In fact, out of its nineteen members, only one was not Montagnard (Pontecoulant). The Parti National, on the other hand, contained Brissot's closest allies. Twenty-four of its thirty-one names are included in Sydenham's Inner Sixty, the core of the Girondins.[14]

Some important conclusions can be drawn from these lists. First, it is clear that the Girondins, or at least those Girondins who directed the Imprimerie du Cercle Social, wanted the public to think of them as the political faction best representing the

---

[13] *Cdm*, January 1793, pp. 78-79.
[14] Sydenham, *The Girondins*, p. 229; Patrick, *The Men of the First Republic*, pp. 317-39.

national interest. In this sense, an Ami de la Vérité was any supporter of the "Parti National," and the *Bulletin des Amis de la Vérité* meant the daily newspaper of the "Parti National's" supporters. At this same time, the *Chronique du mois* stopped listing the names of its own editors on its title page and simply noted that it too was edited by "Amis de la Vérité," suggesting that the name had definite political overtones. Likewise, the Imprimerie du Cercle Social wanted the public to think of the Jacobins as a small group of Paris-based politicians who were conspiring against the nation.

The Imprimerie wanted to portray the Girondins as the party representing the best interests of the Convention against the Commune. "If peace and fraternity reign in the Convention, it will reign in Paris, in all the whole country and in the armies. Then neighboring peoples will unite with you against their tyrants in order to share your happiness." The public was repeatedly urged to support the Convention's more moderate elements. "Unite yourselves from the ends of the universe, in spirit and in truth, to the National Convention of France." The Montagnards were painted as ambitious politicians who used the sans-culottes and the threat of popular insurrection to intimidate the Convention. "Republicans: remember that you have only one evil to fear: anarchy . . . rally yourselves to the Convention. All is there." In contrast to the scorn displayed for the Montagnards, the *Bulletin* repeatedly praised the Girondin leaders of the Convention. Brissot, Gensonné, and Vergniaud exhibited "all the principles of a true republican who respects the sovereignty of the nation."[15]

This Girondin viewpoint was best summarized by Brissot in an article published in the January issue of the *Chronique du mois*.[16] "The patriot party is divided," the article began. "That's how it had to be. Those who fought royalty under the same banner spoke the same language, but internally they did not share the same views nor the same principles." The Girondins

[15] *BAV*, 31 January 1793, p. 1, 5 January 1793, p. 3, 5 March 1793, p. 3, 7 January 1793, p. 2.
[16] Brissot, "De la marche des accapeurs," *Cdm*, January 1793, pp. 46-52.

were the faction trying to develop rational political institutions based upon the ideas of the Enlightenment:

They envision the establishment of the perfection of human reason, and the restitution of life's comforts for the impoverished classes of the people. They envision a perfect equality of rights, yet an equality supported upon laws, upon respect for properties, upon security, upon the submission to the constituted authorities. They envision places conferred by the people to the talented and the virtuous. There they envision public prosperity resulting from this preference.

The Jacobins, on the other hand, were arousing the irrational passions of the lower orders. "The doctrine of these dangerous men can be reduced to this one principle: *to incessantly excite the multitude against its magistrates, and to always place themselves on the side of the multitude.*" Brissot explicitly noted that the Girondins represented the "people," while the Jacobins claimed to serve the "multitude." "But the multitude, which is not the people, is often injurious and misguided."

The Girondins nevertheless half-heartedly tried to persuade this "multitude" to follow them and ignore the Jacobins. In a "New Year's Greeting From the Amis de la Vérité to Sans-Culottes," the *Bulletin* urged Paris shopkeepers and artisans to realize that there was no need for further insurrections, and that political stability could only develop when they gave their full support to the Girondin leadership in the Convention.

Dear sans-culottes! All the roads that lead honest artisans to prosperity are equally open to everyone. ... The basis of social equality is laid; and thanks to the zeal and watchfulness of these immortal geniuses [the Girondins], whose reputations the assassins of September vainly try to stain, the Amis de la Vérité, with sure hope of success, wish good sans-culottes all the best in accomplishing their greatest dreams.[17]

In fact, many of the sans-culottes' dreams would be realized during 1793. But unfortunately for the Amis de la Vérité, those dreams included replacing the Girondins with a Jacobin government whose radical and centralizing policies would be more to the liking of the sans-culottes.

[17] *BAV*, 2 January 1793, pp. 2-3.

These Imprimerie du Cercle Social publications demonstrate that the Girondins wanted the public to see them as the group of political leaders that best represented the Convention. But this does not necessarily mean that the Girondins really were a well-organized political party whose members behaved in a concerted fashion; the evidence presented so far only shows that the Girondins helped perpetuate such a myth. In fact, as the trial of Louis XVI demonstrates, there is little reason to believe that the Convention's Girondin deputies voted as a bloc. Although the Girondins were friends who published together and were often politically active together, they did not organize themselves into a formal party or even into a cohesive faction in the Convention. In contrast to the discipline of the Jacobins, the Girondins' loose structure was one of the principal reasons for their demise.

THE TRIAL of Louis XVI dominated the Convention's attention between November 1792 and January 1793. There were a number of questions that the Convention had to answer: Who should try the king? If found guilty, what should his sentence be? Should the people be allowed to ratify the decision through a popular vote? On these and other issues, Brissot and his friends found no automatic solutions. Their relationship to the king had been ambiguous. During the summer of 1791, they were among the most vociferous republicans, arguing that Louis' flight to Varennes constituted an abdication of the throne. But when they entered the Legislative Assembly, they accepted the monarchist Constitution of 1791, and tried to work with the king. By the summer of 1792 they were even quietly renouncing republicanism in the hope that Louis XVI would reinstate the "patriot" ministers. When the monarchy was overthrown, they became loyal supporters of the republic, but their attitude toward the fate of the king remained ambivalent.[18]

During the trial the Girondins never expected that they would

[18] The following account is based on David P. Jordan, *The King's Trial: Louis XVI vs. the French Revolution*; Michael Walzer, ed., *Regicide and Revolution: Speeches at the Trial of Louis XVI*; Patrick, *Men of the First Republic*, pp. 39-107; Sydenham, *Girondins*, pp. 133-44.

develop a party line, and each Girondin developed his own particular opinion. Some believed that the king had done nothing illegal, since Article 2, Chapter II, of the Constitution of 1791 specifically stated that the "person of the king is inviolable and sacred." Others believed him guilty of treason but thought that executing the king would only antagonize a great part of the French population; still others believed him guilty, but wanted his sentence determined by a national referendum.

In contrast, the Jacobins stood united in their belief that the king must be tried by the Convention and sentenced to death, not only for his treacherous crimes against the nation but also as a revolutionary symbol that the age of monarchy was over. Their unity stood in sharp contrast to the varying views of the Girondins. In many ways, the Girondin-Jacobin conflict over the trial resembles the Feuillant-Girondin struggle of a year earlier over the declaration of war: just as the Girondins had used the war to divide and weaken the Feuillants, so the Jacobins now used the trial to divide and weaken the Girondins. In short, the Jacobins exploited Girondin disunity to win control of the Convention. "Roland and the Girondins," commented one contemporary observer,

seem to be in something of the same situation that the court was in a little before the tenth of August. The party of Danton and Robespierre are as earnest for the destruction of the first as ever they were for that of the second; and they seem preparing to attempt it by the same means.[19]

One of the ways the Jacobins expressed their strength was by continually interrupting and heckling Girondin speakers. The trial was marked by constant disruptions and a general breakdown of parliamentary order. The Girondins thought that these incidents would offend most deputies and strengthen their popularity, and they often responded to Jacobin intimidation by reminding the Convention that the Montagnards were the sup-

[19] John Moore, *A Journal During a Residence in France From the Beginning of August to the Middle of December 1792*, 2: 369-70.

porters of the September Massacres. One early issue of the *Bulletin* even went so far as to describe the Jacobins as "cannibals."[20]

On 9 January the *Bulletin* told readers that "the venerable Dusaulx," one of the deputies closest to the Imprimerie du Cercle Social, "indignant at seeing the Convention forever disgraced by the enemies of the public good, demanded an end to the scandalous disorders. Not being heard, he proposed his resignation." If Dusaulx intended this bluff as a way to quiet the Jacobins, it backfired. Leonard Bourdon, a staunch Jacobin, led a chorus of applause from the Montagnard benches, sarcastically welcoming the resignation. "But this resignation was not accepted," the *Bulletin* stated. "The frenzied Bourdon was called to order, and thanks to his frenzied colleagues, order was reestablished only after a very long time."[21]

Despite the fact that Bourdon was stopped, the Girondins came to realize that the Convention would not tolerate the interruptions if a large number of deputies were not already sympathetic to the Jacobin viewpoint. Curiously, during the second week in January, the *Bulletin des Amis de la Vérité* stopped attacking the Jacobins and tried to reverse the image of a polarized Convention. "You have been told that there are two parties in the Convention," the *Bulletin* stated,

but they probably have not told you that the situation is absolutely not a war for and against truth, nor between royalism and democracy, nor finally between two parties in which one wants the total downfall and the other the complete salvation of the fatherland. Rather, it is a struggle of egoism and stubbornness, unfortunately too common among men, which makes them say: I must have it my way, I want it like this, because in order to come to the same outcome, I will at least have the glory that the benefits will flow from the channel that I dug.[22]

According to this article, the struggle between Girondins and Jacobins was a personal one; on questions of ideology and loyalty to the Revolution there were no differences. This view was in marked contrast to earlier issues of the *Bulletin* and other Imprimerie propaganda. Now, on the eve of the voting over the

[20] *BAV*, 2 January 1793, p. 1.
[21] *BAV*, 9 January 1793, p. 1.
[22] *BAV*, 12 January 1793, p. 2.

trial of Louis XVI, the Imprimerie du Cercle Social wanted the public to believe that "it is certainly not the Brissotins nor the Robespierrois who spread lies among you. It is the aristocrats, and no one else."[23]

This change was not an aberration, but represented a significant and permanent turning point in Imprimerie du Cercle Social propaganda. After four months of attacking the Jacobins for being anarchists, assassins, and dictators, the Imprimerie abandoned this hostile voice, and returned to more neutral and vague attacks against "aristocrats." Unfortunately neither the Imprimerie du Cercle Social nor its Girondin leaders in the Convention gave an explanation for the change. But the reason is clear: the Girondins realized that the Jacobin attempt to use the trial of Louis XVI to weaken the Girondin leadership of the Convention was working.

The Jacobins' growing power was demonstrated during the culmination of the trial, the four days of voting that began on 15 January 1793. Nearly everyone agreed that the king was guilty of treason. But where the Jacobins were almost unanimous in their call for his immediate execution, the Girondins tended to want to save the king's life, either through a national referendum on the question or, if that failed, through a reprieve. But there were many Girondins who voted with the Montagnards, and several who went their own way. For example, of the fifteen Girondin deputies who wrote for the Imprimerie du Cercle Social, only ten voted with Brissot for a national referendum on the king; five voted with the Montagnards against the referendum. If the decision on the referendum was "a test of the effectiveness of Girondin leadership," as some historians suggest, the Girondins partially defeated themselves. Whatever the cause, the majority of the Convention sided with the Jacobins on all of the major issues. Louis was found guilty of treason and sentenced to death without reprieve or referendum.[24]

The outcome of the trial marked a major political defeat for

---

[23] Ibid.
[24] Patrick, *Men of the First Republic*, p. 88. The ten who voted moderate were Brissot, Fauchet, Barbaroux, Kersaint, Dusaulx, Bancal, Louvet, Garran-Coulon, Creuzé-Latouche, and Gensonné. The five who voted with the Montagnards were Condorcet, Mercier, Lanthenas, Paine, and Boilleau.

the Girondins, weakening their leadership of the Convention. Their disunity was underscored by the *Bulletin des Amis de la Vérité*, which offered no editorial comment on the outcome, but briefly reviewed how the leading Girondins had voted. The review gives a good indication of the wide variety of opinions within the Girondins. Barbaroux voted for death and asked that the royal family be immediately banished from France; Gensonné voted for death, but requested that the minister of justice pursue those responsible for the September Massacres; Guadet and Vergniaud voted for death, but hoped the Convention would delay the actual execution; Condorcet's opposition to capital punishment in principle obliged him to prefer the next heaviest sentence; Lanthenas voted for death, but hoped the Convention would later pardon Louis; Brissot and Louvet refused to agree to a regicide until it had been sanctioned by the people in a national vote; and finally, Paine, Mercier, Fauchet, and Garran-Coulon voted against death, hoping to convince the Convention to imprison the king and expel him from France after the war.[25]

The Montagnard victory over the Girondins was brought home on 21 January when the former were able to secure passage of a bill eliminating the Bureau de l'esprit public. For months the Montagnards had attacked the Bureau as little more than a propaganda device for Roland and his friends. With some truth Marat had charged that Roland misused the Bureau's funds for his own political purposes. Roland himself interpreted the vote on the Bureau as a vote of no confidence. The day after its elimination he resigned his post as minister of the interior and retired from politics.[26]

After Roland's resignation the situation for the Girondins deteriorated. Some, like Armand-Guy Kersaint, resigned from the Convention in disgust; while this may have helped soothe his wounded pride, it did nothing for his cause. Others, such as François Lanthenas, had already broken with his old group of friends for personal reasons. In December Lanthenas had found

[25] *BAV*, 19 January 1793, p. 2.

[26] Manon Roland, *Mémoires* 1: 116; Jean Jaurès, *Histoire socialiste de la Révolution française* 3: 599; Charles Le Guin, *Roland de la Platière: A Public Servant in the Eighteenth Century*, p. 110.

himself in love with Madame Roland, his old friend. "You who invoke reason and protest against the passions," wrote Madame Roland to Lanthenas, "be content to be my friend." But the role of friend was not good enough. Lanthenas broke with the Rolands and drifted closer to Jacobin circles.[27]

These setbacks not only affected the Girondins in the Convention, they also had a direct bearing on the Imprimerie du Cercle Social. The Imprimerie had been the most important Girondin mouthpiece and a large beneficiary of the Bureau de l'esprit public. Now, with the Bureau gone and the Girondins weakened, the Imprimerie's future was uncertain. Although the Imprimerie managed to stay afloat for six more months, it significantly reduced the number of pamphlets it published, and in many ways ceased to be a center for Girondin political propaganda.

This important change in the Imprimerie's direction is evident in the *Bulletin des Amis de la Vérité*. After the king's trial, the *Bulletin* refrained from any polemics. It tried to present news more objectively. Whenever Robespierre, Danton, or even Marat were mentioned, the paper simply reported what they had said without editorial comment. In March the *Bulletin* began reporting news of the Commune on a daily basis, again with little editorial comment. On 13 March the paper simply reprinted a declaration from the Section des Quatre Nations attacking Roland, Brissot, Guadet, Louvet, and their allies and announcing the formation of an "insurrectional committee."[28]

In fact, the *Bulletin* began to turn its attention away from controversial partisan struggles altogether. We have seen how in the fall of 1790 the Cercle Social temporarily abandoned a strong political posture after being discredited in the Paris Municipal Revolution. Now during the spring of 1793 a similar phenomenon occurred. The *Bulletin* began to devote more and more space to civil religion and public education, issues that had

---

[27] Patrick, *Men of the First Republic*, p. 86; *Lettres de Mme Roland* 2: 453; C. A. Dauban, *Etude sur Madame Roland et son temps, suivie des lettres inédites de Madame Roland à Buzot*, 1: 336.

[28] *BAV*, 28 March 1793, p. 1, 13 March 1793, p. 2.

always been important to the Cercle Social, but which now took on a special significance.

THE RENEWED interest in educational matters was a conscious decision proclaimed in all three Imprimerie du Cercle Social journals. "We beseech our subscribers to turn all their attention toward public instruction. On this all-too-neglected matter depends the safety of the state, and the happiness of future generations." Indeed, the aim of the *Bulletin des Amis de la Vérité* itself "was especially to prepare public instruction." Despite the importance of economic, military, and political activities, more pages of the *Bulletin* were devoted to educational topics than to any other single issue.[29]

This new focus was not only the result of the Girondins' political failures but was also associated with efforts in the Convention to pass legislation on a national system of public education. The Imprimerie took great interest in the Committee of Public Instruction, which was in charge of formulating a plan for a national system of public education. Discussion within the Committee focused on the plans of two Cercle Social authors, Condorcet and Lanthenas. Both schemes included free elementary education for all citizens and more specialized training in higher education. The system was to be regulated by intellectuals, who would be formed into a National Society for the Arts and Sciences. The Committee accepted all aspects of their plans except for leadership by intellectuals. Many deputies feared that such a system would merely continue the elitist nature of the academies and would subvert any move to democratize culture.[30]

While more pressing political concerns prevented an educational program from getting off the ground, the Imprimerie repeatedly urged the Convention to pass some plan and specifically defended those proposed by Condorcet and Lanthenas. Condorcet himself used the pages of the *Chronique du mois* to

[29] *BAV*, 11 February 1793, p. 2, 19 January 1793, p. 2; see also *Cdm*, February 1793, p. 80; and *Feuille villageoise*, 31 January 1793, pp. 428-429.

[30] On these plans and the Committee's activities see M. J. Guillaume, ed., *Procès-verbaux du Comité de l'instruction publique de la Convention Nationale*, vol. 1.

refute the charge that his plan would lead to "intellectual cor-
porations." The Cercle Social went beyond Condorcet's mild
proposals, suggesting that the government subsidize intellectuals
to write textbooks and hire them as inspectors to ensure the
schools' patriotism and uniformity.[31]

The *Bulletin des Amis de la Vérité* asked three young writers,
Publicola Chaussard, Joseph Lavallée, and François Puthod, to
write a series of articles on public instruction. These authors
insisted that no matter what specific plan was passed, France
could not afford to go another day without some system of public
instruction. "Cannons will win the Revolution, but public instruction will consolidate it: it is the basis of the Revolution."
They sometimes described learning in almost mystical terms:
"When I enter a library, when I open a book, all prejudices
leave me en masse [and new ideas] penetrate through my pores,
arriving victorious in my mind." They argued that there was a
symbiotic relationship between the republic and national education. In the state of nature, formal education was superfluous.
In despotic societies ranging from the Oriental model to the Old
Regime, public instruction became a tool that undermined the
government. But only in a free society, where education "shows
to each what he can and should be," was public education an
absolute necessity.[32]

Closely associated with its efforts in public instruction were
the Imprimerie's renewed efforts to establish a revolutionary
civil religion. The relationship between a system of national
schools and a civil religion is best demonstrated by the eighteenth-century distinction between "instruction" and "education."

Public instruction is only one part of a vast system of national education.
... An education which ... embraces all: religion and the laws (which
must be the same thing), institutions, rituals, customs, letters, arts,
manners, and morality.[33]

---

[31] *Cdm*, January 1793, p. 29; *BAV*, 27 January 1793, p. 3, and 7 March 1793,
p. 3.

[32] *BAV*, 6 March 1793, p. 3, 27 January 1793, pp. 2-3, 7 March 1793, p. 2.

[33] Ibid., 31 March 1793, p. 2; see also Guillaume, *Procès-verbaux*, 1: 205-206.

In other words, "instruction" was a narrower term referring to those subjects that would improve the mind; that is, reading, writing, and arithmetic. An "education," on the other hand, was aimed at the heart as well as the mind. Its purpose was to mould the entire personality of the citizen. "Civil religion," a term the Cercle Social had borrowed from Rousseau, was the generic name given to the formal organization of an educational plan aimed directly at the heart. Cercle Social authors claimed that in a republic like France, civil religion was as fundamental to public life as the constitution, and ultimately originated from the same social compact of the people. "From the sanctity of this act comes *civil religion*; this cult of the law that uplifts the soul, advances thought, gives burning love for the fatherland, conserves beautiful and fraternal harmony between members, and supports the superb edifice of the state."[34]

During the spring of 1793, the Imprimerie published the works of two thinkers who developed very different ideas on civil religion. The first, Sylvain Maréchal, was a notorious atheist, soon to be leader of the Dechristianization movement during the Terror, and one of Babeuf's fellow-conspirators in 1796. Maréchal believed that a new, enlightened revolutionary cult must supplant Christianity. While this new faith would shun the supernatural, it would invent new rituals to preserve the values of the Revolution. In the *Bulletin*, Maréchal published lyrics for patriotic hymns that were actually sung in civic festivals. The Imprimerie also published his *Almanach des républicains*, which developed a set of republican holidays intended to replace traditional Christian holidays.[35]

The other thinker was one of the best-known mystical philosophers in late eighteenth-century France, Louis-Claude de Saint-Martin. As a young man he had studied law in Paris and had become engrossed in the works of the philosophes. Within a few years, however, Saint-Martin had left Paris for Bordeaux,

[34] Antoine-Jean Bonnemain, *Instituts républicains, ou Développement analytique des facultés naturelles, civiles, et politiques de l'homme* . . . (Paris: ICS, 1792), p. 13.
[35] *BAV*, 15 April 1793, p. 4; Maurice Dommanget, *Sylvain Maréchal, l'égalitaire, "l'homme sans Dieu," sa vie-son oeuvre (1750-1803)*, pp. 233-40.

where he became involved in a mystical cult led by Martines de Pasquilly. This group mixed Freemasonry, Occultism, and Christianity into a "new" cosmopolitan and pseudo-philosophical system. When Martines de Pasquilly died in 1774, Saint-Martin became leader of these Martinists. After he moved to Paris in 1792, the Imprimerie published nearly all of his major works.[36]

Martinism opposed what it saw as an overly scientist Enlightenment. "I have been an enemy of science because I have loved mankind," proclaimed Saint-Martin. Philosophes like Condorcet believed that social life could be submitted to the same rationalist method which had been used to discover rules governing inanimate objects. The Martinists rejected this contention. The true essence of man, the "radical and primitive source of all that is perfect" was to be found in a man's inner goodness, innate wisdom, and spirituality, which could only be discovered through experiencing primitive feelings and desires.[37]

In Saint-Martin's mystical system, the French Revolution had been a providential event directed by God at every turn. "I believe that His equitable hand has had for its goal the destruction of those abuses which infected the Old Regime of France." The true prophet of the Revolution was Rousseau, whom Saint-Martin transformed into a Christ: "Jean-Jacques . . . whose heart and pen were so proper for descending truth on earth; this Jean-Jacques whom I regard as a messenger." Saint-Martin hoped the Revolution would develop a new faith, similar to Rousseau's Savoyard Vicar, which would be simple, free from dogma, and based upon the inherent goodness of the human soul.[38]

Neither Maréchal nor Saint-Martin were in any sense Giron-

[36] Mieczylawa Sekrecka, *Louis-Claude de Saint-Martin, le philosophe inconnu: l'homme et l'oeuvre. Acta Universitatis Wratslaviensis*, no. 65.

[37] Louis-Claude de Saint-Martin, Oeuvres posthumes . . . , 2 vols. (Tours: Letourmy, 1807), 1: 23; *Ecce homo* (Paris: ICS, An IV de la liberté [1792]), p. 29.

[38] Louis-Claude de Saint-Martin, *Lettre à un ami ou Considérations politiques, philosophiques et religieuses sur la Révolution française* . . . (Paris: J. B. Louvet, An III), pp. 1, 33; Mieczylawa Sekrecka, "La Nouvelle Vision de la Révolution dans l'oeuvre de Saint-Martin, le philosophe inconnu," *La Littérature des lumières en France et en Pologne. Esthétique. Terminologie. Echanges*, pp. 131-47.

dins, and the publication of their works illustrates the movement of the Imprimerie away from its role as political propagandist. More important, these new writings contradicted the Girondins' own stand on religious issues. Both Maréchal and Saint-Martin wanted a France without any organized Catholic religion. But the Girondins had actively encouraged the development of a constitutional church that embodied a liberal Catholicism under the auspices of a democratic state. Even though some Girondins, such as Brissot and Condorcet, held private views that were frankly anti-Christian, they never proposed dismantling the Gallican Church altogether, believing instead that some sort of Catholicism was necessary for political stability.

The most important Girondin supporter of the Constitutional Church had always been Claude Fauchet, now Bishop of Calvados. Between 1791 and 1793 Fauchet also represented Calvados in the Legislative Assembly and Convention, where he became one of Brissot's closest allies. Fauchet had led the Cercle Social's club, not its publishing company, and he wrote nothing for the Imprimerie during this period. He limited himself largely to speeches in the national assemblies and pastoral letters to his constituents. But during the king's trial Fauchet began his own newspaper, which became very critical of the Imprimerie's new religious position. "The *Bulletin des Amis de la Vérité* presents very useful and agreeable reading," wrote Fauchet in March 1793, "if one excepts some articles where the author subscribes to irreligion and the horror of the priesthood." Fauchet agreed with the Imprimerie's political principles but attacked its distrust of Catholicism and priests. Fauchet correctly charged that where Catholicism was concerned, there was no difference between the Imprimerie du Cercle Social and the Jacobins:

It is above all unnecessary to profess such horror for the maxims of Marat, and then to adopt them concerning the ministers of religion, and to put on every page an article of Maratism against all priests. Yes, my dear Bonneville, *still the priests, and forever and ever the priests*: in order to speak the truth to the philosophes, and to preach to the followers of the gospel of the great *ami de la vérité*. ... When the philosophes will have religion, and the priests will have philosophy, then there will be perfection of teaching on the earth. Until then all principles will be in contradiction, and disorder in morality.[39]

Fauchet's public attack upon Bonneville and the Imprimerie du Cercle Social is an important indication of the disunity that plagued the Girondins during the spring of 1793.

THE NEW MOVES to transform the Imprimerie into something other than a Girondin press were too little and too late. After April, when it stopped publishing the *Bulletin des Amis de la Vérité*, the Cercle Social ceased to play a major role in public affairs, but by this time its fate was tied to the Girondins, whose premier mouthpiece it had long ago become.

The final demise and fall of the Girondins is a familiar story.[40] By the spring of 1793 the struggle between the Girondins and the Montagnards reached a stalemate that prevented the Convention from attending to urgent business. The Girondins had ascended to power by encouraging a swift military victory against the Austrians and by developing laissez-faire economic policies. In both areas their programs were in serious jeopardy. Counterrevolution was erupting in the Vendée, the economy continued to deteriorate, and the great military victories of the previous fall were not repeated. Two political crises further tarnished the Girondins' popularity. First was the treason of General Dumouriez, whose close relations with the Rolands and Brissot implicated the entire Girondin leadership; second, in April the Girondins finally tried to impeach Jean-Paul Marat. Although they secured enough votes for an indictment, a jury acquitted him of all charges, and he retained his seat in the Convention. The affair backfired on the Girondins. It made them look like political opportunists who were out of touch with the popular will, as expressed by the jury.

---

[39] *Journal des amis*, 9 March 1793, p. 458. On Fauchet's role in the Imprimerie see Nicolas Bonneville, *Appendices de la seconde édition de l'Esprit des religions; pour servir à l'entretien, à la propagation des bons principes, et à la Confédération universelle des Amis de la Vérité* (Paris: ICS, 1792), pp. 304-305, and *Bdf*, 23 March 1791, p. 544.

[40] Sydenham, *The French Revolution*, pp. 139-61; Claude Perroud, *Recherches sur la proscription des Girondins*.

Increasingly, the sans-culottes and their Montagnard spokesmen came to see that only another popular insurrection could
break through the stalemate. On 15 April a federation of Parisian
sections called on the Convention to expel twenty-two Girondins,
including Brissot, Louvet, Fauchet, Lanthenas, and Barbaroux.
This petition was approved by the Paris Commune and the
Jacobins. Two weeks later, during the night of 30-31 May 1793,
the sans-culottes organized themselves into a Central Revolutionary Committee, which demanded that the Girondins be purged
from the Convention. The next day Madame Roland and Clavière were arrested by municipal officials. By 2 June the Convention was surrounded by 20,000 armed sans-culottes demanding expulsion of the Girondins. The Convention obeyed their
Parisian masters and voted to arrest twenty-nine Girondin deputies.

The Girondins were now ruined as a political force, and the
Terror had begun. Not all of the Girondins followed Clavière
and Madame Roland immediately into jail, however. Roland
himself escaped Paris and eventually made his way to Rouen,
where friends hid him until November, when he killed himself
soon after learning of his wife's condemnation by the Revolutionary Tribunal. Condorcet, who hid in Paris until the spring
of 1794, may also have died by suicide. Brissot escaped from the
capital, but he was discovered posing as a Swiss merchant in a
provincial town and was brought back to Paris in late June. He
sat in prison for five months before dying under the guillotine
on 31 October. Fauchet was arrested in July 1793 and shared a
prison cell with his friend and fellow bishop, Lamourette, until
both were finally guillotined. Louvet and Bonneville were more
fortunate. Louvet managed to outwit his pursuers, hiding first
in Normandy and then in southwestern France. As for Bonneville, he was arrested in the summer of 1793, spent the year of
the Terror in jail, but managed to avoid his turn on the scaffold.[41]

---

[41] M.C.M. Simpson, ed., *Reminiscences of a Regicide*, p. 155; Archives Nationales, W10, dos. 448, W186, dos. 1.

Needless to say, with its leaders on the run, in prison, or dead, the Imprimerie du Cercle Social collapsed.

THIS BOOK has argued that the Cercle Social was controlled by a group of friends who emerged at the core of the Girondins during the period of the Legislative Assembly. This does not mean, of course, that all of the Girondin politicians who served in the Legislative Assembly and Convention belonged to the Cercle Social. Most of the great orators from the Gironde, such as Vergniaud, Grangeneuve, and Ducos, did not participate in the Cercle Social. What emerges from this study is a group of Paris-based politicians like Brissot, Condorcet, and Bonneville who were connected to one another through an intricate web of old friendships. During the Municipal Revolution they had used the Cercle Social to propagate an ideology of representative democracy. Their club, the Confédération des Amis de la Vérité, allowed them to remain highly visible among French intellectuals and to strengthen ties with the sans-culottes. When they became national leaders the Cercle Social became their most important center of propaganda. The Imprimerie published close to 200 books, pamphlets, and journals, many of them secretly subsidized by the Roland ministry. In essence the Cercle Social was neither a party headquarters nor a club of utopian mystics, but rather a Girondin agency designed to develop a political language to interpret the unprecedented events of the day.

This history of the Cercle Social has also shed new light on the nature and development of the Girondins in at least four ways. First, it has revealed that the concept of a separate Girondin party was not merely a Montagnard myth created in 1792. While the Girondins may never have operated in a disciplined party fashion, they consciously helped to create the myth that they did. During the fall of 1792 Cercle Social publications repeatedly tried to present a united Girondin leadership in opposition to Montagnard anarchists, despite the fact that these Girondin leaders did not vote as a bloc in the Convention.

Second, this book has shown that the links between the Girondins and the sans-culottes were much closer than has been previously recognized. Between 1789 and 1791 the Cercle Social and the Cordeliers club (spokesmen for the sans-culottes) co-operated to a great extent in leading the campaign for a more democratic regime, first during the Paris Municipal Revolution, and then during the crisis surrounding the king's flight to Varennes. In 1792, when the split between the Girondins and the more radical Jacobins surfaced, the Girondins tried hard to retain the support of the sans-culottes through publications like Louvet's *Sentinelle*. Only after the September Massacres did the Girondins finally renounce the sans-culottes movement. Thus while historians generally have viewed the rift between the sans-culottes and the Girondins as inevitable given their differing political and economic ideas, the Girondins, at least until the fall of 1792, believed that some kind of sans-culottes constituency could be maintained.

Third, this book shows that while the Girondins may have been little more than "Brissot's circle of friends," they had joined together in a variety of political causes since 1789. As Louis Namier pointed out over fifty years ago, eighteenth-century politics was often guided by circles of friends or other personal networks rather than by formal political parties. In this respect, the establishment of the Cercle Social itself is the best evidence for demonstrating that a group of friends could carry great political weight in the Revolution.

Finally, this study suggests that the Girondins were more effective as intellectuals than as statesmen. Certainly their notoriously poor political record contrasts sharply with their success as writers and journalists. What Madame Roland wrote of her fellow Cercle Social author, Louis-Sébastien Mercier, on the eve of her execution may apply as well to the rest of the group:

Mercier ... offers new proof that the talent of writing is only one small part of being a legislator. It is easy to moralize about men in ingenious fictional works. It is difficult to change them by wise laws. The good Mercier, easy-going, a more likeable fellow than most men of letters, is nothing but a zero in the Convention.[42]

[42] Roland, *Mémoires* 1: 188-89.

After the Terror

Louis-Sébastien Mercier (1740-1814). Elected to the Convention. *Chronique du mois* editor. Novelist, playwright, essayist, Mercier personified the Cercle Social image of a philosophe turned revolutionary intellectual.
Courtesy of The Newberry Library, Chicago

Honneur à Nicolas! que le chêne civique
En ombrageant son front, des rois soit la terreur
De la liberté sainte il fut le précurseur
Et le tribun du peuple avant la République.

Sylvain Maréchal, *BAV*, 3 January 1793, p. 1.

WHEN Bonneville was released from prison during the summer of 1794, he reestablished the Imprimerie du Cercle Social. But this was not the same organization as before. Instead of representing a tightly knit group of national politicians and writers, it was little more than Bonneville's own business.[1] While this later Imprimerie du Cercle Social managed to publish some very important works, such as the first edition of Laplace's *Exposition du système du monde* and a ten-volume series of the newly-established Ecole Normale, its authors did not think of themselves as a group or political faction, and few of them held any political aspirations. The publishing company itself played a very minor role in the revival of cultural life that characterized the period after the Terror.

The only coterie that can be distinguished among the Cercle Social authors is a small band of Bonneville's closest friends, including Louis-Sébastien Mercier, Nicolas-Edme Restif de la Bretonne, Jacques-Henri Bernardin de Saint-Pierre, and Tom Paine. While Mercier and Bernardin were on the faculty of the Institut (a new academy), they played a minor role. Bonneville socialized with Mercier and other writers at Putode's Café on the rue des Marais. It is quite probable that Restif went there often as well, for Bonneville told a mutual friend that he saw Restif "almost every day during the last twenty years of his life." But this was definitely not a political circle. Here they would gossip about old friends, discuss the activities of the Institut and Ecole Normale, and debate literature and philosophy. Mercier

[1] See, for example, the descriptions of the Imprimerie du Cercle Social in *Bien informé*, 22 January 1798, p. 8; 19 February 1798, p. 4; and 8 March 1798, Supplement, p. 4. For a list of Cercle Social publications during this late period, see Kates, "The Cercle Social: French Intellectuals and the French Revolution," pp. 291-92.

and Bonneville were particularly impressed with Restif's views
on Rousseau, and the Cercle Social published his *Monsieur Nicolas*, which was clearly inspired by Rousseau's *Confessions*. Mercier even nominated Restif to the Institut, but the academicians
rejected him for having little taste or talent.[2]

Bonneville had known Bernardin de Saint-Pierre since before
the Revolution. When the Confédération des Amis de la Vérité
was established, Bernardin had refused to join the club, and the
two men split. Mercier tried to persuade Bernardin to join the
club, but the latter was determined to avoid all clubs and political
affairs. Such an attitude precluded close friendship in the hectic
days of 1792 and 1793, but after the Terror politics was less
important to these thinkers than the more traditional belles-
lettres. Bernardin became a regular contributor to Bonneville's
journal, and the Cercle Social published his very interesting essay
on the relationship between social institutions and morality.[3]

No one was closer to Bonneville in these years than Tom
Paine. The two had been good friends since the early days of
the Revolution when they had met at Roland's salon. Bonneville's
knowledge of English and Paine's ignorance of French had
formed the basis for a close rapport. In 1796 Paine returned to
Paris and stayed with Bonneville. The latter converted his study
into a bedroom, and despite the cramped accommodations, Paine
lived there for the next six years.[4]

Mercier, Bernardin, and Paine helped Bonneville put out two
journals during this period, the *Vieux tribun et sa bouche de fer*,
and the *Bien informé*. The first was styled after Bonneville's
earlier journal of 1789 and contained more reflective essays than
news. In a rambling and often unreadable style, Bonneville gave
his general impressions of the spirit of the age, praised the leaders

---

[2] Michel de Cubières-Palmézeaux, "Notice Historique et critique sur la vie
et les ouvrages de Nicolas-Edme Restif de la Bretonne," in [P. L. Jacob],
Bibliographie et iconographie de tous les ouvrages de Restif de la Bretonne, p. 30;
Charles Nodier, *Oeuvres complètes* 3: 331-34; *Vieux tribun et sa bouche de fer*,
no. 6, p. 291.

[3] On the split see the letter from Bernardin to Mercier of 24 January 1791
in the Bibliothèque de l'arsenal, Ms. 15078 (2c), fols. 189-90; and *Bdf*, 5 July
1791, p. 2.

[4] "The Cobbett Papers," in Moncure Conway, *Life of Thomas Paine* 2: 433-
59.

of the Institut, and dreamed up new projects, such as proposing that all Paris publishers form an association and create a central bank for aiding poor and unknown writers. The *Bien informé*, on the other hand, was a successful daily review of political, social, and literary events, complete with the latest stock prices and weather reports.

Thus the strongest claim that can be made about Bonneville and his friends after the Terror is that they were an informal group of "Romantics" (the term used by Charles Nodier, then a young member of the coterie), with no political pretensions.[5] In fact, when it came to politics Bonneville and his friends had to be quite cautious. When the *Bien informé* once made a swipe at the Director Sieyès, the government suspended the paper. It took Paine's efforts to remove the ban. "I am certain," he told the government, "that Bonneville in inserting that paragraph meant only a witticism and not an injury, and never expected it would be taken seriously."[6]

Bonneville was not so fortunate a few years later when he satirically compared Bonaparte to Cromwell in the pages of the *Bien informé*. This time the government not only shut down the paper but confiscated the Cercle Social presses. Bonneville and his friends realized that this was the beginning of the end for the republic. Paine quickly left for America, and Bonneville soon sent his wife and two sons to him in New York. "At this time, 1802," Madame Bonneville later wrote,

public spirit was at an end in France. The real republicans were harassed by eternal persecutions. ... During the six years that [Paine] lived in our house, he frequently pressed us to go to America, offering us all that he should be able to do for us, and saying that he would bequeath his property to our children. ... Foreseeing a new revolution that would strike personally [at] many of the Republicans, it was resolved, soon after the departure of Mr. Paine, that I should go thither with my children.[7]

[5] Nodier, *Oeuvres* 3: 331; on Bonneville and Nodier see A. Richard Olliver, *Charles Nodier: Pilot of Romanticism*, pp. 30, 92-93, 131.

[6] Cited in David Hawke, *Paine*, p. 334. See also Archives Nationales, AF III* 96, no. 2121.

[7] "The Cobbett Papers," pp. 446-47; *Bien informé*, An VII, p. 4.

Paine took care of the Bonneville family and treated the sons as if they were his own. In his letters he repeatedly urged Bonneville to join them, but Nicolas had waited too long and could not leave the country. Bonaparte's government had "positively identified" him "as an enemy of the government" and he was now subject to harassment and surveillance.[8] Bonneville did not join his family until the Empire fell in 1815. He had always felt a special love for America and had even named his two sons after Franklin and Paine. Benjamin and Thomas Paine Bonneville lived out their lives in the New World. Washington Irving immortalized Benjamin's adventures as an explorer in the Rocky Mountains, and the Bonneville Salt Flats in Utah were later named in his honor.[9] Posterity was not so kind to Benjamin's father. Paine had died in 1809, and Nicolas found few friends in the United States. In 1819 he returned to Paris without his wife. His last years were sad ones. He opened a small second-hand bookstore, but it never amounted to much. Years earlier, when he had been in the center of things, Bonneville had directed one of the most influential publishing houses in France; but now this impoverished relic of a previous era was trying to eke out a living selling used books. "He spent his last days," wrote Tissot, a nineteenth-century philosophy professor,

in a room at the back of a shop (14, rue des Grès), where he had been taken in by an old woman . . . who was almost as poor as he, and who remained his most enthusiastic admirer. . . . Oh! It was so lovely talking with M. Bonneville; to hear him relate the story of his life and read in strange fashion from his collection of patriotic poems. . . . This same year [1828] Bonneville, who was already practically out of this world, left it for good.[10]

[8] Archives Nationales, F7 8083, no. 1196.
[9] Washington Irving, *Adventures of Captain Bonneville or Scenes Beyond the Rocky Mountains of the Far West.*
[10] Cited in Jules Michelet, *Histoire de la Révolution française* 1: 612; on Bonneville's last years see also "Une Lettre de Charles Nodier," *Bulletin du bibliophile*, no. 11, 1847, pp. 487-89.

APPENDIX A

MEMBERS OF THE CONFÉDÉRATION
DES AMIS DE LA VÉRITÉ

BECAUSE no membership list has ever been found, what follows is a reconstructed list based upon information gleaned from the *Bouche de fer* and other sources. For the purposes of this list, a member is defined as anyone who attended one or more meetings of the Confédération des Amis de la Vérité. An asterisk following the name indicates membership in the Directoire du Cercle Social. Where available, birth dates are included with other comments. Following the name and comments is the source of the information and, unless otherwise noted, the dates refer to issues of the *Bdf*. The following have been abbreviated: Deputy to the Paris Communal Assembly (CA), Deputy to the Constituent Assembly (CONST), Deputy to the Legislative Assembly (LEG), Deputy to the National Convention (CONV).

Abauzit, Marc Théophile;[1] Genovese minister.
Amiard, Veuve. 13 January 1791, p. 66.
d'André*. No. 16, October 1790, p. 245.
Arcanger. 21 February 1791, p. 334.
Auger, Athanase; b. 1734, professor. 7 June 1791, p. 7.
Babeuf, François-Noël [Gracchus];[2] famous conspirator.
Balland, C.P.J.; forest administrator. 22 January 1791, p. 133.
Bancal, Henri; CA, CONV. 14 April 1791, pp. 102-3.
Barère, Bertrand*; CONV, journalist. No. 9, October 1790, p. 166.
Baumier; publicist. 10 July 1791, p. 5.
Beaurain, Léon-Charles; CA. 31 May 1791, pp. 3-4.
Beauvallet, François; CA, police commissioner. 27 January 1791, p. 178.
Bernot. 15 March 1791, p. 489.
Biauzat, Jean-François Gaultier de; CONST. No. 9, October 1790, p. 166.

---

[1] Bibliothèque Nationale, Nouvelles acquisitions françaises, 9534, fol. 191.
[2] M. Daline, "Babeuf et le Cercle Social," *Recherches internationales à la lumière du Marxisme*, No. 62 (1970): 62-73.

Billardon de Sauvigny, Louis-Edme; CA, military officer. 3 January 1791, p. 3.

Billot-Philip.[3]

Blondel, Georges-François; architect. 11 May 1791, p. 258.

Blondez; priest. No. 2, October 1790, p. 14.

Boilleau d'Ausson, Jacques; b. 1751, CONV, lawyer. *Journal des clubs,* 15-20 April 1791, pp. 433-39.

Boissy d'Anglas; b. 1756, CONST, CONV. 6 April 1791, p. 60.

Bonneville, Nicolas*;[4] b. 1760, CA.

Bonvallet*; CA, national guard administrator. 24 May 1791, p. 317.

Bonnard, L. G. 22 February 1791, p. 348.

Boucher, René; CA. 31 May 1791, p. 15.

Bourbon, Duchesse. 7 June 1791, p. 2.

Brancas; member Cordeliers club. 31 May 1791, p. 14.

Brie-Serrant, Marquis Clement Alexandre de. 1 February 1791, pp. 209-10.

Brissot, Jacques-Pierre;[5] LEG, CONV.

Brizard, Gabriel; b. 1730, lawyer. 5 May 1791, p. 273.

Castera, Jean-Henri; b. 1749. 5 May 1791, p. 271.

Cerisier; journalist. 29 March 1791, p. 583.

Cerutti, Joachim;[6] CA, priest, journalist.

Chabroud, J.B.C.*; b. 1750, CONST, lawyer. No. 11, October 1790, p. 166.

Chaix, Richard d'Est-Ange; priest. 9 March 1791, p. 433.

Chappon, Pierre*; b. 1749, physician. 1 February 1791, p. 206.

Chaudet, Antoine-Denis; b. 1763, artist. 6 January 1791, p. 20.

Cloots, Anacharsis; b. 1755, writer. *Révolutions de France et de Brabant,* no. 77, pp. 573-74.

Colom; Masonic officer. 12 February 1791, p. 263.

Condorcet, J.A.N. Caritat de; b. 1743, CA, LEG, CONV. 6 April 1791, p. 43.

[3] Bibliothèque historique de la ville de Paris, Mss. 777, fols. 69-75.

[4] Halem, *Paris en 1790,* p. 209.

[5] Although the documents never actually mention Brissot as participating in a Confédération meeting, there is overwhelming circumstantial evidence that he was a member of the group. See especially *Bdf,* 29 March 1791 and 17 July 1791; *Pf,* 8 April 1791, p. 377, 2 May 1791, p. 433, 12 July 1791; 11 August 1791, p. 173, 18 August 1791; *Annales historiques de la Révolution française* 16 (1939): 245; Ellery, *Brissot de Warville,* p. 161; Bibliothèque Nationale, Nouvelles acquisitions françaises, 9534, fols. 200-207.

[6] Etienne Charavay, ed., *L'Assemblée électorale de Paris. 18 novembre 1790-15 juin 1791,* p. 439.

Couard, Nicolas-François; CA, founder of Point central des arts et métiers. 11 May 1791, p. 330.

Cressy, Louis Claude de.[7]

Dansard; founder of *Société fraternelle*. 14 April 1791, p. 101-102.

Desgrange, Louis*. 13 January 1791, p. 66.

Desmoulins, Camille*; b. 1760, CONV, journalist. No. 34, December 1790, p. 532.

Desvignes, Pierre-Hubert; b. 1737, CA.

Dorgement*; municipal officer. 22 January 1791, p. 134.

Dubin. 12 February 1791, p. 262.

Dubut de Longchamps; CA, postal administrator. No. 3, October 1790, p. 482.

Duchosal, M.E.G.; b. 1763, writer. 13 June 1791, p. 4.

Ducros, François;[8] printer.

Dumesnil*. 5 May 1791, p. 277.

Dunouy; engineer, Cordeliers club officer. 24 May 1791, p. 316.

Duplessis. 4 March 1791, p. 423.

l'Epine d'Andilly. 7 June 1791, p. 7.

Eymard; CONST. No. 34, December 1790, p. 532.

Fauchet, Claude*; b. 1744, CA, LEG, CONV, priest. No. 3, October 1790, p. 18.

Gallot, Jean Gabriel; b. 1744, CONST. 3 January 1791, p. 4.

Garran-Coulon, Jean-Philippe; b. 1748, LEG, CONV. No. 4, October 1790, p. 45.

Godard, Jacques; b. 1762, CA, LEG, lawyer.

Gonnet, Jean-Louis; locksmith. 22 February 1791, p. 342.

Goupil de Préfeln, G.F.C.*; CONST, President of Feuillants. No. 34, December 1790, pp. 530-31.

Guéroult, Jean-François; playwright. *Journal des Amis*, Prospectus, p. 3.

Halem, Gerhard Anton von.[9]

Heron; naval officer. 11 May 1791, pp. 271-72.

Hervier, P. Charles.[10]

Lafite. 11 May 1791, p. 332.

Lalande, Luc-François; b. 1732. CONV, priest, professor. 23 March 1791, p. 529.

---

[7] Louis Claude de Cressy, *Discours sur l'abolition de la peine du mort . . . Lu aux Amis de la Vérité* (Paris: Boulard, 1791).

[8] Fr. Ducros, *Réponse . . . à l'errata d'Anacharsis Cloots* (Paris: ICS, [1791]).

[9] Halem, *Paris en 1790*, p. 212.

[10] Avenel, *Anacharsis Cloots*, p. 227.

Lamourette, Andrien; b. 1742, Leg, priest. No. 9, October 1790, p. 119.

Lanoa; carpenter, publicist. 20 April 1791, p. 200.

Lanthenas, François; b. 1754, Conv. 14 April 1791, pp. 102-3.

La Poype, Jean-François*; military officer. No. 7, October 1790, p. 102.

Le Bois; b. 1757, lawyer, member of Cordeliers club. 31 May 1791, p. 15.

Lebrun. 5 May 1791, p. 279.

Lefebure, Louis-Guillaume*; b. 1751, CA, priest, professor. 22 January 1791, p. 132.

Le Gros. 14 April 1791.

Lequinio, Joseph-Marie; b. 1755, Leg, Conv, lawyer. 6 January 1791, p. 18.

Luciot. 27 January 1791, p. 178.

Mailly de Châteaurenard, Antoine*; b. 1742, Const. No. 34, December 1790, p. 529.

Malguin; priest. 23 March 1791, p. 530.

Mandar, Théophile; b. 1759, publicist. 3 July 1791, p. 4.

Mathieu-Mirampel, J.B.C.*; CA, Conv. No. 34, December 1790, p. 533.

Maubach. 27 January 1791, p. 178.

Mercier, Louis-Sébastien; b. 1749, Conv. 21 February 1791, p. 334.

Michel, Jean-François*; physician. 3 January 1791, p. 4.

Mille, François-Bernard; priest. 12 March 1791, p. 481.

Momoro, Antoine-François; b. 1765, printer. 18 July 1791, p. 4.

Montizen; CA, engineer. 14 April 1791, p. 115.

Mourlens. 27 January 1791, p. 178.

Mulot, François-Valentin; b. 1749, Leg, priest. 22 January 1791, p. 130.

Nusse, Jean-François; priest. 6 April 1791, p. 59.

Nicolo. 7 June 1791, p. 8.

Noël. 14 April 1791, pp. 102-103.

Pagnon. 1 July 1791, p. 8.

Palloy.[11]

Palm, Etta d'Aelders; feminist, publicist. 3 January 1791, pp. 4-11.

Perrot, Michel. 20 April 1791, p. 278.

Pio; Italian diplomat. No. 7, October 1790, p. 102.

Plaisant, J.B.E.; CA, lawyer. 27 January 1791, p. 178.

Provent, Nicolas. 25 July 1791, pp. 4-5.

Poulenot. 27 July 1791, p. 128.

Poupart. 31 May 1791, p. 15.

[11] Bibliothèque historique de la ville de Paris, Mss. 777, fols. 69-75.

Raffron du Trouvillet, Nicolas; b. 1723, Conv, professor. 21 May 1791, p. 13.
Reynier, J.L.A.*; b. 1762, botanist. 2 January 1791, p. 130.
Reys-Héron. 24 January 1791, p. 146.
Ricard; CA. No. 30, December 1790, p. 479.
Richardson. 24 February 1791, p. 358.
Roland, Jean-Marie;[12] minister of the interior.
Roland, Manon;[13] wife of minister.
Rousseau, Claude-Louis; feminist writer. No. 22, November 1790, p. 352.
Ruault, Henri*; publicist. 15 March 1791, p. 483.
Rutledge, James; b. 1742, publicist. 10 July 1791, p. 5.
Salm-Salm, Prince E. de; landowner. 6 April 1791, p. 45.
Saint-Christol, J. L. 12 March 1791, p. 467.
Savard*; journalist. No. 34, December 1790, p. 332.
Sergent, François; b. 1751, CA, professor. No. 13, November 1790, p. 195.
Sieyès, Emmanuel*; b. 1748, priest, Const, Conv. No. 16, October 1790, p. 245.
Sussy*. 28 April 1791, p. 248.
Tanevot d'Herbault, Gabriel-Claude*;[14] b. 1724, CA.
Taurin. 27 January 1791, p. 178.
Villette, Charles;[15] publicist.
Volfius; b. 1734, priest, professor. 23 March 1791, p. 531.

[12] Bibliothèque Nationale, Nouvelles acquisitions françaises, 6242, fol. 32.
[13] *Lettres de Mme Roland* 2: 266.
[14] *Annales de la Confédération universelle des Amis de la Vérité*, pp. 31-32.
[15] Bibliothèque historique de la ville de Paris, Mss. 777, fols. 69-75.

APPENDIX B

BIBLIOGRAPHY OF WORKS PUBLISHED
BY THE IMPRIMERIE DU CERCLE
SOCIAL, 1790-1793

SINCE IT IS very possible that books, pamphlets, and especially posters could have gone unannounced at the time of publication and have been lost, the following list is probably incomplete. It is based upon several French, English, and American bibliographical guides, particularly G. Walter and A. Martin, *Catalogue de l'histoire de la Révolution française*, 5 vols. (Paris: Bibliothèque Nationale, 1936-43). Unless otherwise noted, all works are available at the Bibliothèque Nationale.

Adresse à la Convention Nationale présentée par la Commune d'Orly. N.d.

Adresse d'un très grand nombre de citoyens actifs de la ville d'Amiens, département de la Somme, à l'Assemblée Nationale, du 26 juin 1792. ... [1792].

Allimont, Georges-Louis-Chappe. *Discours des jeunes citoyens du bataillon de l'abbaye Saint Germain, partant sur les frontières, à la section des Quatre-Nations. Réponse du président.* N.d.

Les Amis de la constitution de Marseille, à J. M. Roland, ex-ministre de l'intérieur. [1792].

L'Apothicaire patriote, ou Découverte importante d'une Seringue Nationale. ... N.d.

Arrêté de l'Assemblée générale permanente de la section de la Croix-Rouge, concernant le traitement du maire et des membres salariés de la municipalité. Du 28 septembre, l'an I. [1792].

Arrêtés de la section du Théâtre-Français. ... [1792].

Arrêtés de la section du Théâtre-Français, dite de Marseille, du 23 septembre 1792. ... [1792].

Artillerie Nationale Parisienne. N.d.

Auger, Athanase. *Ouvrages posthumes.* ... 1792.

————. *Sur les gouvernements en général, et en particulier sur celui qui nous convient.* ... [1791].

————. *De la Tragédie grecque et du nom qu'on devrait lui donner dans notre langue pour s'en faire une juste idée.* ... 1792.

Avis pressant aux députés de l'Assemblée Nationale. [1792].

Balland, Cl. P. Jos. *Observations sur l'administration de forêts.* With observations by J. L. Reynier. 1791.

Bancal des Issarts, Henri. *Henri Bancal . . . à Anacharsis Cloots, son collègue.* 1793.

————. *Du Nouvel ordre social.* 1792.

Belair, Alexandre-Pierre-Julienne. *Défense de Paris et tout l'empire. . . . L'An IV de la liberté.* [1792].

————. *Extrait du registre des délibérations du club des Cordeliers ou Adresse aux Français sur des objets de la plus grande importance relatives au salut de la patrie.* 1791.

————. *Mémoire sur les moyens de parvenir à la plus grande perfection de la culture et de la suppression des jachères.* L'An II.

Boilleau, Jacques. *Jacques Boilleau . . . à tous les vrais sans-culottes.* [1793].

————. *Surtout, lisez-moi avant de me juger. Justification . . . de Jacques Boilleau . . . accusés d'être les chefs d'une conspiration contre la République. . . . 1793.*

Bonnemain, Antoine-Jean-Thomas. *Instituts républicains, ou Développement analytique des facultés naturelles, civiles et politiques de l'homme. . . . 1792.*

————. *Régénération des colonies ou Moyens de restituer graduellement aux hommes leur état politique et d'assurer la prosperité des nations, et moyens pour rétablir . . . l'ordre dans les colonies françaises. . . . 1792.*

Bonneville, Nicolas. *L'Année M. DCC. LXXIX, ou Les Tribuns du peuple* [1790].

————. *Appendices de la seconde édition de l'Esprit des religions; pour servir à l'entretien, à la propagation des bons principes, et à la Confédération universelle des amis de la vérité.* 1792.

[————]. *La Bouche de fer* [prospectus]. [1790]. Bibliothèque de l'Arsenal, 8° JO 20.207B.

————. *La Bouche de fer* [prospectus]. [1790]. Bibliothèque historique de la ville de Paris, 606020.

————. *La Bouche de fer. Cercle Social. Dixième libraison. Introduction à la partie politique des feuilles de la bouche de fer, ou Tableau analytique des principes constitutionnels décrétés par l'Assemblée Nationale suivi d'une table alphabétique, et d'une récapitulation générale et chronologique de toutes les séances et pièces attachées aux procès-verbaux publiés par son ordre.* 1790.

————. *La Bouche de fer. Cercle Social. Tome II. Première livraison* [prospectus]. [1790].

Bonneville, Nicolas. *Bulletin des Amis de la Vérité, publié par les Directeurs de l'Imprimerie du Cercle Social* [prospectus]. [1792].

———. *De l'Esprit des religions. Ouvrages promis et nécessaire à la Confédération universelle des amis de la Vérité.* 1791.

———. *Histoire de l'Europe moderne, depuis l'irruption des peuples du Nord clans de l'Empire romain, jusqu' à la paix de 1783.* ... vol. 3. 1792.

———. *Nicolas de Bonneville, électeur du département de Paris, aux véritables amis de la liberté.* [1791].

———. *"Nous avons attaché ... ,"* [an untitled prospectus]. [1790]. Bibliothèque historique de la ville de Paris, 604593.

———. *Le Nouveau Code conjugal, établi sur les bases de la constitution, et d'après les principes et les considérations de la loi déjà faite et sanctionnée, qui a préparé et ordonné ce nouveau code.* 1792.

———. *Les Poésies de Nicolas Bonneville.* 1793.

———. *Programme du Cercle Social, pour la Confédération universelle des Amis de la Vérité.* [1791].

———. *Qu'est-ce que la bouche de fer?* [1790].

———. *Tableau analytique des principes constitutionels décrétés par l'Assemblée Nationale, suivi d'une Table alphabétique, et d'une récapitulation générale et chronologique de toutes les séances et pièces attachées aux procès-verbaux publiés par son ordre. Deuxième partie.* 1790.

———. *Le Tribun du peuple, ou Recueil des lettres de quelques électeurs de Paris, avant la Révolution de 1789, pour servir d'introduction aux feuilles de la bouche de fer.* [1790].

Bonneville, François [various engravings of portraits].

Brissot, Jacques-Pierre. *A tous les républicains de France sur la Société des Jacobins.* 1792.

Cambis, Madame de. *Du sort actuel des femmes.* 1791.

Chaussard, Publicola. *De l'Allemagne et de la maison d'Autriche.* ... 1792.

———. *Lettre d'un homme libre à l'esclave Raynal.* N.d.

Chaix d'Est-Ange, Richard. *Serment civique.* [1791].

Clavière, Etienne. *De la Conjuration contre les finances et des mesures à prendre pour en arrêter les effets.* ... 1792.

———. *E. Clavière à l'Assemblée Nationale sur les finances.* [1791].

———. *Du Numéraire métallique, ou De la Nécessité d'une prompte refonte de monnoyes en abolissant l'usage d'en fixer la valeur en livres tournois.* ... 1792.

Club des Cordeliers. ... *Extrait du registre du 22 juin 1791.* [1791]. Archives Nationales, D XXIX b35 no. 365.

Collin, Antoine. *Réflexions sur quelques articles du Code de police correctionelle.* ... 1792.

Collot d'Herbois, J. M. *The Spirit of the French Constitution or the Almanach of Goodman Gerard for the Year 1792.* ... Translated by John Oswald. 1791.

Condorcet, J.A.N. *Des Conventions Nationales.* ... [1791].

———. *Discours sur les Conventions Nationales ... prononcé le 7 août 1791, à l'Assemblée des amis de la constitution.* [1791].

———. *Pièces extraites du recueil périodique intitulé Le Républicain.* L'an IV de la liberté [1792].

———. *De la République, oui Un roi est-il nécessaire à la conservation de la liberté? Discours dont l'Assemblée fédérative des Amis de la vérité à demandé l'impression.* ... [1791].

Considérations importantes sur un des plus précieux monuments de la république françoise. N.d.

Couard, Nicolas François. *Moyens et nécessité absolues d'occuper les ouvriers oisifs et ceux des ateliers de charité à des travaux utiles à l'Etat et à eux-mêmes ... approuvé ... par l'Assemblée fédérative des amis de la vérité.* ... [1791]. Cited in the catalogue for the British Museum, F.R. 481, 3, but not found.

Creuzé-Latouche, Jacques-Antoine. *Lettre ... aux municipalités, et aux habitants des campagnes du département de la Vienne.* [1790].

———. 3rd ed. 1791.

———. *Sur les subsistances.* 1793.

Courtes réflexions sur les décrets de l'Assemblée Nationale constituante, des 28 octobre 1790, et 19 juin 1791, concernant les indemnités à accorder aux princes Allemands, qui ont des possessions en France. N.d.

Constitution françoise, telle qu'elle à été lue à la Convention, le vendredi 15 février 1793. 1793.

De la Convention Nationale. Extrait des délibérations de la Section du Marché des Innocents du 9 août 1792. ... 1792.

Coup d'oeil sur la société en général, en 1792 ... par J.J.H. 1793.

Daubermesnil, François-Antoine. *Extraits d'un manuscrit intitulé "Le Culte des adorateurs," contenant des fragments de leurs différents livres sur l'institution du culte, les observances religieuses, l'instruction, les préceptes et l'adoration.* N.d.

Déclaration que les Princes, frères de S.M. très-chrétienne, et les Princes de son sang unis à eux, font à la France et à l'Europe entière de leurs sentiments et de leurs intentions. [1792].

Les Députés du département des Bouches-du-Rhône à la Convention Nationale, à Marat. N.d.

Discours des jeunes citoyens du bataillon de l'abbaye Saint-Germain, partant sur les frontières, à la section des Quatre Nations. N.d.

Doit-on consulter les départements sur le jugement de l'affaire du roi. N.d.

Doppet, François Amédée, and Boinod. *Réponse de la Légion franche allobroge aux ennemis de la république.* 1793.

Douce. *Circulaire aux citoyens de la section du Bonnet-Rouge.* [1792].

Ducros, François. *Réponse de F. Ducros à l'errata d'Anarcharsis Cloots.* [1791].

Dufour de Saint-Pathus, Julien-Michel. *Projet de loi relatif aux récompenses individuelles, proposé à l'Assemblée Nationale.* . . . 1792.

Dufourny de Villiers, Louis-Pierre. *L'Homme libre aux hommes de l'être.* [1792].

Dupré, Augustin. *Réponse à l'écrit de M. Beyerlé . . . dénonçant la fabrication des pièces de 15 sols.* . . . N.d.

Dutrone La Couture, Jacques-François. *Extrait des mémoires . . . présentés à l'Assemblée Nationale au mois de janvier 1791, tiré du "Journal des colonies."* N.d.

Les Electeurs formant la société en l'Eveché, à leurs commettans. [1791].

Fabre d'Eglantine, Philippe-François-Nazaire. *L'Intrigue épistolaire, comédie en 5 actes et en vers.* . . . 1792.

Fauchet, Claude. *Mandement. . . . Discours prononcé . . . à l'autel de la patrie, pendant la cérémonie de la fédération générale du département . . . près la ville de Caen.* [1791].

———. *Sermon sur l'accord de la Religion et de la Liberté . . . 4 février 1791.* 1791.

Favier, Jean-Louis. *Observations . . . sur les maisons d'Autriche et particulièrement sur le traité de Versailles du 1er mai 1756 entre le roi et l'impératrice-reine de Hongrie.* New ed. 1792.

Feydel, Gabriel. *Sur la loi du mariage, la loi du divorce et le système de l'adoption.* L'An II de la République [1792].

Focard de Château. *Mémoire . . . faisent suite et se référant à un autre . . . sur la nécessité de soulager le trésor public de deux millions environ que coute annuellement le de département de Corse.* . . . 1792.

Follie, Louis-Guillaume. *Voyage dans les déserts du Sahara.* . . . 1792.

Les Forfeits de l'Intoleramie sacerdotale. . . . N.d.

Fourquevaux, Marie-Angélique-Hélène-Felicio. *Aperçu pour la citoyenne Fourquevaux.* N.d.

Frères et amis. . . . N.d.

Galbaud-Dufort, François Thomas. *Observations sur la pétition présentée à la Convention Nationale dans sa séance du 28 octobre 1792.* . . . N.d.

Gallet, Pierre. *Le Véritable évangile.* . . . L'An II. [1793]

Garran-Coulon, Jean-Philippe. *J. Ph. Garran . . . sur le jugement de Louis XVI.* 1793.

La Générale. [1791].

Gerlet. *Le Médecin patriote, ou Ouvrage dans lequel on fait connaitre par les symptômes la nature des maladies, leurs causes, on indique leur préservatif ou les moyens les plus prompts pour y remédier. . . .* N.d.

Gorani, Guiseppe. *Lettre au roi d'Espagne. . . .* [1793].

Le Grand baptême du faubourg Saint-Antoine fait au Cirque national le 18 février de l'an 1791, troisième de la liberté. [1791].

Guéroult, Jean-François. *La Journée de Marathon, ou Le Triomphe de la liberté. Pièce historique en quatre actes, en prose, avec des intermèdes et des choeurs. . . .* 1792.

Hauy, René-Just. *Exposition abrégée de la théorie sur la structure des crystaux. . . .* 1792.

Henriquez, L. M. *Le Diable à confesse.* N.d.

———. *Le Pape traité comme il le mérite, ou Réponse à la bulle de Pie VI.* [1791].

Jallet, Jacques. *Pourquoi ne jurent-ils pas puisqu'ils savent jurer? ou Lettres de J. Jallet . . . à L. E. J. . . .* 2d ed. L'An II de la liberté [1791].

Kersaint, Armand Guy. *De la Constitution et du gouvernement qui pourroient convenir à la République françoise. . . .* 1792.

———. *Moyens proposés à l'Assemblée Nationale pour rétablir la paix et l'ordre dans les colonies. . . .* 2 vols. 1792.

Lacroix, Marie-Sébastien-Bruno de. *Moyens présentés à la section de Marseilles . . . pour établir irrévocablement la liberté et l'égalité. . . .* [1791].

Lanoa. *La Vérité sans fard pour les entrepreneurs, menuisiers et autres qui ont fourni et construit les travaux que toute la France a admiré au Champ de Mars et à la Fédération générale, le 14 juillet 1790.* 1790.

Lanthenas, François. *Bases fondamentales de l'instruction publique et de toute constitution libre, ou Moyens de lier l'opinion publique, la morale, l'éducation, l'enseignement, l'instruction, les fêtes, la propogation des lumières, et le progrès de toutes les connoissances au gouvernement national-républicain. . . .* 1793.

———. *Des Electeurs et du mode d'élire par listes épuratoires. . . .* 1792.

———. *Nécessité et moyens d'établir la force publique sur la rotation continuelle du service militaire et la représentation nationale sur la proportion exacte du nombre des citoyens. . . .* 1792.

———. *Des Sociétés populaires, considérés comme une branche essentielle de l'instruction publique. . . .* 1792.

La Place, P. A. de. *Les Forfaits de l'intolérance sacerdotale, ou Cacul* *moderé de ce que les hérésies, les practiques prétendues pieuses, l'ambition et la cupidité tant des que du clergé, ont produit de victimes humaines dans la chrétienté, par le feu Lord****. N.d.

Lavallée, Joseph, *Voyage dans les départements de la France par une société d'artistes et gens de lettres*. . . . 13 vols. 1792.

Lavicomterie de Saint-Samson, Louis. *Aux Assemblées primaires*. N.d.

———. *La République sans impôts*. 1792.

Le Gangneur. *Réponse au discours des jeunes citoyens du bataillon de l'abbaye Saint-Germain partant sur les frontières*. N.d.

Lequinio, Joseph-Marie. *Les Préjugés détruits*. 2d ed. 1793.

Lettres et pièces intéressantes pour servir à l'histoire du ministère du Roland, Servan, et Clavière. 1792.

Louvet de Couvray, Jean Baptiste. *A Maximilien Robespierre et ses royalistes*. 1792.

Machet-Vélye. *Programme sur la nécessité de construire un canal de navigation, depuis Paris, jusqu'à Dieppe et Rouen, avec l'exposé des moyens d'exécution*. 1793.

Mandar, Théophile. *Des Insurrections, ouvrage philosophique et politique sur les rapports des insurrections avec la prospérité des empires*. . . . 1793.

Manuel, B. E. *L'Etude de la nature en général et de l'homme en particulier considerée dans ses rapports avec l'instruction publique*. . . . 1793.

Marcandier, Roch. *Pétition à la Convention Nationale*. 1793.

Maréchal, Sylvain. *Almanach des républicains, pour servir à l'instruction publique*. . . . 1793.

———. *Correctif à la Révolution*. 1793.

Marsillac, Jean de. *La Goutte radicalement guérie*. [1792].

———. *La Vie de Guillaume Penn*. . . . 2 vols. 1791.

Maxwell, W. *Déclaration . . . relativement à l'Assemblée qui devoit se tenir chez lui à Londres, le 12 septembre 1792, pour ouvrir une souscription en faveur des Patriotes Français*. . . . N.d.

Mercier, Sébastien. *Le Ci-devant Noble*. . . . *1792*.

———. *Fictions morales*. 3 vols. 1792.

———. *Le Vieillard et ses trois filles, pièce en trois actes, en prose*. . . . *1792*.

Milscent, Claude-Louis-Michel. *Du Régime colonial*. . . . 1792.

Mogue. *Mogue . . . à la Convention Nationale*. . . . [1793].

Moreton-Chabrillan, Jacques-Henri-Sébastien-César. *Pétition à l'Assemblée*. 1791.

———. *Pétition à l'Assemblée Nationale . . . le 31 octobre 1791*. [1791].

———. *Précis pour J. H. Moreton*. [1791].

————. *Réclamation contre M. Duportai, ministre de la guerre, adressée à l'Assemblée Nationale . . . le 5 septembre 1791.* [1791].

Nitona Franka et le Sultan Patapouf, ou histoire de la révolution franche, à l'ordre du jour. Traduction libre. L'an IV de la liberté [1792].

Nusse, J. F. *Lettre . . . à un curé qui à preté serment, sur ce que nous attendons de la régénération de l'épiscopat. Lue à l'Assemblée fédérative des Amis de la Vérité.* 1791.

Ordre et marche de la translation de Voltaire à Paris . . . 11 juillet, et sa profession de foi. 1791.

Oswald, John. *The Triumph of Freedom! An Ode to Commemorate the Anniversary of the French Revolution. . . .* [1791].

Paine, Thomas. *Lettre . . . au peuple françois . . . le 25 septembre 1792. . . .* [1792].

————. *Théorie et pratique des droits de l'homme. . . .* Translated by François Lanthenas. 1792.

Palm d'Aelders, Etta. *Appel aux Françoises sur la régénération des moeurs et la nécessité de l'influence des femmes dans un gouvernement libre.* 1791.

————. *Prospectus pour le cercle patriotique des Amies de la verité.* N.d.

Perot, Michel. *Exposition patriotique des droits de l'homme, dédiée à tous les clubs et sociétés de bons citoyens.* 1790.

Un Petit Mot sur la grande affaire du jour. [1792].

Pétition adressée à l'Assemblée Nationale. N.d.

Pétition de la Société des amis des droits de l'homme et citoyen aux Représentants de la Nation. [1791].

Pièces principales remises au comité d'agriculture et de commerce relatives aux concessions et à la propriété des mines de charbon de terre . . . de Rhône et Loire. [1791].

Pierron. *Discours prononcé le 20 brumaire l'an II . . . sur l'autel dressé, rue de Serres, à l'Occasion de l'inauguration des bustes de Marat et de Lepelletier.* N.d.

Poincon. *Pétition à la Convention Nationale.* N.d.

Polyglotte, ou Traduction de la constitution française dans les langues les plus usitées de l'Europe. 3 vols. 1791-92.

Pradel, Henri. *L'Instituteur ou Le Patriote à l'épreuve, comédie en trois actes, en vers. . . .* 1793.

Projet d'Association pour l'encouragement de l'agriculture et des arts agricoles. 1791.

Projet pour un mode d'élection pour les Conventions Nationales et pour les législateurs. 1791.

Questions simples et précises proposées aux 40 sections de Paris, aux conseils généraux de toutes les communes et à tous les citoyens de l'empire, par la Société des amis de la liberté séante à la Croix-Rouge. N.d.

Raimond, Julien. *Correspondance . . . avec ses frères de Saint-Domingue. . . .* An II. [1793].

――――. *Lettres . . . à ses frères les hommes de couleur . . . et comparison des originaux de sa correspondance avec les extraits perfides qu'en ont fait MM. Page et Brulley, dans un libelle intitulé: "Développement des causes des colonies françaises."* An II. [1793].

――――. *Mémoire sur les causes des troubles et des désastres de la colonie de Saint-Domingue, presenté aux Comité de marine et des colonies. . . .* [1793].

Recicourt, François de. *De l'Importance d'une première école générale pour l'éducation des jeunes gens destinés à être employés dans le corps royal du génie.* N.d.

Réponse au No. 69 de Marat . . . par les citoyens soldats des bataillons nationaux, canonés à Paris. . . . [1792].

Roland de la Platière, Jean Marie. *Convention Nationale. Lettre du ministre de l'intérieur à la Convention Nationale, du 30 septembre 1792. . . .* [1792].

――――. *Correspondance du ministre de l'intérieur Roland, avec le Général Lafayette.* L'An Quatrième de la liberté [1792].

――――. *Lettre écrite au Roi, par le ministre de l'intérieur, le 10 juin 1792.* 1792.

――――. *Des Usuriers et des accapareurs.* [1792].

Saint-Martin, Louis-Claude de. *Ecce homo.* L'An IV de la liberté [1792].

――――. *Le Nouvel Homme.* L'An IV de la liberté [1792].

Santerre, Antoine Joseph. *Procès du sieur Santerre, Contre les sieurs Desmottes et Lafayette.* [1791]. Archives Nationales F7 4622 plaquette no. 4.

Section de la Croix-Rouge. [1793].

Section de la Croix-Rouge. Du 5 [sic] aôut 1792. . . . [1792].

Section de Marseille. 16 aôut 1792. . . . Invitation. . . . N.d.

Section de Marseille. Séance permanente. Extrait des déliberations de la section du Théâtre-Français et de Marseille, du 19 aôut 1792. . . . [1792].

Section de Marseille. Du 24 septembre 1792. . . . [1792].

Section des Halles. Extrait des registres des délibérations . . . du 17 septembre 1792. . . . [1792].

Section du Marche des Innocents . . . du 2 juillet 1792. . . . [1792].

Servan de Gerby, Joseph. *Lettre . . . sur le mémoire lu par M. Dumourier, le 13 juin à l'Assemblée Nationale.* [1792].

———. *Lettre* ... *à l'Assemblée National, sur le rapport du Comité des Comptes, et réflexions de l'éditeur à cette occasion.* N.d.

Supplément au manifest des princes. Déclaration des droits de l'Homme et du Citoyen, revue, corrigée, et augmentée par S. A. S. Mgr. le duc ... de Brunswick. ... [1792].

Trimmer, Sara. *Les Rouges-Gorges, ourvrage destiné à l'instruction et à l'amusement des enfants.* ... 2 vols. N.d.

Udin, Jean-Baptiste. *Adresse à l'Assemblée Nationale legislative.* ... N.d.

Varlet, Jean-François. *Projet d'un mandat spécial et impératif, aux mandataires du peuple à la Convention Nationale.* ... 1792.

La Vie du Capitaine Thurot par M.***. 1791.

Williams, David. *Observations sur la dernière constitution de la France, avec des rues pour la formation de la nouvelle constitution.* ... Translated by Maudru. 1793.

JOURNALS

Annales de la Confédération universelle des Amis de la Vérité. Edited by Bonneville. Appeared irregularly. 1791.

La Bouche de fer. Edited by Bonneville. Appeared thrice weekly until 22 June, when it became daily. October 1790-July 1791.

Bulletin de la Bouche de fer. Edited by Bonneville. Appeared irregularly. June-August 1790.

Bulletin des Amis de la Vérité. Edited by Bonneville. Appeared daily. January-March 1793.

Bulletin des Marsellois. Edited by Barbaroux. Appeared daily. 13-16 November 1792.

Cercle Social. Edited by Bonneville. Appeared irregularly. January-June 1790.

Chronique du mois. Edited by Bonneville. Appeared monthly. November 1791-July 1793.

La Feuille villageoise. Edited by Grouvelle and Ginguené. Appeared weekly. Published by the Cercle Social October 1792-October 1793.

Journal d'histoire naturelle. Edited by Lamarck. Appeared biweekly. January-June 1792.

Révolutions de France et de Brabant. Edited by Desmoulins. Appeared weekly. Published by the Cercle Social March-June 1791.

La Sentinelle. Edited by Louvet de Couvray. Appeared irregularly. May-November 1792.

APPENDIX C

AUTHORS OF THE IMPRIMERIE
DU CERCLE SOCIAL, 1790-1793.

THE FOLLOWING list includes all of the writers who wrote books, pamphlets, and/or articles for Cercle Social publications between 1790 and 1793. The only authors deliberately omitted were minor contributors to the *Feuille villageoise*, the *Journal d'histoire naturelle*, and the *Bulletin des Amis de la Vérité*. Where available, birth date and biographical comments follow the author's name.

Allimont, Georges-Louis-Chappe; military officer
Auger, Athanase (1734); professor of rhetoric
Balland, Cl. P. Jos.; forest administrator
Bancal, Henri (1750); Convention—Inner Sixty
Barbaroux, Charles (1767); Convention—Inner Sixty
Belair, Alexandre-Pierre-Julienne (1747); military officer
Bidermann, (1751); financier, government administrator
Bonnemain, Antoine-Jean-Thomas (1756); Convention
Boilleau, Jacques (1751); Convention—Inner Sixty
Bonneville, François; portraitist, N. Bonneville's cousin
Bonneville, Nicolas (1760); municipal politician
Bosc d'Antic, Louis (1759); scientist, postal administrator
Brissot, Jacques-Pierre (1754); Convention—Inner Sixty
Brugières, Jean-Guillaume; scientist
Chaix d'Est-Ange, Richard; priest
Chaussard, Publicola (1766); professor of classics
Clavière, Etienne (1735); minister of finance
Collin, Antoine; administrator, Department of Paris
Collot d'Herbois, Jean-Marie (1750); Convention—Montagnard
Condorcet, J.A.N. (1743); Convention—Inner Sixty
Crivelli
Creuzé-Latouche, Jacques-Antoine (1749); Convention—Inner Sixty
Cubières-Palmézeaux, Michel de (1752); municipal politician
Daubermesnil, François-Antoine (1748); Convention
Desmoulins, Camille (1762); Convention—Montagnard

Doppet, François–Amédée (1753); military officer
Ducros, François; foreman of ICS
Dufour de Saint-Pathus, Julien-Michel
Dufourny de Villiers, Louis-Pierre (1739); engineer, founder of Lycée
Dupré, Augustin; engraver
Dusaulx, Jean (1728); Legislative Assembly
Dussault, Jean-Joseph (1769)
Dutrone la Conture, Jacques-François; physician
Enguehard; physician
Fabre d'Eglantine, Philippe (1755); Convention—Mountain
Fauchet, Claude (1744); Convention—Inner Sixty
Favier, Jean-Louis
Feydel, Gabriel; journalist
Focard de Château
Fourquevaux, Marie-Angélique-Hélène-Felicio
Galbaud-Dufort, François-Thomas (1743); military officer
Gallet, Pierre
Garran-Coulan, Jean-Philippe (1748); Convention
Gensonné, Armond (1753); Convention—Inner Sixty
Gerlet
Gianni, Francesco (1750); Italian poet
Ginguené, Pierre-Louis
Gorani, Giuseppe (1744); Italian
Grouvelle, Philippe
Guérault
Hauy, René-Just (1743); scientist, professor
Henriquez, L. M. (1765); professor
Jallet, Jacques (1732); Constitutional curé
Kersaint, Armand-Guy (1742); Convention—Inner Sixty
Lacroix, Marie-Sébastien Bruno de (1768); lawyer
Lamarck, Jean-Baptiste-Pierre Antoine de Monet (1744); scientist
Lameth, A.
Lanoa
Lanthenas, François (1754); Convention—Inner Sixty
La Place, P. A. de (1707); academician
Lavallée, Joseph (1747); military officer
Lavicomterie de Saint-Samson, Louis (1732); Convention—Montagnard
La Grangneur; municipal politician
Lequinio, Joseph-Marie (1755); Convention—Montagnard
Louvet de Couvray, Jean-Baptiste (1760); Convention—Inner Sixty

Machet-Vélye
Mandar, Théophile (1759); municipal politician
Manuel, B. E. (1760); professor, scientist
Marcandier, Roch (1767); journalist
Maréchal, Sylvain (1750); "L'homme sans Dieu"
Marsillac, Jean de; physician
Maxwell, W. English
Mercier, Sébastien (1740); Convention—Inner Sixty
Milscent, Claude-Louis-Michel (1740); antislavery colonist
Mogue
Moreton-Chabrillan, Jacques Henri Sébastien César de (1752); military
    officer, Paris Jacobin
Nusse, J. F.; priest
Olivier, Guillaume-Antoine; scientist
Oswald, John; English radical
Paine, Thomas (1737); Convention
Palm, Etta d'Aelders; feminist leader
Parent, François Nicolas (1752); priest, Paris Elector 1790
Perrot, Michel; member of Confédération
Pierron; municipal politician
Poincon
Pradel, Henri
Puthod, François
Raimond, Julien; radical colonist
Reynier, Jean-Louis-Antoine (1762); publisher, academician
Ricicourt, François de
Roland, Jean-Marie (1734); minister of the interior
Sabatièr-Labastie
Saint-Martin, Louis-Claude de (1743); Martinist philosopher
Santerre, Antoine-Joseph (1752); municipal politician
Servan de Gerby, Joseph; minister of war
Udin, Jean-Baptiste; farmer
Varlet, Jean-François; the Enragé
Williams, David (1738); English radical

BIBLIOGRAPHY

Note: This Bibliography does not include Cercle Social publications already listed in Appendix B.

UNPUBLISHED PRIMARY SOURCES

Archives de la Seine. 3 AZ 250, 4 AZ 931 and 932. Police Committee documents (1789).

————. 4 AZ 937. Letter from Société fraternelle des anciens représentants de la Commune de Paris.

————. VD 623. "Extrait du Registre des délibérations de l'Assemblée Générale de la Commune de Saint-Roch du 2 octobre 1789."

————. VD 12, "Procès-Verbal du Comité des Vingt-Quatre."

Archives Nationales. AF III*, fol. 96, no. 2121. Letter from Paine to Directory.

————. C 54, fol. 535, no. 1. Letter from Fauchet to National Assembly.

————. CI 1, fol. 95. "Motion de M. Bonneville du 26 juin 1789."

————. F7 4622. Note from Reynier to Brissot.

————. F7 4774, fol. 77, dos. 1, no. 9. Police dossier of J. B. E. Plaisant.

————. F7 8083, no. 1196, Police dossier of Nicolas Bonneville.

————. F17 1348, dos. 1, no. 13. Letter of 19 February 1792 from the Directoire du Cercle Social to the Committee of Public Instruction.

————. T 364, T 1601, and T 1686. Papers of Etta Palm d'Aelders.

Bibliothèque de L'Arsenal. Manuscript 15078 (2c), fols. 189-190. Letter of 24 January 1791 from Bernardin de Saint-Pierre to Mercier.

Bibliothèque historique de la ville de Paris. Manuscript 777, nos. 69-75. Letters from Mme Villot-Philip to M. and Mme Palloy.

Bibliothèque Nationale. Nouvelles acquisitions françaises 6242, fols. 119-121. Letters from Roland to Auger.

————. Nouvelles acquisitions françaises 9533-9534. Papers of Roland.

PUBLISHED PRIMARY SOURCES

Ami du peuple, ou Le Publiciste parisien. Edited by Jean-Paul Marat, 12 September 1789 - 21 September 1792.

Annales patriotiques et littéraires. . . . Edited by J. L. Carra and L. S. Mercier. 3 October 1789 - 16 prairial an V.

Archives parlementaires de 1787 à 1860, première série (1787 à 1799).

Edited by M. J. Mavidel and M. E. Laurent. 2d ed. 82 vols. Paris: Paul Dupont, 1879-1913.

Auger, Athanase. *Catéchisme du citoyen françois, composé de l'esprit et de la lettre de la nouvelle constitution.* Paris: Crapert, n.d.

————. *Discours sur ce sujet: Combien il nous importe d'avoir la paix, quels sont les moyens de nous la procurer? Lu dans la Société des Amis de la Vérité . . . suivi De Quelques réflexions sur la nécessité d'obéir la loi.* Paris: L. P. Couret, 1791.

————. "Droits rigoureaux du peuple, vrais intérêts du peuple." *Tribut de la Société nationale des neuf soeurs*, 14 November 1791, pp. 49-52.

————. *Moyens d'assurer la Révolution . . . avec une adresse à l'Assemblée Nationale et des réflexions sur le pouvoir exécutif.* Paris: Garnery, l'an de la liberté, [1790].

————. *Projet d'éducation pour tout le royaume, précédé de quelques réflexions sur l'Assemblée Nationale.* Paris: Didot l'aîné, 1789.

Auger, Athanase, ed. *Organisation de écoles nationales. . . .* Paris: Imprimerie Nationale, 1791.

Aulard, F. Alphonse, ed. *La Société des Jacobins. Recueil des documents pour l'histoire de club des Jacobins de Paris. . . .* 6 vols. Paris: Jouaust, 1889-97.

Bailly, Jean-Sylvain. *Lettre . . . à Messieurs des districts.* Paris: n.p., 1789.

————. *Lettre . . . à M. le Président de l'Assemblée Nationale . . . le 10 octobre 1790.* Paris: Lottin, 1790.

————. *Mémoires. . . .* Edited by Berville and Barrière. 3 vols. Paris: Baudouin, 1821-1822.

Barbier de Montault, X. "Mémoires de Garran de Coulon." *Revue illustrée des provinces de l'Ouest* 2(1890): 256-64, 3(1891): 31-40, 5(1892): 214-19.

————. "Papiers de Garran de Coulon (1756-1788)," *Revue d'archéologie poitevine* 3(1900): 315-18.

Baumier. *De la Monarchie Française. . . .* Paris: Patriote Français, 1791.

Bernardin, Edith, ed. "Letters de Lanthenas à Bancal des Issarts." *Annales historiques de la Révolution Française* 16(1939): 62-68, 152-66, 245-62.

Bonneville, Nicolas. *A M. le Maire et MM. les officiers municipaux de la ville de Paris.* N.p., n.d.

————. *Choix de petits romans imités de l'Allemand . . . suivis de quelques essais de poésie lyrique. . . .* Paris: Théophile Barrois, 1776 [*sic*] read: 1786.

————. *Histoire de l'Europe, depuis l'irruption des peuples du Nord dans l'Empire romain, jusqu'à la paix de 1783.* . . . vol. 1 Geneva: n.p., 1789.

―――. *Les Jésuites chassés de la Maçonnerie, et leur poignard brisé par les maçons.* 2 vols. London: Orient de Londres, and Paris: Volland, 1788.

―――. *Lettre à M. le Maire et à MM. des districts de Paris, par ***, Réprésentant de la Commune.* N.p., n.d.

Boulard, M. S. *Le Manuel de l'imprimeur.* . . . Paris: Boulard, 1791.

Brie-Serrant, Clément Alexandre de. *Au Cercle Social des Amis de la Vérité.* N.p., n.d.

―――. *Mémoires du peuple au peuple, au rapport de huit des comités de l'Assemblée Nationale.* N.p., n.d.

Brissot, Jacques-Pierre. *Correspondance et papiers.* Edited by Claude Perroud. Paris: Picard et fils, 1911.

―――. *Mémoires.* Edited by Claude Perroud. 3 vols. Paris: Picard et fils, n.d.

―――. *Motifs des commissaires, pour adopter le plan de municipalité, qui'ils ont présenté à l'Assemblée générale des Réprésentants de la Commune . . . suivis du projet du plan de municipalité.* Paris: Lottin 1789.

Chaix d'Est-Ange, Richard. *De l'influence de la religion sur le patriotisme* . . . Paris: Valleyre, 1789.

Charavay, Etienne, ed. *L'Assemblée éléctorale de Paris. 18 novembre 1790–15 juin 1791.* Paris: Jouaust, 1890.

―――. *L'Assemblée électorale de Paris. 26 août 1791–12 août 1792.* Paris: Cerf, 1894.

Chassin, Charles, ed. *Les élections et les cahiers de Paris en 1789.* . . . 4 vols. Paris: Jouaust, 1888-89.

Chronique de Paris. Edited by M.J.A.N. Condorcet et al., 24 August 1789–24 August 1793.

Cloots, Anacharsis. *L'Orateur du genre humain.* . . . Paris: Desenne, 1791.

Collot d'Herbois, Jean-Marie. *Almanach du père Gérard pour l'année 1792.* . . . Paris: Société des amis de la constitution, 1792.

Condorcet, M.J.A.N. *Selected Writings.* Edited by Keith Michael Baker. Indianapolis: Bobbs-Merrill, Library of Liberal Arts, 1976.

Courrier de Lyon. Edited by L. A. Champagneux. 1 November 1789–19 November 1790. Archives Municipales de Lyon, 400006.

Le Courrier de Paris dans les 83 départments. Edited by A. J. Gorsas. 3 August 1790–1 October 1791.

Courrier de Versailles à Paris et de Paris à Versailles. Edited by A. J. Gorsas, 5 July 1789–17 October 1789.

Le Créole patriote. Edited by Claude Milscent. 26 July 1792–28 pluvose an II.

Cressy, Louis Claude de. *Essai sur les moeurs, ou Point de constitution durable sans moeurs.* Paris: Grégoire, 1790.

Creuzé-Latouche, Jacques-Antoine. "Les Grandes Journées de juin et de juillet 1789 d'après le *Journal* inédit de Creuzé-Latouche. ..." *Revue des questions historiques* 123 and 124 (1935):242-64.

Daunou, P.C.F. "Mémoires pour servir à l'histoire de la Convention Nationale." *Documents biographiques sur P.C.F. Daunou,* ed. M.A.H. Taillandier. Paris: Firmin Didot, 1841.

Desmoulins, Camille. *Oeuvres.* ... Edited by Jules Claretie. 2 vols. Paris: Charpentier, 1906.

Dumont, Etienne P. L. *Souvenirs de Mirabeau et sur les deux premières assemblées législatives.* Paris: Gosselin, 1832.

Dusaulx, Jean. "L'Oeuvre des sept jours ...," and "La Prise de la Bastille, discours historiques," in *Mémoires de Linguet sur la Bastille et de Dusaulx sur le 14 juillet* ... eds. Berville and Barrière, 2nd edition. Paris: Baudouin fils, 1821, p. 354.

Encyclopédie méthodique. Jurisprudence. 10 vols. Paris: Panckoucke, 1783-1789.

Fauchet, Claude. *Contre les billets de confession. Motion faite* ... *à l'Assemblée des Représentants de la Commune, le 12 mai 1790.* Paris: Lottin l'aîné et Lottin De Saint-Germain, n.d.

———. *De la Religion nationale.* Paris: Gailly, 1789.

———. *A Discourse on the Liberty of France. Delivered the 5 of August, 1789.* ... Trans. W. Harvest. London: Chalklen, 1790.

———. *Discours sur la liberté françoise, prononcé le* ... *5 août 1789.* ... 2nd ed. Paris: Bailly, 1789.

———. *Discours sur les moeurs rurales, prononcé dans l'église de Surenne, le 10 août 1788 pour la fête de la rosière.* Paris: Lottin, 1788.

———. *Encore quatre cris ou Sermon d'un patriote.* ... Paris: Garnery and Volland, 1789.

———. *Elôge civique de Benjamin Franklin, prononcé le 21 juillet 1790, dans la rotonde, au nom de la Commune de Paris.* ... 3d ed. Paris: Lottin, 1790.

———. *Extrait du procès-verbal de l'Assemblée générale des Représentants de la Commune de Paris du jeudi 11 mars 1790.* ... Paris: n.p., n.d.

———. *Extrait du registre des délibérations de la Société des amis de la constitution séante à Caen, du 27 septembre 1791, l'an III.* Caen: Chalopin, n.d.

————. *Motion faite à l'Assemblée générale des Représentants de la Commune, 20 novembre 1789.* N.p., n.d.

————. *Oraison funèbre de Charles-Michel de l'Epée.* Paris: Lottin de Saint-Germain, 1790.

[Fauchet, Claude, ed.] *Tableaux de la Révolution françoise ou Collection de quarante-huit gravures représentant les événements principaux qui ont eu lieu en France depuis la transformation des Etats-Généraux en Assemblée Nationale, le 20 juin 1789.* Paris: Briffault de la Charprais, n.d.

————. *Troisième discours sur la liberté françoise, prononcé le dimanche 27 septembre 1789. . . .* Paris: Bailly, 1789.

La Feuille du cultivateur. Edited by Broussonet, Dubois, and Lefebvre. 1790-98.

Garran-Coulon, Jean-Philippe. *Notice sur Jacques-Antoine Creuzé-Latouche . . . lue, le 28 Brumaire an IX au Sénat-Conservateur. . . .* N.p., n.d.

Girardin, Mis de. *L'Arrestation de dernier ami de Jean-Jacques Rousseau.* Paris: H. Leclerc, 1919.

Godard, Jacques. *Discours prononcé dans l'église des Blancs Manteaux le samedi 12 septembre 1789, à l'occasion de la bénédiction des drapeaux du District des Blancs-Manteaux.* Paris: Prault, 1789.

————. *Exposé des travaux de l'Assemblée Générale des Représentants de la Commune de Paris, depuis le 25 juillet 1789 jusqu'au mois d'octobre 1790. . . .* Paris: Lottin, 1790.

————. *Réfutation des principes exposés par le M. le Maire de Paris, dans sa lettre à M. le président de l'Assemblée Nationale, par une Société de citoyens légalement réunis . . . au cirque national.* Paris: Imprimerie de la Société, 1790.

Guillaume, M. S., ed. *Procès-Verbaux du Comité de l'instruction publique de la Convention Nationale. . . .* 6 vols. Paris: Imprimerie Nationale, 1891-1907.

Halem. *Paris en 1790. Voyage de Halem.* Translated by Arthur Chauquet. Paris: Chailley, 1896.

Jeudy de L'Houmand. *Le Pain à bon marché, ou Le Monopole terrassé et le peuple vengé.* Paris: Laurens and Cressionnier, n.d.

————. *Les Monopoleurs terrassés ou Le Danger éminent de faire manger au peuple de mauvais pain.* Paris: Laurens, n.d.

Journal d'agriculture à l'usage des habitants de la campagne. Edited by J. L. Reynier. 1 March 1790–15 July 1790.

Journal de la municipalité et des districts de Paris. Edited by F. L. Bayard. 1 April 1790–26 June 1791.

Journal de Paris. 1 January 1777–30 September 1811.

Journal des amis. Edited by Claude Fauchet. 5 January 1793–15 June 1793.

Le Journal des amis de la constitution. Edited by P. Choderlos de Laclos. 7 December 1790–20 September 1791.

Journal des beaux-arts et des sciences. 1768-1775.

Journal des clubs ou sociétés patriotiques. Edited by J. J. Le Roux des Tillets, J. Charon, and D. M. Revol. 20 November 1790–3 September 1791.

Journal encyclopédique ou universel. Edited by P. Rousseau. 1 January 1789–30 December 1793.

Journal des laboureurs. Edited by Joseph-Marie Lequinio. 31 March 1791–18 February 1792.

Journal d'Etat et du citoyen. Edited by Louis Robert. 12 September 1789–1 November 1791.

Journal du club des Cordeliers. 28 June 1791–10 August 1791.

Lacroix, Sigismond, ed. *Actes de la Commune de Paris pendant la Révolution. Première série, 25 juillet 1789 à 8 octobre 1790.* 7 vols. Paris: Cerf, 1894-1898.

————. *Actes de la Commune de Paris pendant la Révolution. Seconde série, 9 octobre 1790 à 10 août 1792.* 8 vols. Paris: Cerf, 1900-1909.

Lalande, Luc-François. *Apologie des décrets de l'Assemblée Nationale sur la constitution civile du clergé.* Paris: Froullé, 1791.

Lamourette, Antoine-Adrien. *Les Délices de la religion, ou le Pouvoir de l'Evangile pour nous rendre heureux.* ... Paris: Merigot jeune, 1788.

————. *Instruction pastorale ... au clergé et aux Fidèles de son diocèse.* Lyon: d'Amable Le Roy, 1791.

————. *Pensées sur la philosophie de la foi, ou le Système du christianisme entrevu dans son analogie avec ses idées naturelles de l'entendement humain.* ... Paris: Mérigot jeune, 1789.

————. *Pensées sur la philosophie de l'incrédulité; ou, Réflexions sur l'esprit et le dessein des philosophes irreligieux de ce siècle.* ... Paris: Simon, 1785.

Lanthenas, François. *Inconvéniens du droit d'aînesse, ouvrage dans lequel on démontre que toute distinction entre les enfants d'une famille entraîne une foule de maux politiques, moraux, et physiques.* ... Paris: Visse, [1789].

Lefranc, François Joseph. *Conjuration contre la religion catholique et les souverains.* ... Paris: Lepetit, 1792.

Lequinio, Joseph-Marie. *Ecole des laboureurs.* ... 2d ed. rev. Vennes [sic: read Rennes], 1790.

Levy, Darlene, et al., eds. *Women in Revolutionary Paris, 1789-1795.* Urbana: University of Illinois Press, 1979.

Logographe. Edited by Le Hodey. 1791-1792.

Louvet de Couvray, Jean-Baptiste. *Emile de Varmont, ou Le Divorce nécessaire et les amours du curé Sevin.* ... 3 vols. Paris: Bailly, 1791.

———. *Mémoires ... sur la Révolution française.* Edited by F. A. Aulard. 2 vols. Paris: Librairie des Bibliophiles, 1889.

———. *Une Année de la vie du chevalier de Faublas.* ... 5 vols. Paris and London: Chez l'autour, 1787.

Mémoires secrets pour servir à l'histoire de la république des lettres en France, depuis MDCCLXII jusqu'à nos jours; ou, Journal d'un observateur. Edited by Louis Petit de Bachaumont. 1777-89.

Mercier, Louis-Sébastien. *Memoirs of the Year Two Thousand Five Hundred* [sic]. Translated by W. Hooper. Philadelphia: T. Dobson, 1795.

———. *De Jean-Jacques Rousseau.* ... 2 vols. Paris: Buisson, 1791.

Mercure de France. Edited by Mallet du Pan.

Mercure National et Révolutions de l'Europe. Edited by Louise and François Robert. September 1790–29 March 1791.

Mille, François-Bernard. *Serment civique sur la constitution du clergé* .... Paris: Grangé, 1791.

Momoro, Antoine-François. *Traité élémentaire de l'imprimerie ou Le Manuel de l'imprimeur.* Paris: Momoro, 1793.

Moniteur universel. Réimpression de l'ancien Moniteur; seule histoire authentique et inaltéré de la Révolution française; depuis la réunion des Etats-Généraux jusqu'au Consulat (mai 1789–novembre 1799). 32 vols. Paris: Plon, 1847-79.

Moore, John. *A Journal During a Residence in France from the Beginning of August to the Middle of December 1792.* ... 2 vols. London: Robinson, 1793.

Mulot, François-Valentin. *Discours sur le serment civique.* ... Paris: Lottin l'aîné et Lottin de Saint-Germain, 1790.

L'Orateur du peuple. Edited by Stanislas Fréron. May 1790–25 thermidor an III.

Paine, Thomas. *Complete Writings.* Edited by Philip Foner. New York: Citadel, 1945.

Le Patriote français. Edited by Jacques-Pierre Brissot. 6 May 1789–2 June 1793.

Prichard, Samuel. *Masonry Dissected.* ... London: Byfield and Hawkesworth, n.d.

Procès-verbaux des séances et déliberations de l'Assemblée générale des

Elécteurs de Paris. . . . Edited by J. S. Bailly and H. Duveyrier. 3 vols. Paris: Baudouin, 1790.

Projet du Plan de municipalité de la ville de Paris. . . . *présenté a l'Assemblée générale des Représentans de la Commune, par ses commissaires, le 12 août 1789.* Paris: Lottin, 1789.

Prônes civiques ou Le Pasteur patriote. Edited by Antoine-Adrien Lamourette. 1791.

Le Républicain, ou Le Défenseur du gouvernement représentatif. Edited by Condorcet, Paine, Duchatelet, [Bonneville, Brissot, or Lanthenas?], 1791.

Révolutions de France et de Brabant. Edited by Camille Desmoulins. 28 November 1789–10 December 1792.

Révolutions de Paris. Edited by L. Prudhomme. 12-17 July 1789–25 pluvoise-10 ventose an II.

Roland, Manon [Philpon]. *Lettres de Mme Roland.* Edited by Claude Perroud. 2 vols. Paris: Imprimerie Nationale, 1900-1902.

———. *Mémoires.* Edited by Claude Perroud. 2 vols. Paris: Plon-Nourrit, 1905.

Rousseau, Charles-Louis. *Essai sur l'éducation et l'existence civile des femmes dans la constitution française, dédié à Mme Bailly.* . . . Paris: Girouard, 1790.

Rousseau, Jean-Jacques. *Oeuvres complètes.* Edited by Gabriel Brizard. Paris: Buisson, 1788-93.

———. *The Social Contract and the Discourses.* Translated by G.D.H. Cole. New York: Dutton, 1950.

Saint-Martin, Louis Claude de. *Lettre à un ami ou Considérations politiques, philosophiques, et religieuses sur la Révolution française.* Paris: Louvet, an III.

———. *Oeuvres posthumes.* . . . 2 vols. Tours: Letourmy, 1807.

Sieyès, Emmanuel. *What Is the Third Estate?* Translated by M. Blondel. London: Pall Mall, 1963.

Simpson, M.C.M., ed. *Reminiscences of a Regicide. Edited From the Original Mss. of Sergent-Marceau.* . . . London: Chapman and Hall, 1889.

Tanevot-d'Herbault, Gabriel-Claude. *Discours prononcé . . . au nom du club fraternel des ci-devant représentants provisoires de la Commune, invitant à la fête religieuse et civique que ce club se propose de célébrer chaque année, le 4 février.* Paris: N.p., n.d.

———. *Discours de M. Tanevot, président de la Société fraternelle des anciens Représentants de la Commune de Paris, à M. l'Evêque du Calvados.* . . . Paris: Caisse d'Epargnes, 1791.

Tribun du peuple. Edited by Nicolas de Bonneville. 1789.

Tribut de la Société nationale des neuf soeurs. Edited by E. Cordier de Saint-Firmin. July 1790–August 1792.

Volfius, Jean-Baptiste. *Discours prononcé le 18 mai 1790 à la cérémonie du serment fédératif.* ... Dijon: Causse, 1790.

Wright, D. I. *The French Revolution. Introductory Documents.* St. Lucia, Queensland: Queensland University Press, 1974.

Young, Arthur. *Travels in France During 1787, 1788 and 1789.* Edited by Jeffrey Kaplow. Garden City, N.Y.: Anchor, 1969.

SECONDARY SOURCES

Abensour, Léon. *La Femme et le Féminisme avant la Révolution.* Paris: N.p., 1923.

Abray, Jane. "Feminism in the French Revolution." *American Historical Review* 80(1975): 43-62.

Aldridge, Alfred Owen. "Condorcet et Paine. Leur rapports intellectuels." *Revue de littérature comparée* 32 (1958): 47-65.

————. *Man of Reason: The Life of Thomas Paine.* Philadelphia: Lippincott, 1959.

Alexeev-Popov, V. "Le Cercle Social (1790-1791)." *Recherches soviétiques,* no. 4 (1956): 89-150.

Amiable, Louis. *Une Loge maçonnique d'avant 1789, la G . ∴ L . ∴ les neuf soeurs.* Paris: Alcan, 1897.

Aulard, F. Alphonse. *Le Culte de la raison et le culte de l'être suprême (1793-1794). Essai historique.* Paris: Alcan, 1892.

————. "Danton au club des Cordeliers et au département de Paris." *Révolution française* 24(1893): 226-46.

————. "Danton au district des Cordeliers et à la Commune de Paris." *Révolution française* 24(1893): 113-44.

————. "Le Féminisme pendant la Révolution française." *Revue bleue,* 4th series, 9(1898): 361-66.

————. *The French Revolution: A Political History, 1789-1804.* 4 vols. Translated by Bernard Moll. New York: Charles Scribner's Sons, 1910.

Avenel, Georges. *Anacharsis Cloots: L'Orateur du genre humain.* Paris: Editions Champ Libre, 1976.

Baker, Keith Michael. *Condorcet: From Natural Philosophy to Social Mathematics.* Chicago: University of Chicago Press, 1975.

————. "Scientism, Elitism, and Liberalism: The Case of Condorcet." *Studies on Voltaire and the Eighteenth Century* 55 (1967): 129-65.

Baltot, J., et al. *Dictionnaire de biographie française.* . . . Paris: Letouzey et Ané, 1933- . Incomplete.

Barny, Roger. "Jean-Jacques Rousseau dans la Révolution." *Dix-huitième siècle* 6 (1974): 59-98.

Bellanger, Claude, et al. *Histoire générale de la presse française.* . . . 4 vols. Paris: P.U.F., 1969.

Benetruy, J. *L'Atelier de Mirabeau: Quatre proscrits génévois dans la tourmente révolutionnaire.* Paris: A. & J. Picard, 1962.

Bernardin, Edith. *Jean-Marie Roland et le ministère de l'intérieur.* Paris: Société des Etudes Robespierristes, 1964.

Berthe, Leon. "Grégoire, élève de l'abbé Lamourette." *Revue du Nord* 44 (1962): 40-46.

Billington, James H. *Fire in the Minds of Men: The Origins of the Revolutionary Faith.* New York: Basic Books, 1981.

Bouchary, Jean. *Les Manieurs d'argent à Paris à la fin du xviiie siècle.* 3 vols. Paris: Rivière, 1939.

Bourdin, Isabelle. *Les Sociétés populaires à Paris pendant la Révolution.* Paris: Recueil Sirely, 1937.

Bourne, Henry E. "Improvising a Government in Paris in July 1789," *American Historical Review* 10(1904-1905): 280-308.

———. "Municipal Politics in Paris in 1789." *American Historical Review* 11(1905-1906): 263-86.

Boursin, Elphège. *Dictionnaire de la Révolution française.* Paris: Jouvet, 1893.

Bouvier, Jeanne. *Les Femmes pendant la Révolution.* Paris: Figuiere, 1931.

Braesch, F. "Les Petitions du Champ de Mars." *Revue historique* 143(1923): 192-209; 143(January-April): 1-37; and 143(May-August): 181-97.

Brinton, Clarence Crane. *The Jacobins: An Essay in the New History.* New York: Russell and Russell, 1961.

Brucker, Gene A. *Jean-Sylvain Bailly, Revolutionary Mayor of Paris.* Urbana: University of Illinois Press, 1950.

Buchez, P.J.B., and Roux, P. L. *Histoire parlementaire de la Révolution française.* . . . 40 vols. Paris: Paulin, 1834.

Cahen, Léon. *Condorcet et la Révolution française.* Paris: Alcan, 1904.

———. "La Société des amis des noirs et Condorcet." *Révolution française* 50(1906): 481-511.

Carlyle, Thomas. *The French Revolution. A History.* New York: Burt, 1900.

Caron, P. "La Mission de Loyseau et Bonneville à Rouen." *Révolution française* 86(1933): 236-58, 326-44.

Censer, Jack Richard. *Prelude to Power: The Parisian Radical Press, 1789-1791*. Baltimore: Johns Hopkins University Press, 1976.

Challamel, J. B. *Les Clubs contre-révolutionnaires*. Paris: Cerf, 1895.

Charrier, Jules. *Claude Fauchet. Evêque constitutionnel du Calvados, député à l'Assemblée legislative et à la Convention, 1744-1793*. 2 vols. Paris: Champion, 1909.

Chevallier, Pierre. *Histoire de la Franc-Maçonnerie française*. Vol. 1. *La Maçonnerie: Ecole de l'égalité 1725-1799*. Paris: Fayard, 1974.

Clifford, Dale, and Decker, Jane. "District Sovereignty and the Parisian Soldat-Citoyen, 1790: The Struggle Over Permanence" (abstract), *The Consortium on Revolutionary Europe: Proceedings*. Athens, Georgia: University of Georgia Press, 1979.

——. "July to September: the Critical Months of the Parisian Municipal Revolution" (unpublished).

Conway, Moncure D. *The Life of Thomas Paine*. 2 vols. New York: Putnam, 1893.

Cook, Mercer. "Julien Raimond." *Journal of Negro History* 26(1941): 139-70.

Cubières-Palmézeaux, Michel de. "Notice historique et critique sur la vie et les ouvrages de Nicolas-Edme Restif de la Bretonne." [Jacob, P.L.], *Bibliographie et iconographie de tous les ouvrages de Restif de la Bretonne*. New York: Burt Franklin, 1971.

Curtin, Philip D. "The Declaration of the Rights of Man in Saint-Domingue, 1788-1791." *Hispanic American Historical Review* 30(1950): 157-75.

Daline, V. M. "Babeuf et le Cercle Social." *Recherches internationales à la lumière du Marxisme,* no. 62 (1970): 62-73.

Darnton, Robert. *The Literary Underground of the Old Regime*. Cambridge: Harvard University Press, 1982.

Dard, Emile. *Le Général Choderlos de Laclos*. Paris: Perrin, 1936.

Dauban, C. A. *Etude sur Madame Roland et son temps, suivie des lettres inédites de Madame Roland à Buzot*. 2 vols. Paris: Baudouin, 1864.

Debien, Gabriel, *Les Colons de Saint-Dominque et la Révolution: Essai sur le Club Massiac, août 1789–août 1792*. Paris: A. Colin, 1953.

Dejace, André. *Les Règles de la dévolution successorale sous la Révolution (1789-1794)*. Paris: n.p., 1957.

Delsaux, Hélène. *Condorcet journaliste (1790-1794)*. Paris: Champion, 1931.

Dictionary of the History of Ideas. Edited by Philip P. Weiner. 4 vols. New York: Charles Scribner's Sons, 1973.

Di Padova, Theodore. "The Girondins and the Question of Revolutionary Government." *French Historical Studies* 9(1976): 432-50.

―――. "The Question of Girondin Motives: A Response to Sydenham." *French Historical Studies* 10(1977): 349-52.

Dommanget, Maurice. *Sylvain Maréchal. L'Egalitaire, "l'Homme sans Dieu," sa vie—son oeuvre 1750-1803.* Paris: Lefeuvre, 1950.

Dorigny, Marcel. "Recherche sur les idées économiques des Girondins." *Actes du colloque Girondins et Montagnards (Sorbonne, 14 décembre 1975) sous la direction d'Albert Soboul.* Paris: Société des Etudes Robespierristes, 1980.

―――. "Violence et révolution. Les Girondins et les massacres de septembre." *Actes du colloque Girondins et Montagnards (Sorbonne, 14 décembre 1975) sous la direction d'Albert Soboul.* Paris: Société des Etudes Robespierristes, 1980.

Dorimon. "L'Abbé Claude Fauchet, membre de la Commune de Paris." *Revue de la Révolution* 10(1887): 148-70.

Doyle, William. *The Origins of the French Revolution.* Oxford: Oxford University Press, 1980.

―――. "Was There an Aristocratic Reaction in Pre-Revolutionary France?" *Past and Present*, no. 57, (1972): 97-122.

Du Boff, Richard B. "Economic Thought in Revolutionary France, 1789-1792: The Question of Poverty and Unemployment." *French Historical Studies* 4(1966): 434-51.

Duhet, Paule-Marie. *Les Femmes et la Révolution française 1789-1794.* Paris: Gallimard, 1971.

Dulaure, J. A. *Histoire physique, civile, et morale de Paris.* 7th edition. 4 vols. Paris: Fournier, 1839.

Edelstein, Melvin. *La Feuille villageoise: Communication et modernisation dans les régions rurales pendant la Révolution.* Paris: Bibliothèque Nationale, 1977.

Egret, Jean. *The French Pre-Revolution, 1787-1789.* Translated by Wesley D. Camp. Chicago: University of Chicago Press, 1977.

Ellery, Eloise. *Brissot de Warville: A Study in the History of the French Revolution.* New York: Vassar College, 1915.

Ellis, Aytoun. *The Penny Universities: A History of the Coffee-Houses.* London: Secker and Warburg, 1956.

Espezel, Pierre d'. *Le Palais Royal.* Paris: Calmann-Lévy, 1936.

Foner, Laura. "The Free People of Color in Louisiana and Saint-Domingue." *Journal of Social History* 3(1970): 406-30.

Forado-Cunéo, Y. "Les Ateliers de charité de Paris pendant la Révolution, 1789-1791." *Révolution française* 86(1933): 317-42, and 87 (1934): 29-61, 103-23.

Furet, François. *Interpreting the French Revolution.* Translated by Elborg Forster. Cambridge: Cambridge University Press, 1981.

Gallois, Léonard. *Histoire des journaux et des journalistes de la Révolution française (1789-1796).* . . . 2 vols. Paris: Société de l'industrie fraternelle, 1845-1846.

Garrigues, Georges. *Les Districts parisiens pendant la Révolution française.* Paris: Editions Spès, 1931.

Gay, Peter. *Voltaire's Politics: The Poet as Realist.* New York: Vintage, 1965.

――――. *The Party of Humanity: Essays in the French Enlightenment.* New York: Norton, 1963.

Gliozzo, Charles A., and Friguglietti, James. "The Personal Enemy of Jesus Christ: Anacharsis Cloots, an Irreligious Revolutionary of the Eighteenth Century." *Eighteenth Century Life* 3(1977): 80-84.

Godechot, Jacques. *Les Institutions de la France sous la Révolution et l'Empire.* 2nd ed. Paris: P.U.F., 1968.

――――. *The Taking of the Bastille, July 14, 1789.* Translated by Jean Stewart. New York: Charles Scribner's Sons, 1970.

Hampson, Norman. *A Social History of the French Revolution.* Toronto: University of Toronto Press, 1963.

――――. *Danton.* New York: Holmes and Meier, 1978.

Hamy, M.E.T. "Note sur diverses gravures de Bonneville, représentant des Nègres (1794-1803)." *Anthropologie* (1900): 42-46.

Hardenber, H. *Etta Palm: Een Hollandse Parisienne 1743-1799.* Assen: Vern Gorcum & Comp., 1962.

Harris, J. E. *The Assignats.* Cambridge: Harvard University, 1931.

Hatin, Eugène. *Histoire politique et littéraire de la presse en France.* . . . 8 vols. Paris: Poulet-Malassis et De Broise, 1859-1861.

Hawke, David Freeman. *Paine.* New York: Harper and Row, 1974.

Hertzberg, Arthur. *The French Enlightenment and the Jews: The Origins of Modern Anti-Semitism.* New York: Columbia University Press, 1968.

Hoeffer. *Nouvelle Biographie générale depuis les temps les plus reculés jusqu'à nos jours.* . . . 42 vols. Paris: Firmin-Didot, 1857-1862.

Hufton, Olwen. "Women in Revolution, 1789-1796." *Past and Present,* no. 53 (1971): 98-121.

Irving, Washington. *Adventures of Captain Bonneville or Scenes Beyond the Rocky Mountains of the Far West.* . . . Revised edition. New York: Putnam, 1851.

Janssens, Jacques. *Camille Desmoulins: Le Premier Républicain de France.* Paris: Perrin, 1973.

Jaurès, Jean. *Histoire socialiste de la Révolution française.* Edited by Albert Soboul. 7 vols. Paris: Editions Sociales, 1969-1973.

Jordan, David P. *The King's Trial: The French Revolution vs. Louis XVI.* Berkeley: University of California Press, 1979.

Joynes, Daniel Carroll. "Jansenists and Ideologues: Opposition Theory in the Parlement of Paris, 1750-1775." Ph.D. dissertation. University of Chicago, 1981.

Kates, Gary. "The Cercle Social: French Intellectuals and the French Revolution." Ph.D. dissertation. University of Chicago, 1978.

Kennedy, Michael L. *The Jacobin Clubs in the French Revolution. The First Years.* Princeton: Princeton University Press, 1982.

Koppius, W. J. *Etta Palm ... Nederland's eerste Feministe.* Zeist: J. Ploegsma, 1929.

Kulstein, David I. "The Ideas of Charles-Joseph Pankoucke, Publisher of the *Moniteur universel* in the French Revolution." *French Historical Studies* 4(1966): 304-19.

Kuscinski, A. *Dictionnaire des conventionnels.* Paris: Société de l'histoire de la Révolution, 1916-1918.

Lamartine, Alphonse de. *History of the Girondists.* . . . 3 vols. Translated by H. T. Ryde. London: Bohn, 1856.

Lefebvre, Georges. *The French Revolution. From Its Origins to 1793.* Translated by Elizabeth Moss Evanson. New York: Columbia University, 1962.

———. *The Coming of the French Revolution.* Translated by R. R. Palmer. Princeton: Princeton University Press, 1947.

Le Guin, Charles A. *Roland de la Platière: a Public Servant in the Eighteenth Century.* Philadelphia: American Philosophical Society, 1966.

Le Harivel, Philippe. *Nicolas de Bonneville: Pré-Romantique et révolutionnaire.* Oxford: Oxford University, 1923.

Lichtenberger, André. *Le Socialisme et la Révolution française. Etude sur les idées socialistes in France de 1789 à 1796.* Paris: Alcan, 1899.

———. "John Oswald: Écossais, Jacobin, et socialiste." *Révolution française* 22(1897): 181-95.

Liébaut, Achille Pierre. *Lamourette, prêtre et évêque assermenté.* Nancy: Voirin et Kreiss, 1894.

Ligou, Daniel. *Histoire des Franc-Maçons en France.* Toulouse: Privat, 1981.

Lough, John. *An Introduction to Eighteenth Century France*. New York: McKay, 1960.

McClelland, C. A. "The Lameths and Lafayette: The Politics of Moderation in the French Revolution, 1789-1791." Ph.D. dissertation, University of California, Berkeley, 1942.

McDonald, Joan. *Rousseau and the French Revolution, 1762-1791*. London: University of London, Anthlone Press, 1965.

McManners, John. *The French Revolution and the Church*. New York: Harper and Row, 1969.

Maier, Hans. *Revolution and Church: the Early History of Christian Democracy 1789-1901*. Translated by Emily M. Schossberger. South Bend: University of Notre Dame Press, 1969.

Marion, Marcel. "Un Révolutionnaire très conservateur: Creuzé-Latouche." *Revue d'histoire moderne* 11(1936): 101-34.

Martin, Gaston. *La Franc-Maçonnerie française et la préparation de la Révolution*. Paris: P.U.F., n.d.

Marx, Karl. *The Holy Family or Critique of Critical Criticism*. Translated by R. Dixon. Moscow: Foreign Language Publishing House, 1956.

Mathiez, Albert. *Le Club des Cordeliers pendant la crise de Varennes et le massacre du Champ de Mars*. Paris: Champion, 1910.

————. "La Fortune de Lanthenas." *Révolution française* 11(1919): 264-65.

————. *The French Revolution*. Translated by Catherine Alison Phillips. New York: Grosset and Dunlap, 1964.

————. *Girondins et Montagnards*. Paris: Firmin-Didot, 1930.

————. "La Lecture des décrets au prône sous la Constituente." *Annales Révolutionnaires* 1(1908): 223-43.

————. *Les Origines des cultes révolutionnaires, 1789-1792*. Paris: Bellais, 1904.

————. "Reponse aux articles de M. Braesch." *Revue historique* 144(1923): 87-91.

————. "Sur le titre du journal *La Bouche de Fer*." *Annales Révolutionnaires* 9 (1917): 685-90.

————. *La Vie chère et le mouvement social sous la Terreur*. 2 vols. Paris: Payot, 1973.

Mège, Francisque. *Le Conventionnel Bancal des Issarts. Etude biographique. Suivi de lettres inédites*. Paris: Champion, 1887.

Menozzi, Daniele. *"Philosophes" e "chrétiens éclairés:" Politica e religione nella collaborazione de G. H. Mirabeau e A. A. Lamourette (1774-1794)*. Brescia: Plaideia Editrice, 1976.

Michaud. *Biographie ancienne et moderne*. . . . New ed. 45 vols. Paris: Delagrave, n.d.

Michelet, Jules. *Histoire de la Révolution française*. Edited by Gérard Walter. 2 vols. Paris: Galimard, Bibliothèque de la Pléiade, 1952.

Monglond, André. "Nicolas de Bonneville: à propos du livre de M. Philippe Le Harivel." *Revue d'histoire littéraire* 1(1926): 408-15.

Murry, W. J. "The Right-Wing Press in the French Revolution, 1789-1792." Ph.D. dissertation, Australian National University, 1971.

Nemours, Luc. "Julien Raimond, le chef des gens de couleur et sa famille." *Annales historiques de la Révolution française* 23(1951): 257-62.

Nodier, Charles. *Oeuvres complètes*. . . . Geneva: Slatkine, 1968.

————. "Une Lettre de Charles Nodier." *Bulletin du bibliophile*, no. 11 (1847): 487-89.

Olliver, A. Richard. *Charles Nodier: Pilot of Romanticism*. Syracuse: Syracuse University Press, 1964.

Patrick, Allison. *The Men of the First Republic: Political Alignments in the National Convention of 1792*. Baltimore: Johns Hopkins University Press, 1972.

————. "The Montagnards and Their Opponents: Some Comments." *Journal of Modern History* 43(1971): 293-97.

————. "Political Divisions in the French National Convention, 1792-1793." *Journal of Modern History* 41(1969): 421-74.

Payne, Harry C. *The Philosophes and the People*. New Haven: Yale University Press, 1976.

Perroud, Claude. "Brissot et les Rolands. Collaboration des Rolands au *Patriote français*." *Révolution française* 34(1898): 404-20.

————. "Projet de Brissot pour une association agricole." *Révolution française* 42(1902): 260-65.

————. "A Propos de l'abolition du droit d'aînesse." *Révolution française* 54(1908): 193-202.

————. "Le Premier Ministre de Roland." *Révolution française* 42(1902): 511-28.

————. "Roland et la presse subventionnée." *Révolution française* 62(1912): 206-13, 315-32, 396-419.

————. "La Société française des amis des noirs." *Révolution française* 10(1916): 122-47.

————. *Recherches sur la proscription des Girondins 1793-1795*. Paris: Alcan, 1917.

Pertué, Michel. "La Liste des Girondins de Jean-Paul Marat." *Annales historiques de la Révolution française* no. 245 (1981): 379-89.

Phillips, Roderick. *Family Breakdown in Late Eighteenth Century France. Divorces in Rouen 1792-1803.* Oxford: Oxford University Press, 1980.

Poisson, Ch. *Les Fournisseurs aux armées sous la Révolution française ... J. Bidermann, Cousin, Marx-Berr.* Paris: Margraff, 1932.

Quinney, Valerie. "Decisions on Slavery, the Slave-Trade, and Civil Rights for Negroes in the Early French Revolution." *Journal of Negro History* 55(1970): 117-30.

————. "The Problem of Civil Rights for Free Men of Color in the Early French Revolution." *French Historical Studies* 7(1972): 544-58.

Rabbe, Alphonse. *Biographie universelle et portative des contemporains. ... 4 vols.* Paris: V. de Boisjuslin, 1830.

Ravitch, Norman. "The Abbé Fauchet: Romantic Religion During the French Revolution." *Journal of the American Academy of Religion* 42(1974): 247-62.

————. "Catholicism in Crisis: The Impact of the French Revolution on the Thought of the Abbé Adrien Lamourette." *International Journal of Economic and Social History* no. 9 (1978): 354-85.

Reinhard, Marcel. *La Chute de la royauté, 10 août 1792.* Paris: Gallimard, 1969.

————. *Nouvelle Histoire de Paris: la Révolution 1789-1799.* Paris: Hachette, 1971.

————. "Les Drapeaux de la Garde Nationale parisienne." *Mélanges offerts à Victor L. Tapié.* Paris: Sorbonne, 1971.

Resnick, Daniel P. "The Société des amis des Noirs and the Abolition of Slavery." *French Historical Studies* 7(1972): 558-69.

Rivers, John. *Louvet: Revolutionist and Romance-Writer.* New York: Brentano's, 1911.

Robertson, George M. "The Society of the Cordeliers and the French Revolution, 1790-1794." Ph.D. dissertation, University of Wisconsin, Madison, 1972.

Rodmell, Graham E. "Laclos, Brissot, and the Petitions of the Champ de Mars." *Studies on Voltaire and the Eighteenth Century* 183(1980): 189-222.

Rose, R. B. *The Making of the Sans-Culottes: Democratic Ideas and Institutions in Paris, 1789-1792.* Manchester: Manchester University Press, 1983.

————. "Socialism and the French Revolution: The Cercle Social and the Enragés." *Bulletin of the John Rylands Library* 41 (1958-1959): 139-64.

Rosenfield, Lenora Cohen. "The Rights of Women in the French

Revolution." *Studies in Eighteenth Century Culture.* Vol. 7. Madison: University of Wisconsin, 1978.

Rudé, George. *The Crowd in the French Revolution.* New York: Oxford University Press, 1959.

Sagnac, Philippe, and Caron, Pierre. *Recueil de documents sur l'abolition du régime seigneurial.* Paris: Imprimerie Nationale, 1907.

Seeber, Edward Derbyshire. *Anti-Slavery Opinion in France During the Second Half of the Eighteenth Century.* Baltimore: Johns Hopkins University Press, 1937.

Sekrecka, Mieczyslawa. *Louis-Claude de Saint-Martin, le philosophe inconnu. L'Homme et l'oeuvre.* Warsaw: Acta Universitatis Wratislaviensis, 1968.

————. "La Nouvelle Vision de la Révolution dans l'oeuvre de Saint-Martin, le philosophe inconnu," *La Littérature des lumières en France et en Pologne. Esthétique. Terminologie. Echanges.* Warsaw: Panstwokwe Wydawnictwo Naukowe, 1976.

Soboul, Albert. *The French Revolution 1787-1799. From the Storming of the Bastille to Napoleon.* Translated by Alan Forest and Colin Jones. New York: Vintage, 1974.

————. *Les Sans-Culottes parisiens en l'an II.* La Roche-sur-Yon: Henri Patier, 1958.

Söderhjelm, Alma. *Le Régime de la presse pendant la Révolution française. 1900-1902.* Reprint ed. (2 vols. in 1.) Geneva: Slatkin, 1971.

Sydenham, Michael J. *The French Revolution.* New York: Capricorn, 1965.

————. *The Girondins.* London: University of London, Athlone Press, 1961.

————. "The Girondins and the Question of Revolutionary Government: A New Approach to the Problem of Political Divisions in the National Convention." *French Historical Studies* 10(1977): 342-48.

————. "The Montagnards and Their Opponents: Some Considerations on a Recent Reassessment of the Conflicts in the French National Convention." *Journal of Modern History* 43(1971): 287-348.

Tackett, Timothy. *Priest and Parish in Eighteenth-Century France: A Social and Political Study of the Curés in a Diocese of Dauphiné, 1750-1791.* Princeton: Princeton University Press, 1977.

Taylor, George V. "The Paris Bourse on the Eve of the Revolution, 1781-1789." *American Historical Review* 63(1962): 951-977.

Thompson, J. M. *The French Revolution.* New York: Oxford University, 1966.

————. *Leaders of the French Revolution.* New York: Harper and Row, 1967.

Walter, Gérard. *Histoire des Jacobins.* Paris: Aimery Somoby, 1946.

Walter, Gérard, and Martin, André, eds. *Catalogue de l'histoire de la Révolution française.* 5 vols. Paris: Bibliothèque Nationale, 1940-55.

Walzer, Michael, ed. *Regicide and Revolution: Speeches at the Trial of Louis XVI.* Cambridge, Eng.: Cambridge University Press, 1974.

Williams, David. "The Politics of Feminism in the French Enlightenment." *The Varied Pattern. Studies in the Eighteenth Century.* Edited by Peter Hughes and David Williams. Toronto: University of Toronto Press, 1971.

Williams, William Hayes. "The Priest in History: a Study in Divided Loyalties in the French Lower Clergy From 1776 to 1789." Ph.D. dissertation, Duke University, 1965.

Library of Congress Cataloging in Publication Data

Kates, Gary, 1952-
The Cercle social, the Girondins, and the French Revolution.

Revision of thesis (Ph.D.)—University of Chicago, 1978.
Bibliography: p.
Includes index.
1. Cercle social (Paris, France) 2. Girondists.
3. France—History—Revolution, 1789-1799. I. Title.

DC158.8.K38 1985   944'.3604   84-42890
ISBN 0-691-05440-1